OPERATION PEDRO PAN

OPERATION PEDRO PAN

The Migration of
Unaccompanied Children
from Castro's Cuba

JOHN A. GRONBECK-TEDESCO

POTOMAC BOOKS

An imprint of the University of Nebraska Press

Library of Congress Control Number: 2022002092

Set in Minion Pro by Laura Buis.

For displaced children everywhere

CONTENTS

List of Illustrations   ix

Acknowledgments   xi

A Note on Language   xiii

Introduction   1

1. Takeoff   13

2. Landing   22

3. From Camps to Resettlement   43

4. Americanize a la Cubana   55

5. The "Other Miami"   65

6. Operation Pedro Pan in Cuba   84

7. A Brief History of Intimate Ties   99

8. A National Test   105

9. Cold War Childhood   115

10. For God and Country   133

11. Abuse   147

12. Vaults of Oblivion   152

13. Bittersweet Reunions   162

14. Putting the Program to Bed   172

15. The Politics of Exile Identity   180

16. The Return   189

Conclusion   196

Notes   203

Index   253

ILLUSTRATIONS

1. Cuban girl holding her dolls   24
2. Cuban Refugee Emergency Center registration card (front)   27
3. Cuban Refugee Emergency Center registration card (back)   27
4. Group portrait of Cuban Boys' Home residents   30
5. Florida City housing   31
6. Opa-locka dormitories   32
7. Boys at Camp Matecumbe   41
8. Monsignor Walsh visits Cuban boys   45
9. Social worker at Camp Matecumbe   47
10. Father Bryan O. Walsh at Camp Matecumbe   48
11. The Oberweiser family   49
12. Cuban boys playing baseball at St. Joseph's Home   57
13. Demonstration against Frank Legree   74
14. Representatives greet Cuban high school students in Montana   86
15. Card advertising *The Cuban Confusion*   107
16. Front page of *Resettlement Re-cap*   109
17. Residents of St. Joseph's Home   145
18. Mercedes Diaz Dash and Rosario Diaz Juliano   159

ACKNOWLEDGMENTS

This project began as an odd appendage in my doctoral dissertation that turned into an insatiable curiosity. While researching this topic, I have been struck by how many people have told me they know a Pedro Pan. It is a testament to the impact these more than fourteen thousand people have had on everyday life in the United States. Over the course of researching and writing this book, I had the good fortune of finding many individuals who helped me along the way. Pedro Pans near and far entrusted me with their stories, memories, and emotions, and in the process taught me more about familial bonds as I was becoming a new father myself. Eloy, Gerardo, Jay, José, José Antonio, Mario, Mayda, Mercedes, Pury, Raul, and Roberto took generous time out of their lives to impart their recollections. The *muchachitas de Villa Maria* I met at Marilyn Borroto's house fashioned an unforgettable night of storytelling and merriment, which informed my writing of this history. And I will always cherish the two remarkable conversations I had with two non–Pedro Pans, Marvin Dunn and T. Willard Fair, whose insights gave the manuscript a new direction.

This work could not have been accomplished without the assistance of mentors, colleagues, and a slew of folks kind enough to respond to my emails and phone calls. Michelle Chase, Chris Dietrich, Karen Dubinsky, Michael Koncewicz, Iraida López, Paul Mishler, Lisandro Pérez, Luis Roniger, James Shrader, Nena Torres, and Elaine Tyler May read, advised, and reflected on my work. Jay Weaver of the *Miami Herald* also gave me important feedback. Clint Attebery was an eleventh-hour hero when he shared information on his research on Pedro Pans in Helena, Montana, and Laura Ferguson at *Montana Magazine* helped me track down permissions for key images. Father Jeff at the Diocese of Helena set aside his many sacred demands to help this researcher from out east.

A bevy of experts in the archival and publishing worlds assisted me directly and indirectly. Dominique St. Victor and Ximena Valdivia were unfailing in navigating me through the Pedro Pan archives at Barry University. The staff at Florida International University, the National Archives and Records Administration, the State Library and Archives of Florida, and the University of Miami's Cuban Heritage Collection also deserve luminous praise. I am also indebted to my agent, Lane Heymont, and to Tom Swanson and Taylor Rothgeb at Potomac Books. At home, Karuna and Nisha sustained me through this process as only they know how to do. Finally, this book is dedicated to the millions of children who live today as forcibly displaced people. Uprooted, they are made to confront circumstances not of their design yet still manage to sprout in their adopted countries.

A NOTE ON LANGUAGE

The reader will notice that I have elected to include racist language from the period under examination in its entirety rather than having it abbreviated. I have not made this choice lightly. To grasp this history more fully, I feel it is important to convey the violence of racism that Cubans and African Americans confronted, and using original language helps to make these scenarios more vivid.

INTRODUCTION

Will it reach the clear surface of my consciousness—this memory, this old moment which . . . has come from so far to invite, to move, to raise up from the deepest part of me?

—MARCEL PROUST, *Swann's Way*

At the outset, it was a modest proposal: transfer two hundred unaccompanied Cuban children to Miami to save them from communism. The time apart from their parents would be short, only until Fidel Castro fell from power by the result of U.S. force, Cuban counterrevolutionary tactics, or a combination of both. Families would reunite in a matter of months. A plan was hashed, and it worked. But soon it ballooned into something unwieldy, so that within two years the modest proposal erupted into the largest migration of unaccompanied minors to the United States to date.

Mercedes Diaz Dash remembers the day her parents prepared her exit. Living in the posh Havana neighborhood Marianao, her father was an accounting professor and her mother a homemaker. Fearful of losing their children to communism, they secured visa waivers and sent Mercedes, her sister, and her cousin—nine, eleven, and five years old, respectively—on a Pan American Airways flight filled with children scattered throughout the cabin. It was January 25, 1962. In her home today, several papers, photographs, and mementos document that time, including the doll her parents gave her the day before she boarded the plane.[1]

Common in the days leading up to all the children's departure was a sudden increase of activity in the household. With little to no warning, neighbors and family members would scurry in and out, and there was an unexpected gravity to the situation. Children learned that they would be traveling to the United States to attend school for a short time. Many were told that they had earned a special scholarship. When the day arrived, they went to the Havana airport and saw their parents for the last time in months, sometimes years, and, in some rare cases, forever.

Such a memory will forever be seared into José Azel's consciousness. In Cuba he was a student at a Marist Brothers school and lived an upper-middle-class life. When Fidel Castro took over Cuba and set his sights on the Catholic Church, the precocious child found himself in the ranks of the underground opposition, engaging in acts of sabotage. The Marists were known for their political militancy. When Castro closed private schools, José's father became more worried. Surely the trip would be brief, he thought. Staying behind to take care of the family's possessions, he sent his thirteen-year-old boy to West Palm Beach in June 1961 on a cargo ship chock-full of seminarians. That would be the last time they saw each other. One of the things José regrets most today is that he and his father never had an adult conversation.[2]

Where do our memories reside in our consciousness, and why and when do they "raise up from the deepest part" of ourselves? It was a question that mesmerized Marcel Proust in his multivolume collection *Remembrance of Things Past*. In the opening book, *Swann's Way*, the narrator bites into a madeleine and in doing so releases a flood of bittersweet recollections. He is electrified with evidence that memories can lie dormant until resuscitated in the most mundane yet vivid of moments. Roberto Rodriguez Diaz remembered his awakening in a similar fashion later in life. It was on a flight to Houston in 1994 when he unexpectedly broke into tears. His mind was abruptly alive with uncontrolled yet vivid flashbacks to his childhood in Texas, a time of harrowing isolation in a foreign land not of his choosing.[3]

Thousands of such stories "reach the surface of consciousness" in uneven, conflicted ways, told by participants of the Unaccompanied Cuban Refugee Children's Program. The project known as Operation Pedro Pan, which existed between 1960 and 1962, was the coordinated effort to relocate and care for over fourteen thousand children in the United States between 1960 and 1981. The program relied on a vast network of federal and state offices: the Department of Health, Education, and Welfare (HEW); the U.S. State Department; and the Florida State Department of Public Welfare, to name a few. A long list of nonprofit church groups, child welfare agencies, and airlines aided and abetted the cause, as did embassies, parochial schools, and a solid counterrevolutionary network in Cuba. Children without immediate family support in the United States—more than half of the Pedro Pans—received group and foster care through the Catholic Welfare Bureau (CWB) and other religious, governmental, and nongovernmental organizations as the young Cubans were dispersed throughout the country. By 1968 more than 8,300 Cuban children had received assistance.[4] Of these children, the Catholic Church had assumed responsibility for 7,346 of them.[5]

In our own era, we stand witness to a constant flow of unaccompanied children at the U.S. border. Fleeing primarily Honduras, Guatemala, Mexico, and El Salvador, they are sent by their families or are separated from them in the crossing, in desperate search of refuge from violence and of newfound economic opportunity. In 2014 President Barack Obama's administration had to contend with sixty-eight thousand unaccompanied minors attempting to enter the United States. Donald Trump's administration, in an effort to promote "zero tolerance," made child separation a strong feature of the border crisis. In 2019 Customs and Border Protection commissioner Kevin McAleenan called the migrant swell a "breaking point."[6] But more children have arrived, with reports of nineteen thousand unaccompanied minors crossing in March 2021 alone. By year's end, the United States would count an unprecedented 122,000 children in shelters separated from their parents.[7]

But in 1960 it was another reality. Cuban refugee children were thought about in a very different way, with their reasons for coming and their manner of arrival being distinct from those in the headlines today. Parents willfully put their most prized possessions on planes to Miami. The U.S. government aided these ventures and aggressively extended federal resources to reunify the families. Similar to today, however, throngs of Americans decried the incoming waves of Cubans. Were there communists in these masses? Why should taxpayers shoulder the hefty financial burden? Yet topping these critical voices was an overall willingness both to accept the children in the name of national security and to make good on America's long-storied tradition of offering sanctuary and freedom.

The Cold War made such realities seem reasonable. After the triumph of the Cuban Revolution in 1959, Cubans of a particular station became gripped with fear of what Fidel Castro was doing to their country. So strong was this panic that one family sent eight children to Miami.[8] They belonged to the larger deluge of refugees landing on U.S. shores between 1959 and 1962. Such was the push factor, while opportunities in the United States provided ample pull. Operation Pedro Pan flourished among the changes in religion, familial well-being, and racial identity that were transforming the United States. The Cold War boiled down to a simplified contest; a line in the sand neatly divided the world between the Soviet sphere of influence and America's. In a matter of months, Castro's Cuba stood as a proxy of the "Red menace," a mere ninety miles from U.S. shores, and its status disrupted not only the long-standing ties between Havana and Washington but also destabilized the hemispheric neighborhood that the United States had dominated since the Monroe Doctrine of 1823.

In the West during the Cold War, saving the world from communism was of utmost importance in the battle for hearts and minds. Children became symbols with political import tied to strong religious commitments to refugees. Some Pedro Pans were taken in by Protestant, Jewish, and secular organizations. But above all, the Catholic Church made up the nucleus of the Cuban Children's Program. At its helm was Father Bryan O. Walsh, an Irish priest who had recently relocated to Miami and embraced his mission with gusto. He labored at a time when Catholic laity found new life and prestige in postwar America with the election of the first Catholic president, John F. Kennedy. The children's program nearly consumed Walsh, but the young priest was bent on growing Miami's Catholic community. Together, the church and the Cubans did just that. When Walsh lit out for Miami in 1958, the city glistened as a newly minted diocese, and a decade later it would boast its own archdiocese.

Father Walsh quickly ascended the ranks of the church, becoming a monsignor in 1962.[9] When poring over his robust archive, one sees a storied career of religious leadership laden with relentless humanitarian involvement. He worked at a breathtaking pace through a variety of demands, but nothing occupied his attention in his forty-two-year career as much as the children's program. He later conceded: "I conceived of my job of helping Cuban refugees, and in particular, Cuban children, as an opportunity given to me by Divine Providence to combat communism." Walsh saw his role in terms of battle, what he called a "holy war for God and country."[10] He was not alone. His work depended on dozens of Catholic centers in nearly every state to secure temporary care for Cuban young people in foster families and group homes.[11] In a moment when Cuban authorities were isolating and banishing Catholic leaders, the church in the United States opened its doors to them.

Walsh's success also entailed a special partnership with the government and nonprofit organizations working to save Cubans from communism. The unique collaboration effectively dissolved the First Amendment's division between church and state in favor of humanitarianism and national security. In its day, the Cuban migration was the largest, single-nation refugee crisis the United States had confronted. Facilitated by federal, state, and municipal institutions and incalculable heavy lifting by everyday residents, it became a national first and elevated test for U.S. democracy. The goal was to absorb exiles escaping political and religious persecution, communism, and godlessness, which were among the country's fiercest anxieties. Their religious dedication and fear of losing their way of life prompted Cuban parents to make the agonizing decision to send their children away. They were terrified of "communist indoctrination" and baseless rumors that the Cuban state would dispossess them of their parental rights.

When the children arrived, they found an America in the throes of the most consequential movement of the twentieth century—the struggle for civil rights. As the country's abysmal record on racism reached a violent reckoning, Cuban kids were ensnared in these tectonic forces. Because they were anti-communist heroes, mostly light skinned, and to a large degree from middle- and upper-class backgrounds, they benefited from an exceptional refugee status that permitted faster avenues toward gaining residency and eventual U.S. citizenship. Yet Cubans were also marked as outsiders who did not fit within traditional racial understandings in Miami and other U.S. communities, people who for the most part were neither Black nor white but inhabitants of a new racial space that slipped in and out of these established demarcations.

In this light, Pedro Pan children suddenly embodied two polarizing extremes: on the one hand, they were champion tokens of militant

anti-communism, while on the other hand they represented controversial non-white exiles threatening the white-majority nation. Living
on a new hyphen, alchemizing aspects of both *cubanidad* (Cubanness)
and U.S. "Americanness," they negotiated identities that could not be
separated from their value as political symbols.[12] The production of
Cuban America required the enlistment of U.S. residents to accept
refugees and shelter unaccompanied children. The task required ample
effort to strengthen the nation's image as a bastion of multiculturalism
at a time when evidence of brutal violence directed at the civil rights
movement appeared in print and on screens around the world. This
visible violence undermined Washington's credibility as the foremost
authority of liberty and equality. As Cuban children were scattered
throughout the United States—Dubuque, Iowa; San Antonio, Texas;
Helena, Montana—with them came the mandate to assimilate them
in the name of an enlightened antiracist democracy.

The absorption of Cubans was paramount to America's strategy
for defeating the Union of Soviet Socialist Republics (USSR). But the
country's prestige was in peril of dismantling as Jim Crow segregation
eviscerated cities such as Birmingham and Memphis. It was a public
relations nightmare for the State Department. Cuban refugees, and
particularly children, were, in the words of the government, a "national
responsibility." Seymour Samet, the executive director of the American
Jewish Committee in Miami, echoed what many Americans realized
when he testified: "Miami and its Cuban refugee situation are in the
spotlight of the nation, and, in fact, of the world. Our ability in Dade
County . . . to accept those refugees and to provide for their successful
integration into our society can serve either as a showcase for democracy, or, if we are unsuccessful, as a propaganda tool for our enemies.
We really have no choice."[13]

But some Miamians and many Americans believed the country did
have a choice and that accepting so many Cubans would have disastrous consequences. Successful integration would indeed come, but
the birthing process was slow.

The crowded Havana–Miami channel transformed the modest U.S.
southern city into a major Pan-American destination and place of
notoriety. However, it also was undergoing its own difficult civil rights

journey. The majority of the nearly 250,000 Cubans entering the United States between 1959 and 1962 changed the demography of a locale on its way to becoming the capital of Cuban America.[14] The Cubanization of Miami gave locals the opportunity to fulfill the creeds of anti-communist Christianity and racial tolerance, and, in doing so, herald themselves as part of a new cosmopolitan South. But the making of modern Miami necessitated weeding out the nettles of racism, a task that was complicated by the presence of exiles. The Cubans prompted suspicion by whites as well as bitter resentment from African American community leaders who deplored the federal assistance offered to refugees when many Blacks needed money and jobs. Pedro Pans and their exile community were accused of taking up spaces in public schools and positions of employment that would have better served the country's non-white citizens.

It may have been the largest, but it was not southern Florida's first encounter with Cubans. Creoles living under Spanish colonialism traipsed north in the nineteenth century. But contemporary history parses postrevolutionary waves into four periods: 1959–62, 1965–73, 1980, and the mid-1990s. Though the majority of unaccompanied children arrived between 1960 and 1962, the Cuban Children's Program lasted in some form until 1981. In the early 1960s, the "refugee problem," as it was often referred to, was meant to have a temporary solution. Once the revolutionary government was toppled, the Cuban exiles would return home. But weeks turned into months and then to years. The conversion from refugee to permanent resident to citizen turned into an unforeseen reality. In these decades, the exiles hewed into symbols thick with political meaning and fashioned a highly influential enclave of Cuban Americans. Between 1959 and 1980, eight hundred thousand Cubans ventured to the United States. In 2013 nearly 2 million out of 53 million Latinos counted themselves members of the island's diaspora.[15]

The ultimate success of the program depended on an improvised matrix of organizations and, most importantly, everyday people to "save children from communism." Most of the figures who appear in this book are evidence of the accidental elements of history; they are the occupiers of a significance not of their own choosing. These myriad mid-level women and men worked tirelessly in government offices, orphanages, churches, airline desks, social work agencies, classrooms, shelters, and many community corners where seemingly inane duties actually produced history. This tale does not grant magnanimity to a Lyndon B. Johnson or Martin Luther King Jr. Instead, it centers on ordinary folks who followed their beliefs and instincts in their daily lives and in the process ended up shaping events of lasting momentousness. Foregrounded are the subjects who are often overlooked in Cold War assessments—children—and the reality that regular routines of work, church, and school can thrust people into durable prominence.

What is it to put children at the center of history? As Karen Dubinsky has observed, "The protagonists are children, but the social and political dramas they express are always created by and about adults."[16] Children are molded into citizens, but so, too, does the nation construct itself through its youngsters. One of the problems with placing children's historical agency is that they "leave few literate traces," writes Paula Fass. A major hurdle in working with the history of children is that their thoughts and behaviors are often mediated by adult interpretations.[17] Navigating between adult memories of childhood and archival records has produced the details that follow. Pinpointing the facts of the Cuban Children's Program can be a nettlesome affair, for any journey into its history necessarily involves official and unofficial accounts, government documents, anecdotes, rumored speculation, and, of course, the holdings left by its largest orchestrator, Monsignor Walsh. Even in Walsh's veritable archive, the details can vary greatly.

Take, for example, the question of how many children made the journey alone. The number often used is 14,048, the number Walsh said arrived between January 3, 1961, when Cuba and the United States broke diplomatic relations, and October 22, 1962, when flights between the countries ceased during the Cuban Missile Crisis.[18] Later, a 1963 fact sheet by the Catholic Welfare Bureau stated that 14,124 Cuban youths had entered the United States by that time. Of those children, 10,611 had reunited with parents or relatives.[19] Yet a report by the Florida Department of Public Welfare indicated that even before the program was officially launched, "many teenage boys escaped by small boats" but encountered no fit reception in the United States. Whether these children are counted among official tallies is not clear.[20] For its part, HEW counted 14,072 children between December 26, 1960, and February 11, 1963.[21] The numbers can climb from there. In a letter penned in 1965, Walsh cited the total as 14,130 children.[22] But in an interview later in life, he said 15,000 kids arrived between December 26, 1960, and October 23, 1962.[23] Leaping even higher, the *New York Times* asserted in the priest's obituary that he aided over 16,000 unaccompanied children between 1960 and 1964, most likely an overstatement but in the end unverifiable.[24]

Such is the untidy nature of this story. Part of the problem deals with nomenclature. Operation Pedro Pan was never an official term and often fails to appear in agency documents, unlike its proper name, Unaccompanied Cuban Children's Program, which formally began in February 1961. Operation Pedro Pan is generally defined as the clandestine effort to transfer and care for Cuban children between December 1960, when Walsh started, and late October 1962, when flights between the nations halted. But most public commentators, writers, and participants themselves have used the phrase "Operation Pedro Pan" to denote the whole phenomenon of unaccompanied Cuban children regardless of chronology.[25]

To wade into this history, therefore, is to confront inconsistencies. Memories resuscitated from decades ago rest alongside written documents of the day. Pedro Pans remember with fondness and grief, nostalgia and regret. As adults, they process the past differently than they did as children. We all do. Memory morphs as we age because our frameworks for understanding the past change. Truth and memory are bound in a double helix whose separation can be a troublesome or foolhardy errand. But what is distinct about the Cuban case is that a refugee memory can serve a political purpose as well as a social identity. When picking apart the dominant public strands of this memory, one finds it is still firmly attached to a Cold War framework, which will hold for many Pedro Pans as long as Cuba is a communist country.

While most are U.S. citizens now, many Pedro Pan adults still self-identify with the unstable realm of refugee life. Overwhelmingly they are thankful that their parents sent them, and they are unable to imagine an alternative life in Cuba. Even the exercise of trying to do so is unbearable. Yet across the board, they attest they never would have sent their own children if given a similar predicament. What is it to be thankful for an act that you could never do yourself? Familial separation of this kind, especially at a very young age, often breeds a type of trauma, one that settled into the foundation of the Pedro Pans' memories and their Cuban American identities. Although they became prized U.S. residents, Cuban children were forced to maneuver conditions that were more precarious than the entitlements granted to them by law. Though the Cold War has become a faded relic of the past, the Cuban case still offers an exceptional example in U.S. immigration history. The children who were saved from communism were afforded a pre-eminence in the nation not bestowed on other immigrants, one that still generates social and political meaning in their adult lives.

Critically, following the threads of Operation Pedro Pan leads to the larger tapestry of Cuban America. For a considerable portion of this population, the Cuban government is the same enemy it has been for decades. The revolution robbed the exiles of their nation, while the United States still remains their heroic savior. As a political bloc, Cuban Americans have crafted a narrative that continues to uphold U.S. triumphalism and refugee victimhood, even as the long twilight struggle has withered by other measurements. Wading into this varied community splashes up endless political conversations and even heated arguments.

Doing research in both countries invites its own politics. For those who study Cuban history, one of the recurring claims is that state censorship restricts the type of history that can be written. It has the same heroes and villains, triumphs and failures, and to deviate from the acceptable version is to invite investigation from authorities in Cuba. There is much merit to this assertion. Yet just as the revolution produced a set of truths that make up official accounts, the creation of modern Cuban America sponsored a framing that, until much later, was very difficult to diverge from or counter. This is the so-called line of the "Miami Cubans." In the United States, a similar inflexibility around discussing Cuban refugee history also has adhered to a narrow collection of ideas. To be sure, opinions about U.S.-Cuban politics differ substantially depending on where one watches the evening news, Havana or Miami.

Yet this investigation concludes that these long-held maxims have also changed over time. The voluminous stories shared by the Pedro Pans disclose that these individuals have been affected differently. Many have reassessed their relationship to the U.S.-Cuban divide with a forgiving air of reconciliation, signaled by their returning to Cuba to "feel" Cuban once again. To be sure, the production of Cuban America has created something more than a singular community of conservative, anti-communist patriots. Pedro Pan children instead attest to the dizzying life on the hyphen, as products of both U.S. Americanness and cubanidad that remade their childhood and, as with other identity formations, that are fraught with ambivalence and complexity.

1 | TAKEOFF

As passengers deplaned from her flight in Miami, Silvia Wilhelm recalled a State Department official boarding the aircraft, reading a list of names, and taking her and other children to a special room in the airport. There she met a man named James Baker.[1] After a period of processing, she was sent to Buffalo, New York.[2] On another route, future U.S. senator Mel Martínez (R-FL) had left behind his family and Cuba in the thick of adolescence. Reaching cruising altitude, a flight attendant said, "You have just left Cuban airspace. . . . You are free." At that point, everyone cheered.[3]

It is doubtful, however, that many unaccompanied children shared in the revelry. To reconcile the joy that surrounded them with the feelings of detachment they unexpectedly encountered must have been impossible. Their parents sent them away out of love, but all around were the painful signposts of abandonment. Agonizing separation, although temporary for most, was the price of freedom. Wrested from their families and forced to become wards of a foreign government and its attending institutions, Pedro Pans would falter but find their way as momentous inheritors of a new nation.

In his frequent recounting of Operation Pedro Pan, Monsignor Walsh often began with a Cuban man who approached him in Miami and implored the Catholic Church to help a fifteen-year-old unaccompanied boy named Pedro Menéndez.[4] It was November 1960. The Catholic Welfare Bureau (CWB) and representatives from local welfare agencies met with the Dade County Welfare Planning Council to contemplate the growing refugee crisis. Reports of unattended minors were in their files. Pedro was one of them, as were two children taken to Key West by their mother, who petitioned a juvenile court judge to find them safe harbor. The judge put the siblings in foster care, and the mother returned to Cuba to wage battle against Fidel Castro.[5]

Children had landed elsewhere earlier. The month before, long-time *New York Times* correspondent Ruby Hart Phillips wrote about a group of Cuban girls resettled in an Ursuline school in New Orleans.[6] Around the time Walsh learned about Pedro, the priest was put in contact with James Baker—then in Cuba—who was the rector of Ruston Academy. Ruston was a private American school in Havana for elite Cuban and American students. Baker had followed the revolutionary tide of the country in opposing Fulgencio Batista, but then things abruptly changed. That November parents began asking him for *becas* (scholarships) for their children to study in the United States. He went to Miami along with members of the American business community in Havana. Someone mentioned Walsh's name, and in December the two spoke and came up with a plan.[7]

"I felt very happy and thought that my government was doing incredible work," Baker later remembered. "I felt that way because we had Communism 90 miles away, and here people were arriving from there with their problems, and as a democracy we had the responsibility to help them."[8] For their scheme to work, Baker and Walsh first needed to coordinate with appropriate childcare agencies. The CWB was perfect. It could ensure housing and schooling once children were in Miami. Parents would obtain student visas from the U.S. Embassy or a consulate in Cuba, and Coral Gables High School or a similar school would furnish the proper scholastic paperwork in Miami. The I-20 forms necessary for foreign students to obtain visas would be sent to Havana. All these documents would circulate between Walsh and Baker via diplomatic pouch with the assistance of the U.S. Embassy. Walsh could ensure that his bureau would facilitate the placement and education of the children upon their arrival.[9]

It seemed workable. In mid-December Walsh wrote Chargé d'Affaires Daniel Braddock in Havana to discuss what he called the American Chamber of Commerce Plan.[10] The chamber in Havana and other generous donors had pooled money to transfer the children. Many of the chamber's members and friends wanted to rush their children out of the country. Esso Standard Oil Company, Freeport Sulphur Company, and Shell Oil Company were among the major contributors. Loads of cash were making their way to Father Walsh from Cuba. The money flowed, with some of it, according to Baker, coming directly from the U.S. government. The Cuban Catholic Church also sent money. At one point, Walsh was dispatching between $10,000 and $15,000 worth of money orders to Cuba, and Baker believed he raised as much as $20,000 in the first few months of the operation.[11]

The W. Harry Smith Agency in Havana handled the airline tickets, which cost $25 each. The first list of children's names dropped into Walsh's possession on December 15, 1960, and on December 26, Pan American Airways flight 422 landed in Miami with two teenagers, Sixto Aquino and his sister Vivian, aboard.[12] They were taken to St. Joseph's Villa, where they lived for two months. Then they transferred to the home of their mother's cousin in Hialeah. Their mother came five months later, and their father arrived six months anon. Sixto would go on to earn a degree in economics at Georgetown University in 1969 and work for the Inter-American Development Bank.[13]

Other children trickled in. Walsh coordinated with the U.S. Immigration and Naturalization Service at the Miami airport to identify unaccompanied minors. But curiously, none possessed the student visas as planned.[14] Alternately they had to rely on tourist visas because the embassy in Havana was stalling on the student variety. This posed a potential problem because it was not clear that Walsh could legally process the minors without the appropriate visas.[15]

Walsh would go on to provide slightly different versions of this story over his lifetime. In one instance, he recalled receiving a call from Frank Auerbach, the assistant director of the Visa Office in the U.S. State Department, who told Baker that he had from the U.S. Embassy in Havana a list of the names of two hundred children whose parents wanted to get them out of Cuba. The State Department could not okay this request without a proper child welfare agency safeguarding the children's well-being. Would Walsh do it?[16] But in a letter to Auerbach in late December 1960, Walsh indicated that Baker had called the priest on December 30 to ask about the hold-up. It is not clear if this was the first or second time Walsh made contact with the assistant director. In his letter, Walsh asked for 250 student visas in Havana and gave his assurance that the CWB would be the agency responsible for the children's well-being.[17] Either way, Auerbach had a different idea in the end. He said the government would issue two hundred visa waivers.[18] No longer would minors need student visas. Walsh broached the topic with his superior, Bishop Coleman Carroll, who tersely replied, "Take them all."[19]

Initially the only sponsoring airline, Pan American (Pan Am) Airways estimated that as many as one-third of its passengers from Cuba were children. If a family had the waiver and a ticket plus $10 for the Cuban exit tax, the parents could obtain a seat for their child. Just as this new strategy got underway, however, portents of change were afoot. Baker urged haste because of an ominous rumor that no children would be allowed to leave Cuba after January.[20] That rumor moved closer to fact when, on January 3, 1961, Washington and Havana broke diplomatic relations. The next day, Baker and his wife broke their own ties with the island and headed for Miami. Confusion and unpredictability led to first-of-a-kind conventions. In the midnight hour, as the embassy was closing and its staff was burning papers, Baker was allowed to stamp the passports of twenty-five children himself.[21]

But a valid visa was still needed for entry into the United States. On January 8 Walsh repaired to Washington to meet Auerbach and Robert F. Hale, the director of the State Department's Visa Office. After receiving the blessings of the State and Justice Departments, visa waivers became a permanent practice. The State Department gave the priest blanket authority to issue waivers to all children between the ages of six and sixteen years old. Other nations stepped up to assist with the ruse. If unable to fly directly from Havana to Miami, children could follow rerouted avenues via a third country. Still under British rule, Jamaica was a top choice because visas could be granted by the British Embassy in Havana or the consul general in Kingston, and from there children could proceed to Miami. On January 10 Walsh went to Kingston to talk with Catholic leadership, immigration authorities, and Robert McGregor, the U.S. consul general. Representatives from Pan Am and KLM Airlines were also present. In Havana, the British ambassador had agreed to grant visas for children going to Nassau via Miami, where the children would simply stay. The Dutch followed suit and instructed KLM and their embassy in Havana to comply with the operation's needs.[22]

There were other routes. Some children arrived via Puerto Rico, while others came on boats to Key West.[23] The CWB helped kids ambling through a third country to obtain a resident visa. Spain was a top choice, and with regularity young people flew in from Madrid. A parallel program transferred thousands of Cuban children to the Spanish capital. Estimates of their numbers vary, from two thousand to three thousand to Walsh's one-time estimate of fifteen thousand children. Wherever they sent them, parents preferred to send their sons of military age. But they had no control once their children landed; it was dreadfully worrisome when Walsh's staff would find children wandering around Miami's airport without chaperones.[24]

Children falling in the allowable age range faced no hurdles upon arrival. Those aged sixteen to eighteen years old, however, needed clearance from the Federal Bureau of Investigation (FBI).[25] Baker protested the age restriction, believing older children were more at risk to be sucked into the postrevolutionary violence.[26] Raul Alvaro was seventeen when he flew to Miami on a Pan Am flight. Over the loudspeaker at the airport were commands routing boys ages sixteen years old and older to a specified location and from there to Opa-locka, a former military base and later a camp with the Cuban Children's Program (CCP). At Opa-locka, Alvaro met with federal agents. He was lucky to complete processing expeditiously; some young men had been waiting months for approval.[27]

On Valentine's Day 1961 Walsh wrote Auerbach and let him know the plan was "functioning very smoothly." Demand in Cuba was growing. Walsh pushed his ally to increase the number of waivers and to admit children older than sixteen. But the U.S. government held firm for fear of Castro's agents slipping through.[28] Walsh tested his luck and solicited five hundred additional waivers, and the Visa Office complied by authorizing a "blanket visa waiver," which freed him up even more.[29] Bundles of such waivers were smuggled into Cuba via the diplomatic pouches of participant nations.[30] Each month Walsh could count on a report from the Visa Office on the number of visas applied for and granted. In June 1962, for example, a total of 3,100 visas for Cuban applicants were approved, with 395 going to children.[31]

It was only a matter of time until the program became unmanageable. Children younger than six years old began to appear. Pedro Pan Elly Chovel said she saw two-year-olds arrive.[32] One report contended that some mothers sent their newborn babies.[33] Parents flooded the airport in Havana and begged officials and even random passengers to take their children.[34] In 1963 Wisconsinites learned from their local news that a four-year-old boy turned up with his name and his mother's Brooklyn address sewn to the back of his shirt. In another case, a woman boarded a plane in Havana and gave a social worker an eighteen-month-old who had been given to her by a woman on the cusp of being detained by Havana police.[35]

In 1962 Frank M. Craft, the director of the Florida State Department of Public Welfare, penned an anxious letter to the Children's Bureau saying his department had custody of five children under the age of three. All had been processed in a juvenile court before transferring to CWB foster care.[36] Walsh bristled at such exceptions. He prided himself on running a tight ship, and the news that toddlers possessed waivers alarmed him. At least once he returned a waiver to the State Department, declaring it a fake and the child designee as underage. But the program had billowed beyond his control. Counterfeit documents were everywhere, and children were entering Miami without caregivers.[37] And still the voices of support rang out. FBI director J. Edgar Hoover quipped, "The communists always went after the youth first and we ought in this country to see if we can't place these young people into schools and indoctrinate them with democracy."[38]

Influencing nations deemed unstable or unfit with U.S. democracy lay at the heart of America's Cold War mission. Filling federal filing cabinets were policies that affirmed the country's dedication to the world's dispossessed. The Displaced Persons Act of 1948 had opened America's doors to 200,000 refugees, including 3,000 war orphans. Five years later, the Refugee Relief Act brought 214,000 people along with 4,000 orphans under the age of ten from Europe and East Asia, with a preference for Koreans racked by the U.S.-led war.[39] The showdown with the Soviet Union made these priorities more urgent. But something more was needed for the present emergency. In October 1960 the Cuban Refugee Committee, a conglomeration of Miami business and civic leaders, appealed to the White House for relief. President Dwight (Ike) Eisenhower sent Tracy S. Voorhees to look into the mounting situation. Voorhees was a veteran on the subject. In 1956 he had headed the Hungarian Refugee Relief Program at Camp Kilmer, New Jersey. There he worked with Bryan Walsh, then a young up-and-coming priest in Miami, to help thirty-eight thousand Hungarians attain asylum. Fifty million dollars were spent on sheltering and resettling the newcomers, a thousand of whom were unaccompanied children.[40]

While the Hungarian situation was the model, the Cuban case proved different. The number of Cubans dwarfed the Hungarian total. Hungarians came though Austria, whereas Cubans came directly, making the United States the country of first asylum.[41] Voorhees did not mince words when he blamed the situation on "evil events . . . which have subjugated Cuba to communism." The people's relief, he surmised, was "both a national responsibility and a national opportunity," another test of American will and might.[42] He made a series of recommendations to the president regarding the refugees' health, employment training, and resettlement.[43] Eisenhower responded with an allocation of $1 million drawn from the Mutual Security Act. With the money, the Cuban Refugee Emergency Center was founded at Freedom Tower on Biscayne Boulevard in Miami, vaulting the city to the helm of national relief efforts.

John F. Kennedy (JFK) inherited the humanitarian challenge. As a candidate, he had promised to get tougher on communism while appreciating U.S. prestige in the world. Midway through his inaugural year, in a letter to Congress JFK fastened the importance of the U.S. mission to accept those adrift: "From the earliest days of our history this land has been a refuge for the oppressed and it is proper that we now, as descendants of refugees and immigrants, continue our long humanitarian tradition of helping those who are forced to flee to maintain their lives as individual, self-sufficient human beings in freedom, self-respect, dignity and health. It is, moreover, decidedly in the political interests of the United States that we maintain and continue to enhance our prestige and leadership in this respect."[44]

To make good on this mission, Kennedy created the Cuban Refugee Program (CRP) under the Department of Health, Education, and Welfare (HEW). Kennedy entreated HEW secretary Abraham Ribicoff to see the Cuban matter as part of the greater duty to freedom: "I want to re-emphasize most strongly the tradition of the United States as a humanitarian sanctuary, and the many times it has extended its hand and material help to those who are 'exiles for conscience's sake.' In the presently troubled world, we cannot be a peacemaker if we are not also the protector of those individuals as well as nations who cast with us their personal liberty and hopes for the future."[45]

In a matter of weeks, Ribicoff had the CRP up and running. It had provisions for financial assistance, resettlement, job training and placement, health services, education, food distribution, and unaccompanied children.[46] Drifting in and out in the opening years, the program's directors were dedicated government bureaucrats who wound up in Miami through different avenues. The program's first, Dillon S. Myer, had been the director of the War Relocation Authority that oversaw the internment of 120,000 Japanese nationals and Japanese Americans during World War II. He later served as the contentious commissioner of the Bureau of Indian Affairs.[47] Locally, Arthur Lazell was the director of the Cuban Refugee Center in Miami. Over its inaugural year, the center grew from a staff of fourteen to three hundred people.[48] Kennedy allotted to the program additional assistance worth $4 million, which bumped the total federal investment to $5 million. By February 1961 half of the estimated sixty-six thousand Cuban refugees in the United States were in the Miami area.[49]

To leave their country, Cubans needed a government exit permit, a U.S. visa or waiver, an airline ticket, and a passport. Most of their money and valuables stayed behind. Beginning in 1960, they had to purchase their tickets in Cuba in dollars, and they faced an ever-increasing trail of paperwork and tireless waiting for seat vacancies. At the time of their closing, the U.S. Embassy and consulate in Cuba were issuing a thousand visas per week. Visa waiver requests also flew in at the rate of 1,200 per day by late 1961. Two-thirds were approved. After the Bay of Pigs invasion on April 17, 1961, U.S. visa requirements were eased so Cubans no longer needed a valid passport when applying for visas.[50] Waivers were not just for children. José Miró Cardona, Cuba's prime minister for roughly six weeks, came with one, as did Manuel Ray Rivero, the onetime minister of public works in Castro's young government. But there was legal uncertainty with an adult waiver. Children were a different matter.[51]

If leaving on or after January 1, 1959, most Cubans could easily earn refugee status from the U.S. government with the exceptional designation "parole."[52] They pocketed identification cards and in due time were eligible to become permanent residents of the United States.[53] The reigning logic was that exiles enjoyed privileges as temporary guests, with the expectation they would return once conditions in Cuba were amenable.[54] As time wore on, however, the government grew even laxer with Cuban entries.[55] By one count, Washington had furnished four hundred thousand waivers by 1962.[56] The voyage that was thought to be temporary was winding up to be interminable.

Mayda Riopedre and her sister landed on April 7, 1961, and were sent to the Kendall Children's Home, or simply Camp Kendall.[1] Sitting on what is today Kendall Indian Hammocks Park, the shelter on sw 79th Street between sw 107th and sw 117th Avenues was leased to the cwb from Dade County for a dollar per year. Originally the segregated Dade County Children's Home—a reformatory, school, and hospital for troubled youth—the rebranded Kendall now hosted Cuban children. With space for 140 boys and girls, the five-acre facility contained classrooms and an administration building. Fernando Pruna and his wife were among the first house parents. Several Catholic orders passed through the shelter's doors over its lifespan, including the Ursuline Sisters, Piarist Fathers, and Marist Brothers until March 1963, when it was reclaimed by the county's Welfare Department.[2]

In Cuba Mayda had been a fifteen-year-old student at American Dominican Academy in Havana, an extension of the school run by the Dominican Sisters in Elkins Park, Pennsylvania. The nuns who surrounded her were all Americans. When the mother superior in Pennsylvania beckoned the nuns to return to the United States, Mayda's parents decided that sending their daughters as well would not be a bad idea. Her departure transpired in a haze of goodbyes without her parents actually telling her where she was going. Her life in Cuba, she thought, was "very American." She took classes in English and studied U.S. history, heard American shows on the radio, and watched them on television. *Hit Parade* was a favorite.

After one month at Kendall, she and her sister ended up at St. Mary's Home in Dubuque, Iowa, along with three other Pedro Pans. There Mayda went bowling for the first time. One month later, the girls were sent to Signal Mountain, Tennessee, outside of Chattanooga, and lived with Miguel Caballero and his family for two years. She retains some very pleasant memories of her time there. Her family had known the Caballeros through her grandparents in Cuba. They spoke Spanish in the Caballero home, and the family took care of the girls and arranged visas for their parents. The sisters were separated from their parents for two years, and at times it was rough. Mayda had a favorite outdoor spot where she could "look at the mountains and cry my eyes out."

She later reflected that "it was very hard because we were upper-middle-class girls." Access to ballet and piano lessons, and a French tutor had made her a "pampered" child. Mayda had to learn that in the United States one did not send clothes out to be laundered; cleaning and ironing were chores she now performed. They also faced no shortage of degrading Cuban stereotypes. "They were expecting darker," she reminisced. In line with custom, the Cuban girls already had their ears pierced, which sent shudders up the spines of Americans. Mayda dealt with her own surprises. The woman who collected the siblings at the local airport near Dubuque was pregnant and doing the errand on her own. "Shocking" is the term Mayda uses to describe her impression. The Cuba she knew would not have tolerated a pregnant woman doing such a task by herself. In the end, Mayda considers herself "lucky" and will be "forever grateful" for the Caballero family in Tennessee.[3]

For a good number of Pedro Pans, the process of leaving Cuba began in a disorienting nimbus of frightening uncertainty. Common to many is the memory of entering *la pecera* (fishbowl), a transparent glass holding room in the Havana airport, where they saw their relatives for the last time.[4] Many believed their trip north was a scholastic opportunity, that they had earned a scholarship to study in the United States. It was not unheard of; by the time of the revolution, some 1,100 Cubans were enrolling in U.S. colleges and universities each year. But Pedro Pans quickly learned that the trek demanded their sifting through truths and untruths to survive in a new environment governed by unusual norms and expectations.[5]

At the Miami airport, many had been instructed to "ask for George" after landing. Himself a Cuban American, George Guarch had lived in the United States since 1947 and worked at the CWB. He enjoyed special permission to welcome children before they entered the immigration area.[6] This gave him and other officials time to alter their documents

1. Cuban girl holding her dolls, circa 1961. Courtesy of the State Archives of Florida.

if needed. If the arrivals were too old or young for admission, spilling coffee on their papers or burning holes in them with cigarettes turned out to be an effective way to change birth dates.[7]

If unclaimed by relatives or authorized caregivers in Miami—a reality for more than half of the Pedro Pans—children entered the world of shelters and group and foster homes. Walsh's CWB joined the Children's Bureau and the Jewish Family and Children's Service (JFCS) in the triad of essential agencies for child entrants.[8] The Florida State Department of Public Welfare came onboard in February 1961 when HEW designated it the local captain of relief efforts. When the Family and Children's Division of the Miami Welfare Planning Council met to discuss unaccompanied children, it established three placement agencies: the CWB (part of the National Catholic Welfare Conference), the Dade County Children's Bureau, and the JFCS. The Child Welfare Division within Florida's Department of Public Welfare drew up custodial contracts with these organizations in addition with the United Hebrew Immigrant Aid Society (UHIAS).[9]

As the web of need sprawled, more organizations signed up. The International Rescue Committee, the Church World Service, the Catholic Relief Services, and the Protestant Latin American Emergency Committee (affiliated with the Church World Service) entered into contracts with the federal government. Their volunteers and employees met the planes, assumed temporary custody of children, and ensured that food, lodging, and limited financial assistance were available.[10] Locals were indispensable. Walsh counted five hundred people working in the program in Miami, and all but a handful were of Cuban origin.[11] Eloisa Fajardo was one such worker. She and her husband arrived from Cuba in 1962, and together they helped manage the welfare of seven hundred children between 1963 and 1965.[12]

Children were primarily placed by their religious affiliation. Most were Catholic and thus found respite under Father Walsh's organization, but placement was an interfaith effort, with requests pouring in from religious facilities around the nation. The Children's Bureau handled nonsectarian and Protestant children—some 283 were in its foster care by November 1962—while Jewish children became wards of the JFCS and the UHIAS.[13] One source estimates that a thousand Jewish children were handed over to the UHIAS, but this statistic seems dubiously high.[14] It was true that many Cuban Jews were coming to the United States as refugees, and some of them were tied to the waves that had headed to Cuba while fleeing Nazi violence in the 1930s and 1940s. The Jewish community in Cuba counted fifteen thousand people during the revolution.[15] Victor Triay estimates that Miami's Jewish community aided two-thirds of the ten thousand Cuban Jews who had gone into exile by 1962. In terms of unaccompanied minors, his numbers indicate that the JFCS and the UHIAS placed 145 children in Jewish foster homes, with 117 of them going outside Miami.[16] Not all who went to these families were Jewish themselves, however, as was the case of Yale professor Carlos Eire.[17]

Refugee care mushroomed into a byzantine government project. At the federal level, funding the Cuban Refugee Program fell on the shoulders of HEW's Social Security Administration and its Bureau of Public Assistance (later the Bureau of Family Services). Florida was to assume "responsibility for the administration of assistance and services for Cuban refugees," including child welfare. The state's Department of Public Welfare, led by Frank Craft, arranged care for unaccompanied children in contracts with licensed child-placing agencies. The federal wing began reimbursing the department for its expenditures in February 1961.[18]

Before receiving their new charge, Craft's people already had been preparing for their consequential assignment. On December 15, 1960, just as Operation Pedro Pan was getting underway, HEW held a planning conference with his office. Frances Davis, director of the Child Welfare Division within the Welfare Department, contacted the Children's Bureau after two Cuban children had appeared in a juvenile court in Miami. The court sent the pair to live with a family, but it signaled something larger was about to unfold in the Sunshine State.[19]

Craft ran his office out of Jacksonville, but HEW's regional office was in Atlanta under the authority of Wave L. Perry.[20] The purse strings of the Unaccompanied Cuban Refugee Children's Program were tied between the two. The flow chart elongated by the day. Dorothy McCrary ran the "Cuban Unit" within the Child Welfare Division, and she reported expenditures to the federal offices of the Bureau of Public Assistance and the Children's Bureau in Washington. All had been approved by the Social Security Administration's commissioner William Mitchell. The Florida Department of Welfare kept extensive communication with Walsh's CWB, the Children's Bureau of Dade County, the UHIAS, and the JFCS under the executive directorship of Leon Fisher.[21] Walsh was the fulcrum of all the major players going all the way up to Katherine

CUBAN REFUGEE EMERGENCY CENTER
223 N. W. 3rd AVE. • MIAMI, FLORIDA

CARRY THIS CARD ON YOUR PERSON
AT ALL TIMES

THIS REGISTRATION CARD IS TO BE USED FOR OFFICIAL PURPOSES ONLY
AND IS NOT TO BE USED AS AN ENDORSEMENT OF THE CHARACTER OR
INTEGRITY OF THE BEARER.

ADC BUSINESS FORMS • MIAMI, FLA.

2. Cuban Refugee Emergency Center registration card (front). Courtesy of the State Archives of Florida.

REGISTRATION CARD   FILE NO
NAME
LOCAL ADDRESS   Phone No.
DATE INTERVIEWED   Interviewer
RESETTLEMENT AGENCY VISITS:

COOPERATING AGENCIES:

Signature

3. Cuban Refugee Emergency Center registration card (back). Courtesy of the State Archives of Florida.

Brownell Oettinger, the director of the Children's Bureau in Washington DC, who regularly extolled his work.[22]

Into this labyrinthine bureaucracy entered the Cuban refugees, lone children included. Adults needed to verify their financial resources and family status, undergo a medical examination, and speak with a social worker. Fulfilling these requirements led to the coveted blue card certifying their registration at the Cuban Refugee Emergency Center and made them eligible for assistance.

The mammoth venture relied on untold thousands of volunteers and professionals of varying licensure and motivations—statisticians, teachers, churchgoers, clergy, file clerks, switchboard operators, health care personnel, and swarms of pencil pushers and schleppers in churches, schools, offices, processing centers, and neighborhood associations—all dedicated to throwing a life raft to refugees.[23]

Unclaimed unaccompanied children went in another direction. Of these refugees, the CWB took in the lion's share. At the end of 1965, 7,956 children had received either temporary or extended shelter. The CWB had served 6,971; the Children's Bureau, 347; the JFCS, 117 (many of whom were later transferred to the UHIAS); the UHIAS, 28; and the Florida Department of Public Welfare, 493.[24] By December 31, 1965, the Department of Public Welfare's ledger had spent more than $25 million on children in foster care and group homes, and an additional $1 million on special services and transportation. Frustrating was the fact that the department could not tally accurate figures on the total number of children it had serviced; instead, it only could cast a wide estimate of between 13,000 and 15,000.[25]

The sizable web of CWB transit centers laid most of the groundwork for the entrée of children into their new lives. When they arrived the day after Christmas in 1960, the Aquino siblings were taken to St. Joseph's Villa at NW Seventh Street and Twenty-Ninth Avenue. Other children followed. Staffed by the Sisters of St. Joseph, the center housed children under the age of twelve until 1970.[26] A few days later, Walsh sent boys to the Ferré House, named for Maurice Ferré, the future mayor of Miami, who donated one of his father's properties for lodgers. Alternatively known as the Cuban Boys' Home and Casa Carrión, named eponymously for the Cuban couple Angel and Nina Carrión who later settled in as its house parents, the Ferré House furnished twenty-six beds when it opened at 175 SE Fifteenth Road. The former Ruston rector James Baker and his wife were its first guardians. They watched over young boys whom they themselves collected from the airport.[27]

Some of the camps and homes were comfortable, while others were horrendous, especially as the number of children grew. The shelter Mayda Riopedre and her sister went to—Camp Kendall—was, by some measures, dreadfully inhospitable. It was crowded and had lines for the showers and toilets. "There was no privacy," remembered one inhabitant, "so I did not defecate until I went out on weekends. I would hold it in."[28] But Kendall was quaint compared to the most infamous camp for boys that opened in July 1961, Camp Matecumbe. Named for Florida Native Americans who converted to Christianity in the eighteenth century, the 150 acres of land had been purchased by Archbishop Joseph Patrick Hurley in 1954 and sat at 137th Avenue and SW 120th Street amid a pastoral backdrop of forests and sprawling tomato fields. The La Salle Brothers, headed by Father Francisco Palá, took direction of the camp. Matecumbe was designed to be a modest abode for up to a hundred boarders, but it soon hemorrhaged, forcing the Department of Public Welfare to approve the camp's use of army tents for the masses of children, whose numbers swelled to five hundred. High school courses were available as was an Olympic-sized swimming pool. When the tents and excruciatingly long lines for showers became unbearable, a new building was erected. It closed in October 1964, when Bishop Carroll ordered all shelters for teenage boys—St. Raphael's Hall, Jesuit Boys' Home, and Matecumbe—to be consolidated into Opa-locka.[29]

Matecumbe's reputation was unequivocally one of disrepute. Twelve-year-old Carmen Valdivia classified it as a "savage place" after her transport dropped boys there while taking girls to Florida City.[30] Hazing was frequent. There were weighty disciplinary rules and no phone calls to Cuba. The tents operating as makeshift classrooms reached temperatures of 110 degrees in April. Truancy was common, and at least one Pedro Pan joined Mexican laborers picking tomatoes nearby to make extra money to pay for his parents' visas.[31]

Ed Canler kept horrid recollections of Matecumbe into adulthood. Initially separated from his brother at age ten, his early days at the camp were spent crying "uncontrollably for hours." Things improved when the brothers were reunited at an orphanage in Lansing, Michigan, where he could write to his parents and speak to them by telephone. The family would be complete again in Los Angeles in 1962 just before the missile crisis.[32]

The Matecumbe shelter was also taxing for Walsh. All kinds of negative reports and requests lined his desk. It lacked biology and English offerings, gave out insufficient homework, and meted questionable discipline.[33] The pall of Matecumbe even reached HEW secretary Ribicoff's desk, when he learned of the camp's insufficient bathroom facilities and the little protection it offered from the outside elements.[34]

As more children arrived, the terrain of shelters expanded. In September 1961 the Jesuit Boys' Home opened under Walsh's direction with sixty beds. The home's name changed to Whitehall and accommodated long-term placements. In June 1966 the shelter was once again renamed the Cuban Boys' Home and made room for displaced Jesuit boys. To abate some of the overcrowding, thirty-five kids were moved to St. Raphael's Hall.[35]

4. Group portrait of Cuban Boys' Home residents, 1961. Father Bryan Walsh is the priest on the left. Courtesy of Barry University Archives and Special Collections, Miami Shores, Florida.

In October 1961 Florida City opened at 155 NW Fourteenth Street. A cluster of eighty apartments leased by the CWB, it first lodged girls and boys under the age of twelve. Licensed from the Florida Welfare Department and roomy enough to quarter seven hundred children, Florida City had its own elementary school staffed by the Sisters of St. Philip Neri from Cuba. But here, too, space became tight. Yvonne Conde estimates that the facility bulged to more than 1,100 children. It closed in June 1966 when most children had aged out of the program or had been reunited with family members or authorized caregivers.[36] A 1962 proposal to survey its conditions reveals that the camp contained a population split into four groups: boys ages six to nine and ten to thirteen years old; and girls ages six to eleven and twelve to eighteen years old. But there were cases of caring for children younger than six and older than eighteen years old.[37] As was custom, fresh residents

5. Florida City housing, circa 1961. Courtesy of Barry University Archives and Special Collections, Miami Shores, Florida.

had their documents and health examined, and they received immunizations if necessary.[38]

Elly Chovel and her sister endured the camp for three and a half months, and they remembered twelve girls sharing a single room. Chovel, a founding member of the Operation Pedro Pan Group, previously had never been separated from her parents. From the camp, she and her sister were assigned to a foster home of a Costa Rican woman in Buffalo; then they went to another foster home until they saw their parents again three and a half years later.[39]

In the van that took her from the airport to Florida City, Pury Lopez Santiago thought she was going to the jungle. Her instincts took over. "You gotta go with the program here," she told herself. Thick skin was needed. Some young people did not adjust well. Impossible to ignore was the open grief and worry that permeated the atmosphere. Etched into Pury's memory is the day her bunkmate found out her father had died in Cuba. The inconsolable grief kept Pury up at night.[40]

6. Opa-locka dormitories. Courtesy of Barry University Archives and Special Collections, Miami Shores, Florida.

In 1964 the CWB consolidated its boys' shelters into Opa-locka, a stretch of Seminole land that in the twentieth century was reconfigured into a military site. The Central Intelligence Agency (CIA) had used its airfield in the operation to bring down President Jacobo Árbenz Guzmán of Guatemala in 1954, and the U.S. government mulled over enlisting it again for the Bay of Pigs invasion in 1961. When it became a shelter in 1963 for boys in the seventh to eleventh grades, it was still an active air force base. Pedro Pans were expected to conform to military rules and were restricted in their movements. Opa-locka was a controversial selection. After the missile crisis, Father Walsh wanted to distribute the children to fewer shelters, but Bishop Carroll preferred one large camp. Opa-locka enclosed six buildings that could domicile five hundred people. Unpopular with most, including Walsh, it lacked dignity and functionality due to its barracks-style open showers and dormitories.

When it closed in June 1966, the remaining twenty-five residents moved to the leased apartment of the Cuban Boys' Home. There, Father Walsh later watched over its inhabitants until the program's closing in 1980.[41]

Camp capacity was a chronic problem. The Dade County Health Department directed the shelters to cap their totals at just over 1,500 residents.[42] But the numbers kept changing. Walsh believed the collective limit to be 1,200 children. The buildings were only to house kids temporarily, but then reality set in.[43] Camp life took a direction of its own, constantly abuzz with volunteers, social workers, state officials, church representatives, and anywhere from dozens to hundreds of children making their way between Spanish and English. It was a strange dichotomy of benevolence and hardship. Cuban minors received care and attention, but corporeal punishment was also a fixture. The Latin music singer Willy Chirino remembered that St. Raphael's boarders were paddled when they misbehaved.[44] Siblings were sometimes split up, and relatives and friends had limited visiting rights.[45] Eight-year-old María Dolores Madariaga wound up in Florida City, while her brother was routed to Matecumbe. Like Ed Canler, she cried intermittently for a week.[46]

Of the rolling roster of staff and volunteers, Walsh was the only permanent member of the program.[47] Following Catholic protocol, he implemented a taxing regimen of behavioral control in his Americanization project. Every hour of a Pedro Pan's day was planned. At Matecumbe, kids woke up to attend Mass at 6:30 a.m. and afterward could expect a period of sports and recreation. The boys attended classes on-site, and the day ended with the holy rosary and lights out at 10 p.m.[48] Children received handbooks of dos and don'ts in Spanish and English that stipulated the rules prescribed by the CWB and the Florida Department of Public Welfare. The handbook at the Cuban Boys' Home stressed "self-discipline" and "self-control," and reminded children that they were the benefactors of divine intervention: "In the Providence of God, you have been separated from your parents and loved ones. In His Providence also, you have been given the opportunity, unknown to so many of your countrymen today, of growing up in a free country, where you may be educated in the knowledge and love of God and learn to live as a free man."[49]

Cuban children were to be the modern Pilgrims. One sees hints of earlier sermons on the divine errand waged by God's elect, reminiscent of when John Winthrop intoned such a mission onboard the *Arbella* and told his followers in 1630 that they would birth a New Israel, a "City upon a Hill" for Europe to follow. Anti-communist refugees were the new Israelites in America.

Molding children into proper proselytes meant following religious ideals and conforming to standards of Cold War propriety. Regulation took several forms. Godliness and discipline were sacrosanct, but so, too, were exhibiting model behavior in public spaces and understanding gender norms of young men and women. Exceedingly important was exercising self-control of one's sexuality. Throughout Pedro Pan records are noted concerns of sexual immodesty and abnormality. One Matecumbe administrator clamored that some of the boys' weekend jaunts ended with them wearing "very tight trousers and red shirts which are not furnished by our Program." Fearing the clothes were "being provided by homosexuals," the administrator urged the CWB to investigate what the boys were doing on their weekends, just as Florida City was keeping tabs on its girls.[50] Queer intimacy was an ongoing worry. Data recorded by social workers, administrators, and health care professionals lies mostly occluded from public visibility. But there is evidence in routine correspondence of sensitive topics, and above all homosexuality raised red flags. When one professional recommended hormone injections for boys displaying "feminine characteristics," for example, Walsh promptly sent an advisory to shelters that such "remedies" were not to be administered unless under specific orders by a physician.[51] Another camp regulator bade that Matecumbe boys be disallowed to take showers during school hours or late at night. The mandate might have been an attempt to minimize truancy and regulate sleep schedules, or it was restraint of another kind, possibly to deter trysts between residents.[52] A priest from Matecumbe notified Walsh that some boys were spending their weekends at a drugstore on Flagler Street, where they were "misbehaving" and "associating with undesirables."[53] All the CCP's director of social services Dorothea Sullivan could do was suggest greater clarity on weekend privileges.[54]

Camps mounted a level of surveillance that would have been newly intrusive to most of the Pedro Pans, who were obliged to follow standards of white, middle-class heterosexuality grounded in religious morals. Camp officials expressed Cold War anxieties of the day in which homosexuality was viewed as a form of perversion, sexual deviance, and psychological illness. In addition to reports that mentioned problems with theft and even attempted suicide at Matecumbe, for instance, there were also "homosexual incidents" that included young people dressing in drag. Elsewhere are notes on the children's physical and cognitive abnormalities. "Low-dangling ears, back of head flat appearing of a slight somewhat microcephalic type, may point out that he is an organic mentally defective boy," scribbled one profiler. The substandard IQ, the document continues, may have been caused by the use of forceps during childbirth. The patient was treated at a clinical school in Miami, but before long he ran away, only to be detained by police. After displaying "low intelligence" and "schizoid temperament," the boy went to a residential treatment center in Texas.[55]

Frances Davis of the Florida Department of Welfare wrote the Child Welfare League of America in December 1964 for help with placing Cuban children with "severe adjustment problems." Specifically, wrote Davis, the CWB was trying to "find resources for six boys who are deeply involved in homosexual activities." Four had undergone psychiatric evaluation, and the bureau was looking to foster care as an option. But for another fifteen-year-old, Davis wanted to locate a "treatment institution," which may have meant corrective therapy to "cure" homosexuality. The boy had been arrested in the company of gay men and had admitted to extensive same-sex intimacy. Now he was in county detention while the CWB searched for alternatives. It considered the Devereux School in Victoria, Texas, where other Cuban children now lived. Another option was Lincoln Hall in Lincolndale, New York, a boys' home since 1863 when the U.S. Civil War was producing swaths of orphaned children. Complicating the issue for the department and the league was the language barrier and the fact that neither institution could guarantee "resources for treatment of boys with such extreme overt homosexual problems."[56]

House parents, social workers, doctors, and psychologists studied their residents' habits and thoughts, especially those of the young men. Continually under microscopes were the children's whereabouts and their behavior. Punishment came in multitiered forms, from corporeal methods to losing one's allowance. At St. Raphael's Hall, if a boy was absent from prayers, he then had to pay a ten-cent fine.[57] Arbitrary rules became codified at the whims of staff. Sullivan wrote Walsh expressing alarm over punitive fines, for it was not clear where this money went. "Apparently considerable sums have been collected over the past two years and there are dark rumors among the employees as to where this money goes," she exclaimed.[58]

Behavioral excellence was paramount, for at any moment a child could be transferred to another institution.[59] Attire had to be "clean at all times." T-shirts, jeans, and other casual wear were frowned upon.[60] The dictates of 1950s parochialism made a curious connection between morality and clothing, and Walsh avowed that "psychologists have found that a high standard of appropriate clothing results in a correspondingly high standard of behavior."[61] It extended to appropriate hairstyles, too. Sullivan informed Walsh that one judge had sentenced three Opa-locka boys to haircuts.[62]

Arbiters of adjustment placed weighty importance on cultural excursions, for proper public conduct was a measure of appropriate assimilation. One social worker was optimistic about refugee children when she beamed: "On the whole, they no longer do these things which so disturbed the audiences at first but behave most properly."[63] Girls were subjected to routine oversight in their quests to fit in. After hearing complaints of obese children, the program conducted a study and found that one-third of the girls living at Florida City were overweight. Too much food and not enough exercise were to blame. Their health was a worry, but so, too, was their appearance.[64] In 1973 adolescent residents at the Cuban Girls' Home were told to "dress properly and adequately avoid extremes in style and make-up," which meant donning an "attractive fashion." Mass was still compulsory, and their phone calls were limited to fifteen minutes. The young women could not own cars but were able to sign up for driving lessons. Prohibited from outings on weekdays, except in rare instances, the young coeds required chaperone escorts on weekends and were to be home by 11 p.m.[65]

Shelter authorities enjoyed indomitable power to determine where a child went and how he or she was handled. Children gauged "underdeveloped," "maladjusted," or "educationally backward" were sent to special facilities at the recommendation of the administration.[66] From

Opa-locka, Brother Maximiliano Mediavilla warned Walsh about violence at the camp and blamed religious waywardness: "One who is morally lost is a responsibility of unlimited proportions." Perturbed by some unruly "delinquents," Mediavilla recommended their institutionalization elsewhere.[67] Walsh pushed back by saying that the program needed to provide for all. "If one bad boy is going to contaminate 100 good boys, then the 100 good boys are very weak," he reasoned. Walsh also had misgivings about how such dismissals would affect the health of the church. "Every time that a Catholic school expels a boy, that boy and often his family is lost to the Church. I think Catholic schools have a very bad history in this regard," he retorted.[68]

While there were staff members with professional training, much of the perennial operations landed on the plate of untrained volunteers. Showdowns were always on the horizon. When Miguel Estades Navarro, a houseparent at Kendall and later Opa-locka, raised a red flag about shelter conditions, he received only a consolatory response from Chancellor (later the auxiliary bishop) John J. Fitzpatrick of the Miami Diocese.[69] There were also mounting inter-order disputes among the Catholic religious. The Cuban Marist Brothers stationed at Kendall and Matecumbe stumbled upon such deteriorating conditions to the extent that rampant "immorality" and "corruption" prevented them from wanting to go on teaching. Walsh heard from the group. "Abuses" were also made evident in the boys' letters. Specifics were not mentioned but were "grievous" enough to be taken into account. (More on what these abuses might have been is detailed in chapter 11.)[70]

Three years later, the Marists moved from Kendall and Matecumbe to Opa-locka, where they meted out strict punishments. But at the camp they must have ruffled too many feathers, because in short order they were scuttled from the Miami Diocese and replaced with Jesuits. Walsh wanted the Marists gone from Opa-locka and left a check for travel expenses. The facts surrounding this excommunication are unknown. It may have been a simple administrative change. In September 1964 Walsh also closed St. Raphael's and moved those lodgers to Opa-locka, and the Jesuits also joined the population of 240 boys. This was part of the move to consolidate the shelters as the number of children diminished. When the Marist Brothers left, some of the boys protested, going as far as to smash lightbulbs and windows in demonstration.[71] The dismissal of the Marists earned protests from the group Alumni of Marists in Exile regarding the slander and defamation the priests had suffered. Walsh attempted to mitigate the anger by explaining that the camps had merged, requiring structural adjustments. The Marists themselves had wanted to leave, he pointed out, and when they later changed their minds, it was too late.[72]

Meanwhile, among the meeting minutes are mentions of salaries, priorities for special needs children, and questions surrounding learning aptitude and behavioral adjustment. There are medical analyses and commentary on serious conditions, such as the profiles of two Pedro Pan brothers who ate "compulsively." Staff further feared that one of the brothers may have developed testicular cancer. The contracting agency returned the pair to Miami and contacted their father in Cuba about a possible operation.[73] The CWB worked closely with public health professionals, pediatricians, psychologists, and social workers who surveyed all lodgers and recorded their disabilities and their emotional and behavioral difficulties. There is the occasional mention of "crippled children," "speech defects," and an unsettling frequency of "mentally retarded" children. One psychologist said the numbers of afflictions were in line with averages in the greater population, but the rate of emotionally disturbed cases in Cuban children was higher.[74]

Social work was a burgeoning field available to women, who became fixtures in relief agencies, orphanages, and government organizations such as the Children's Bureau.[75] Carolina Garzón was a social worker at Opa-locka. Her papers give us a peek at what camp professionals dealt with and how they made sense of it. Originally an educator in Cuba, Garzón received her master's degree in social work from Florida State University in 1965 after working with the CWB. She was an ally of Walsh's in his handling of the refugee children, but some of the treatment she witnessed bothered her tremendously.[76] She took exception when one boy complained of the public shaming he endured when a counselor made him stand in front of a wall for a prolonged period because he had stood up without permission during study hour.[77] Other boys lost their daily meals. When punishments of this type became more common, children sought her advocacy. She recommended "humane"

methods of reprimand that would "not leave rancor in a boy's soul."
It was worrisome that some of her fellow counselors, in an effort to
curry favor with upper-level administrators, had no compunction
about excessive castigation.[78]

The footprints left by Garzón lead to some of the dark corners seques-
tered behind the veneer of success that the Cuban Children's Program
wanted to project. There is the report of one boy who arrived on a Pan
American flight on February 28, 1962, along with his sister and two
younger brothers, one of whom died due to a preexisting illness in
the Florida City shelter. The boy and his surviving brother went to a
foster home in Peoria, Illinois, but then the boy returned to Opa-locka
in May 1963 because of his congenital heart condition.[79] Garzón also
noted a sixteen-year-old Afro-Cuban from Banes in eastern Cuba.
Upon arrival on August 18, 1962, he went to Matecumbe and from there
transferred to Helena, Montana, but was later returned to Miami and
assigned to Opa-locka. He had a father in Cuba and a mother in New
York City, but she did not have the money to care for her son because
she was consumed with tending to his sister. The boy wanted to stay
in Montana, Garzón wrote, and after three weeks in Opa-locka, he
briefly fled with a friend, only to return the following day. He came
back in an "emotional state" with "some paranoic [sic] features with
aggressive tendencies."[80]

The social sciences had yet to develop appropriate models for dealing with unaccompanied children caught in the fluctuation of parental
separation and adjustment. Young people were diagnosed with conditions and prescribed treatments that today would seem grievously
erroneous to most childhood professionals. Too often the children's
lack of English and cultural literacy translated to their being deemed
"underdeveloped." Eighteen-year-olds sat in sixth-grade classrooms.
Children appearing "very nervous" automatically received medication.[81]
One clinical psychologist warned against the growing practice of glue
sniffing because it represented a "serious psychological problem" whose
"only possible solution is deep psychotherapy."[82]

One random evaluation of seventeen boys from Matecumbe found
only four to be "of mental capacity and vocational aptitudes." Three displayed "acting out behavior" such as running away, theft, or "abnormal

sexual behavior," and ten demonstrated behavior ranging from "poor adjustment to camp" to "school failure."[83] Matecumbe had other problems. There were complaints to Reverend Francisco Palá, the camp's director, that the dining services were "undesirable" due to the lack of hot meals and the staff's rude behavior toward the boys.[84] The young men made their grievances known in a self-published pamphlet titled "Forja," a creation Walsh tolerated but did not much like.[85]

Losing contact with one's parents and being thrown into overcrowded camp conditions could torment a young refugee. It was impossible to predict how a child would react. How to adjust? How to deal with the absence of familial love now affecting their emotional health? Studies on such displacements were just beginning to materialize. Most administrators had the best intentions for the children, but they were taxed with burdens and duties without proper training and knowledge. Some Cubans were defiant. The 125 Matecumbe boys in 1964 visited the camp's infirmary 1,115 times in January of that year alone. With an average of nearly ten visits per resident, the infirmary was a way to veer from the day's drudgery or maybe escape from something unwelcome.[86] They also offered resistance to the forced American parochialism. Feeling out of place with the new constraining credos of social rectitude, the children lashed out.

Growing one's hair, skipping school, or breaking curfew were acts of a great refusal to embrace circumstances not of their own making or to succumb to emotions they could not fully flush out because there was no framework for understanding them. Defiance was cathartic.

Despite the overall pall of the shelters, a great many Pedro Pans retain fond memories and associations. Jay Castano, for example, was in the seventh grade when he arrived in 1962. In Cuba he attended the all-boys' Felipe Poey School near the University of Havana, one mile from his family's house. Originally from the province of Las Villas, the family moved to Havana after his father died to be close to his older brother. They gravitated toward the promises of Fidel Castro as the Batista regime was coming to an end. But when the regime closed schools and confiscated businesses, the family saw Castro as a "wolf in sheep's clothing." At Castano's public school, a teacher tried to recruit him to serve the neighborhood watch group, Committee for

7. Boys at Camp Matecumbe performing a gymnastics routine, circa 1962–64. Courtesy of Barry University Archives and Special Collections, Miami Shores, Florida.

the Defense of the Revolution. Castano was only eleven years old. The teacher persisted and promised Castano's mother that if he worked diligently, the young Castano could study in the Soviet Union. He devoted himself to the mission, thinking "the motherland needs to be defended by all of us against the Yankee Imperialism." At this point, his mother began gathering the necessary documents to transport him to Miami. Communist brainwashing was a fear of hers as was the daily imprisonment and executions of the *Batistianos* (Batista's supporters) airing on television.

Castano accepted his fate in Miami with more ease because his mother and brother told him they would come soon, and if he stayed in Cuba, he might never see them again. Armed with a CWB waiver bearing Walsh's signature, the young Cuban traveled to Miami and went to Kendall.

The staff was friendly. A Marist Brother from Spain lisped with an accent that reminded the boy of his recently deceased father, who had moved to Cuba in 1936 during the Spanish Civil War. Kendall's cluster of buildings was clean and inviting. The infirmary had a doctor's office that doled out aspirin, Alka-Seltzer, and Bengay cream to relieve mosquito bites. The boys went to Matecumbe once a week to go swimming, and Castano treated himself to milk and cookies on a near-nightly basis.[87]

3 | FROM CAMPS TO RESETTLEMENT

On Valentine's Day in 1962, Pury Lopez moved from a Miami shelter to a foster home in a working-class Italian American neighborhood in Utica, New York. She was different from many of her compatriots. She loved the snow. "I made a splash; they had never seen a Cuban," she recounted. Her foster mother was Cuban born, so there was some Spanish in the home. Still, Pury was an outsider. To this day, she is mystified by her new neighbors' giddiness in showing her how to use ketchup, as if she had never used the condiment in Cuba.[1] As refugees continued to inundate Florida, their resettlement outside of the state turned into a high priority. Children needed proper homes.

There is no consensus on why Pedro Pan was the chosen moniker for the secretive initiative or why "Peter" became "Pedro." Most link the tale about the "boy who could fly" to the Cuban children's leaving aboard airplanes. Father Walsh credited the Miami broadcaster Ralph Renick with using the term as a code word when discussing the program.[2] Walsh and the U.S. government tried to keep Operation Pedro Pan under wraps, but in February 1962, it floated into the public's consciousness in an article from the *Cleveland Plain Dealer*. Then on March 8, readers of the *Miami Herald* learned of "Operation Exodus" when it told the "dramatic story of the flight of Cuban children." Now "80 normal, well-adjusted Cuban teenagers" were living in St. Raphael's Hall. Another 37 had wound up in Portland, Oregon, with some in foster homes and others at St. Mary's Home for Boys and similar boarding houses owned by Catholic Charities. The following day, the *Herald* adopted the name that would stick—Operation Pedro Pan—in reference to the well-known story. It seemed an appropriate allusion to describe the children's flight from "Castro's Red Cuba" to the elysian fields of Miami or Evansville, Indiana. It turns out a good number of children went to Indiana. Thirty had made their way to St. Vincent's Orphanage in Vincennes, a town flanked by the Wabash River along the Indiana-Illinois border. The *Herald* was optimistic: "God willing, they will not stay too long."[3]

Word quickly spread that everyday Americans were pitching in to succor Cuban children.[4] Until now, media outlets had mostly complied with the bid by Walsh and HEW to keep the program clandestine to protect the identity of the children and of their families in Cuba. Reporters avoided photographing or directly interviewing the children, and when they did, they omitted details of their passages.[5] But evidence of a blooming program cropped up in local news stories across the nation. One outlet featured a handful of Cuban teenage boys in Don Bosco Boys' Home in Cottonport, Louisiana. Careful to block out their faces in the photograph, the article hailed Cottonport's "superior educational advantages," with the boys acquiring rural skills of caring for chickens and cows, and transporting eggs, butter, and milk from farms to homes.[6]

But word of mouth spiraled beyond control, and the media did not always respect the policy of secrecy.[7] Walsh and Secretary Ribicoff had no choice but to draw up a press release appealing to Americans to care for the unaccompanied children. With more national attention came additional funding from Washington. In June 1962 Congress allotted $38.5 million to the Cuban Refugee Program. The following year saw a bump to $70 million, with one-fifth of it apportioned for unaccompanied minors. Walsh was receiving over four thousand weekly requests for visa waivers when U.S. airspace closed in October 1962. Though impossible to verify, as many as fifty thousand children may have been stranded with waivers in hand. In March 1963 the *New York Times* reported that 14,072 children had made the solo trek.[8]

The camps were designed to be a temporary solution. They were, after all, "transitional shelters." Distributing children across the country belonged to the larger project of resettling Cubans both to ease the burden on Florida and to Americanize the newcomers far from Miami's Little Havana. Between 1961 and 1968, the CRP relocated nearly 206,000 people, with over half of them going to New York, New Jersey, and California.[9] Not all refugees received entitlements; one first had to register in Miami. We know that some older unaccompanied children were excluded from these benefits. There were also reports of kids who

8. Monsignor Walsh visits Cuban boys studying at St. Benedict's College in Kansas, 1964. Courtesy of Barry University Archives and Special Collections, Miami Shores, Florida.

received immediate care from a relative upon arrival and were later ineligible for subsidies when the relative could no longer keep them.[10]

The thousands of youngsters who did go through the proper channels were sent to contracted childcare facilities in two hundred cities across forty-eight states and U.S. territories.[11] Much of this work fell on the shoulders of Monsignor Walsh. Within days, weeks, or months of touching down, children under the CWB became wards of Catholic Charities anywhere from Brooklyn to Ashtabula, Ohio.[12]

Contracts were drawn up between the Florida State Department of Public Welfare, acting on behalf of HEW, and participant agencies, which permitted the sheltering of children until the age of nineteen. Each month the CWB received a government check for the days of care rendered the previous month at a fixed per diem rate.[13] Accredited homes initially earned $6.50 a day per child in group care, while foster families could depend on $5.50 a day to cover board, room, clothing, medical and dental care, and incidental expenses. As the program wore on, compensation rose, so that by 1972 the going rate reached $9.00 and $6.00, respectively.[14] Once a young person reached her or his nineteenth birthday, the payments ceased.[15] Shifting a child from foster to group care would alter the line item on the bill to the government.[16] As the number of children in care decreased, agencies ended their participation. By 1964, for example, none existed in Arkansas, so families petitioning that state to foster the children were denied.[17]

Over five thousand children would be relocated outside of Florida.[18] Disseminating them throughout the country's towns and cities promised to relieve the burden on the state's assistance programs and advance the cause of anti-communist democracy and racial tolerance. Refugees were future Americans. Newsstands and mailboxes filled with testaments to their triumphant dispersal and success stories. The CRP called on U.S. residents to sponsor Cubans and "fulfill their faith in freedom." During one Thanksgiving holiday, the program thanked Americans for aiding the refugees in their "escape from the oppressions of communism."[19] Through the Cubans' testimonials, Americans learned of their country anew. They saw the photograph of a Cuban girl wearing a cowboy hat in Farmers Branch, Texas, who was fully resettled thanks to Christ Methodist Church.[20] Another refugee in Sigourney, Iowa, was thankful that the town had "opened its arms," gushing that "people there are my friends" and promising that because refugees had "first-hand experience" with communism they knew "how best to defend democracy."[21]

The *Nevada Register* ran an exposé on thirty-nine children in Reno under the supervision of Reverend Charles Shallow, the director of the local Catholic Charities. Forced to live initially in a high school gymnasium, the young settlers ranged from ages ten to fifteen years old and were enrolled in area schools.[22] Walsh asked churches across the country to "involve themselves in such a gratifying Christian endeavor." He encouraged clergy to insert a blurb about Cuban children in their sermons.[23] Enthusiasm spread. The superintendent of Catholic schools in Green Bay, Wisconsin, beseeched: "Tell them to send us a lot more of those children; we love them."[24]

And so they came. But as so often happens, the plans looked better on paper than they did in practice. Communication fell through

9. A social worker talking with two boys at Camp Matecumbe, 1962. Courtesy of Barry University Archives and Special Collections, Miami Shores, Florida.

the cracks. Walsh was frustrated that some agencies failed to notify the bureau when they switched a child from a foster home to a group home or vice versa. Sometimes the only way to know of the shift was the change in billing. Frighteningly, it was not always clear where a boy or girl was in a given moment.[25] Homes and orphanages also were made to deal with newfound difficulties. The placement of Cubans often called for the hiring of a bilingual social worker and additional professionals trained in multiple child health services.

Some agencies failed in their agreements and returned the children to Miami, a practice Walsh firmly discouraged. The goal was to have young persons "removed without damage," but when resettlement did not work out, the kids went back to the shelters.[26]

In one instance, Brother Mediavilla advised Walsh that boys coming back from Allentown, Pennsylvania, appeared "nervous and confused." On another occasion, boys returning from Alexandria, Virginia, told of situations bordering on criminal, where the presence of knives and guns were an everyday matter.[27] Criminality roosted closer to home

10. Father Bryan O. Walsh (*center, smiling with glasses*) at Camp Matecumbe, circa 1961. Courtesy of Barry University Archives and Special Collections, Miami Shores, Florida.

too. Walsh lamented to Bishop Carroll that several Matecumbe residents had been involved "in minor scrapes with the law."[28] The young priest tried to improve the camp's environment by piling on additional restrictions. Young men were to attend class with shaved or combed hair while wearing polished footwear and collared shirts. Out of the question were T-shirts and tennis shoes.[29]

Minor roadblocks in moving the children could descend into havoc. Such was the case when welfare authorities in Montana remitted children to a family home lacking proper certification. The director of the Catholic Charities in Helena, Monsignor Daniel B. Harrington, was accused of negligence, and the complaint reached the desk of Senate majority leader Mike Mansfield (D-MT) and Secretary Ribicoff. Incredibly, only one social worker was tasked with overseeing some one hundred children.[30] James Flanagan of Montana Catholic Charities welcomed the young refugees as the diocese urged its fifty thousand parishioners across Helena, Anaconda, and Whitefish to accommo-

11. The Oberweiser family of Anaconda, Montana, fostered Reinaldo Fong (*back, second from left*) and Oscar Fong (*front, far right*). Courtesy of the Diocese of Helena.

date them. Walsh's titanic Catholic network assumed responsibility of more than 80 percent of the unaccompanied children, and the church had a massive communications apparatus, with newspapers delivering headlines to 25 million readers across the nation. In Helena, Monsignor Harrington petitioned residents to take up the cause: "To hearken to the need of these Cuban youths at this critical time is not only a real act of charity, but true patriotism at its best." In the state capital, most children found refuge at St. Joseph's Home or Brondel Hall. Oscar and Reinaldo Fong were in this group. Their father was a Chinese immigrant who found stable work in Cuba's hotel industry at the end of World

War I. Oscar and Reinaldo were taken in by the Oberweiser family in Anaconda, where they learned to play baseball and football.[31]

Two hundred miles north, however, the people of Whitefish were more averse to the impulsive and Spanish-speaking Cubans they found in their midst. Seventeen-year-old Oscar Torres and two other Cuban teenagers lived with the Bernardi family, which had lost its license to operate a care center. The foster mother cracked down on the boys' behavior and curtailed their privileges. Occasionally they were relegated to the supervision of their teenage foster sister. They complained about their shoddy circumstances. After his high school graduation, Torres was sent back to Matecumbe saddled with accusations of orneriness. The Whitefish High School principal Russell Giesy—a decorated World War II veteran with a Bronze Star and a Purple Heart—intervened on the young man's behalf and wrote Monsignor Harrington and Senator Mansfield. Upon his return to Matecumbe, Torres discovered a completely different atmosphere. The camp had surged from 140 to 431 children, and he now had to sleep on the floor under a tent besieged by mosquitoes. He wrote a friend and implored, "Try to help me please."[32]

The history of Operation Pedro Pan is rife with such tales, but the voluminous catalog of memories is mixed. Many remember the program with fondness and admiration even though they had to contend with extraordinary adjustments. One experienced exhilaration as well as sadness upon landing in Helena and seeing snow for the first time. Tears would immediately freeze. María Cristina Romero associated Colorado with the wild west because it bordered Kansas and Oklahoma. Her new home in the Queen of Heaven Orphanage in Denver was run by the Missionary Sisters of the Sacred Heart. Thoroughly inculcated with images from Hollywood westerns, Romero was "petrified" at the thought of happening upon Indians. As a blonde-haired, blue-eyed girl, she was convinced she would be scalped. But it was she who became the outsider, one of thirty resettled in May 1962. The nuns had steeled the other children by telling them that Cubans were "wild" and "black," and "didn't know how to wear shoes."[33]

In more dire instances, some Pedro Pans landed in institutions reserved for what caregivers in the 1960s called emotionally disturbed or delinquent children. There was the Randall House in Chicago, Baker

Hall in Buffalo, and the Devereux School, which had sites across the nation, many under Catholic control.[34] Walsh claimed that no children were placed in such buildings. "This," he wrote, "would not have been permitted under state law."[35] But Cuban children did bob up in such locales. Onboard a KLM flight destined for Jamaica but with a layover in Miami, the future artist Ana Mendieta and her sister, Raquel, landed on September 11, 1961. Their paperwork indicated they were going to study in Jamaica, but that was never the plan. They were told they would see their parents again in one year. After a relatively pleasant period at Kendall, they were sent to St. Mary's orphanage in Dubuque, Iowa, run by Franciscan nuns. Raquel remembered a lot of ignorance in the Midwest. They thought "people in Cuba lived in trees and didn't wear clothes and didn't have television and had never seen a ballpoint pen."

Then they learned their new home was an institution for children with histories of crime and violence. Some had faced abandonment, and others displayed problematic behavior, earning the attention of authorities. It was not easy to move from a middle-class home to an orphanage with girls who had experienced knife fights, gas station robberies, or the trauma of rape. The sisters were not allowed to eat meals together. Their mail was censored, and for punishment they were locked in closets for long periods. They felt themselves becoming violent. From there, they were transferred to a German American foster family with eight kids, where they carried the tag "dirty Cuban refugees." After six months of living as servants who cleaned the house and washed dishes, the sisters petitioned to return to the orphanage. Their nomadic existence continued. They went to a private school run by nuns, followed by a state orphanage in 1965. Raquel next enrolled in a university, and Ana, now alone, soldiered on through two more families until she graduated high school. Ana did not see her mother until 1967 and her father, who was a political prisoner in Cuba, until 1979.[36] She went on to become a prolific artist whose aesthetic inspiration came from her identity as a Cuban American woman. Her visits to Cuba were part of this evolving identity, but her life tragically ended when she died under suspicious circumstances in 1985.

Lissette and Olguita Alvarez joined the Mendieta sisters in Dubuque. They were daughters of a famous singing duo in Cuba, and their father was imprisoned for his underground activity. A Chinese American nun warned Lissette that the pair would never see their parents again and that soon communication, including mail, would be totally cut off. The nuns interpreted the girls' lack of English as simply a refusal to speak, for which they were punished. Lissette and Olguita had to deal with their own cultural translation problems. They found odd the home's practice of bathing only once a week; in Cuba, the norm was daily.[37]

When Nelson Valdés thinks back to that time, he is convinced that the program was beset by much more than what its orchestrators predicted. They were ill prepared for the cultural and psychological adjustments the thousands of children were facing. Some rebelled. Valdés remembers a hunger strike at Kendall. At age fifteen, he left Cuba just days before the Bay of Pigs invasion, having obtained his passport and plane ticket through his godfather's Masonic lodge in Havana. One of a few unaccompanied children on the KLM flight, Valdés carried a British visa along with an address and telephone number of a place to stay in London, all courtesy of the British Embassy in Havana. From Kendall he went to Albuquerque, where, because of his lack of English, the fifteen-year-old was enrolled in fifth grade. There he stayed and later became a professor of sociology at the University of New Mexico.[38]

Seven-year-old Alfredo Granado landed in Miami in 1962 along with Betty, his sister, who was nine. Their parents told them that they would come in two weeks, which turned into five years. The siblings lived in tents in Florida City; then they were presented a map and asked where they wanted to be placed. "Texas sounded fun," Alfredo thought, but "Utah sounded like a bad word in Spanish." The pair chose Colorado because they figured a lot of people spoke Spanish given its name (it means "red" or "colored" in Spanish). Within days they were in Denver, at which point Alfredo broke his ankle in an accident. Church leaders requested a humanitarian visa for his parents by exaggerating the seriousness of the injury, saying he was going to lose his leg. The petition was granted, and the family reunited in Miami in 1967.[39]

For others, resettlement meant confronting violence for the first time. Some of it was considered standard in American discipline in the 1960s, especially in parochial schools. Mario R. García hated the physical reprimand he withstood when he did not comply with English commands he did not understand.[40] Others suffered more excessive treatments. One woman said a nun punished her brothers by smacking their heads against the wall. She was replaced by a nun who disciplined boys by dressing them in girls' clothing. Another affirms that a nun grabbed her little brother's throat as if to choke him. José Arenas was thrown into tumultuous circumstances at the Mission of the Immaculate Virgin in Staten Island at Mount Loretto, New York. Placed among young men who had criminal records, it was the first time he had met anyone who wanted to kill his own father. To protect himself, Mario feigned mental problems and secured a copy of *The Rise and Fall of the Third Reich*, which had a swastika on its book cover, so people left him alone.

What was it to move from a space of safety and love to a threatening environment? To shift from a place of security to planning defenses for survival? Orphanages such as Mount Loretto were run like the military, and indeed some of its administrators were veterans. Crime and punishment were part of the daily routine, and hazing was common, as was behavior that today would qualify as abuse. When he broke curfew, Emilio Soto was made to stand outside with his arms in the air for two hours in the middle of the night. Haunting was the numbness in his feet brought on by standing in the snow.[41]

After some time in these conditions, the writing on the wall was clear: there would be no imminent return, and reconnecting with parents would be pending indefinitely. Castro had survived. The magnitude of the program was straining resources. Seventy percent of the unaccompanied children were boys older than twelve.[42] Monsignor Walsh was biting his lip in search of lodging for this group. Placement agencies were closing their doors to young men. There was no option but to relocate some in homes for delinquents even if the children exhibited no such behavior.[43] Just under 4,000 children were still in the program as of March 1, 1963, in 108 communities in thirty-nine states, Washington DC, and Puerto Rico.[44] By September the total lowered to 1,914 children in group care and 1,569 with foster families. The cost of replanting children across the nation had climbed upward of $300,000.[45]

With escalating expenses, Walsh faced congressional accountability. Ever faithful in his creditworthiness, he reported to Congress late in 1964 that his organization had served a total of 14,142 children while maintaining tight fiduciary order. He kept meticulous financial records, but he was drained. The federal guidelines had been unclear, and the per diem rate lacked consultation with HEW and the Florida Department of Public Welfare. Some had accused the CWB of mismanaging public monies to the tune of $152,000 over budget. Walsh acknowledged "errors of judgment were made" but charged that more frugality had been impossible and that, if reasonably stipulated, the CWB was keen to observe all rules going forward.[46] It was difficult, but Walsh was defiant. Clear to him was the higher calling that required him to remain steadfast in his faith. The odyssey of caring for Cuba's children was turning out to be much longer than expected.

4 | AMERICANIZE A LA CUBANA

For José Azel, becoming American was connected to the automobile. Registering for a driving permit at the green age of fourteen years old was pure elation. American football and rock 'n' roll also brought the young refugee into American adolescence, as did smoking.[1] At the time, mid-century professionals wagered that the best inoculation against the refugees' homesickness was their "rapid orientation to American ways."[2] Though touted as universally enviable, the American way was disorienting, forcing the children to rearrange the expectations they held prior to leaving Cuba.

Preflight impressions were mined from U.S. popular culture. Pury Lopez regularly watched *The Rifleman* dubbed in Spanish, while Carlos Eire found his USA in Mickey Mouse, Laurel and Hardy, and the Lone Ranger.[3] Over the difficult yet exhilarating course of learning English, Eire always felt out of place because of his accent, so he learned to imitate the language of *The Beverly Hillbillies* and *The Andy Griffith Show*. His perpetual out-of-place feeling caused him to take up writing, because on the page, he has observed, one loses his accent.[4] Gerardo Simms was also a fan of cowboy stories. The code of conduct of a Roy Rogers, Hopalong Cassidy, Lone Ranger, and Tonto made sense to him. He is not sure when he began to "feel" American, but at some point, he stopped translating between English and Spanish in his head. Unforgettable was the ritual of becoming a citizen, when his American identity became legalized: "It was formal, signifying the official beginning of a new chapter. Cuba never becomes the past, but I think that when I got my first job, after graduating from college, I probably realized that I would not be establishing a future or a career in Cuba. And because, more importantly, Communism was still the ruling doctrine, returning was not an option."[5]

Something similar happened to José Arenas, who became an American citizen on July 4, 1986, at the Orange Bowl, along with fourteen thousand others in a nationwide naturalization ceremony led by Chief

Justice Warren Burger via a newsfeed from Ellis Island. Soviet ballet dancer Mikhail Baryshnikov and comedian Yakov Smirnoff were among those taking the oath of citizenship. During the ceremony, José could not bring himself to cross his heart. He identifies as Cuban American, but at the core, he said, "I'm Cuban."[6]

That the influence of the United States was felt everywhere in Cuba before the revolution meant the American way had etched itself into the children before they left. But a lot was still unfamiliar; they had to adjust to the food, the language, the social cues, and the habits. Age played a key role in their reorientation. Research tells us that younger children suffer psychological hardship to a greater degree than older children do when separating from parents because, as we age, we accrue emotional resources to help cope with distance. Whereas younger children are only able to withstand short separation periods before permanent difficulties set in, older juveniles retain memories of their parents for longer, and that ability often—though not always—forges pathways to better cope with the loss. Some scholars have argued that compared with other populations in similar predicaments, Cuban children acclimated quite well.[7]

Where one ended up was also hugely significant. Did one land in Miami or Helena? Carlos Portes was fostered by the Hocketts in Marshalltown, Iowa, where he thrived in sports, theater, and other pastimes. He gravitated toward the Catholic Church and proudly prepared to be an altar boy. "And all of a sudden I started becoming the all-American boy," he later commented. Portes made Iowa his home. He became a successful businessman and later won the prestigious Ellis Island Medal of Honor.[8]

Upon arrival, even though he was not yet sixteen years old, Eloy Cepero and his older brother went to Opa-locka for mandatory clearance. Afterward, they joined Eloy's younger brother at the home of the rich Florida business magnate McGregor Smith, where the three boys would be fostered. There, the boys abruptly found themselves serviced by a butler, a maid, and a chauffeur. Cepero remembers that pushing a button at the table would summon the staff. He began intensive English classes over the summer before enrolling in school in the fall. There he excelled at basketball but needed a Puerto Rican translator during

12. Cuban boys playing baseball at St. Joseph's Home. Courtesy of the Diocese of Helena.

practices. A star athlete at Coral Gables High, he later attended the University of Miami on a track scholarship. The Smiths arranged for Eloy's parents to come through Mexico in 1965 and bought a house for them in Tampa.[9]

Whereas Cepero discovered his new nation in the fashionable environs of Coral Gables, Mario García found it by more humble means. Born in Las Villas, García and his family moved to Havana, where he became a child actor. Of his overhaul in the United States, he says wryly: "I went from being in a telenovela on a Monday to being a bus boy on a Thursday." On February 28, 1962, he boarded a Pan American flight full of Pedro Pans. In Miami the searching fourteen-year-old resided with his uncle, who was a barber. His parents joined him two years later by way of Mexico. His father saved money and bought a jewelry store.

In Cuba García saw the United States as a land of fast cars, open spaces, and big highways. Scenes from the 1950s series *Highway Patrol*, he thought, typified the country. *Davy Crockett* and *I Love Lucy* rounded out his early impressions. But he had been exposed to U.S. materialism earlier in Cuba when he would shadow his uncle who fixed used pianos from the United States and resold them on the island. The young García would find coins, dolls, and other knickknacks in the instruments. Incredulous that people would discard or lose items in such a way, García later pictured it as his "introduction to American capitalism."[10]

Among the larger adjustments Cuban children had to make was settling into their new class status as refugees. Children of means now wrestled with the searing sensation of losing the privilege they had back home. At Matecumbe, one boy clung to his silk pajamas but was shocked to sleep in a cot because no bunk bed was available. In Cuba even his dogs had beds; in due course a proper bunk materialized. Now bereft of parents and house staff, young refugees made their own beds and cleaned bathrooms. Nuns regularly confiscated possessions to hide the extravagance from other children. In addition to remapping class stature, the children were made to handle an unfamiliar racial landscape, including newfound racism. While with a foster family in Orlando, Julio Nuñez and Tony Ardavin stared down prejudice. Julio wanted to date an Irish girl, but her father forbade it because he was a Cuban "orphan."[11]

The Cuban racial framework did not translate to the American one. Cubans of all racial types were now grappling with Americans' racism and puzzlement with where to put Cubans—especially those well off—in the social spectrum. Most Cubans of this generation identified as white. In 1960 less than 7 percent were Black or mulatto; in 1970 the number was a mere 3 percent. Both Cuba and the United States are countries with deep histories of granting privilege to whiteness, but that comfort in Cuba disappeared in the United States. As refugees, Cuban bodies were marked non-white by their class as well. Refugee status took away their whiteness and augmented their "Latinness." Entering the U.S. South in the 1960s exerted even more pressure for one to pass as white, to put oneself above African Americans on the social ladder.

Being Black and Cuban presented its own set of difficulties. One Afro-Cuban boy sent to Peoria, Illinois, faced a more difficult time fitting in than did other Pedro Pans.[12] In Louisiana some children were housed in homes for delinquents and segregated by skin color, with dark-skinned Cuban boys sent to a colored group home, light-skinned ones to a white one.[13] Integration was a hot button issue for the CWB, which demanded that Cuban children find refuge where there was "acceptance of Negroes . . . South of the Mason-Dixon line."[14]

Carlos Eire has discussed how his identity changed in the new racialized caste system. "It would take only a brief plane ride to turn me from a white boy into a spic," he writes.[15] People from Homestead Air Force Base called Eire "spic" and told him to "go back to where he belonged." Children who were white in Cuba became part of the non-white minority in the United States. At a later point, he and his brother were asked to sit at the back of a bus in Miami.[16] "Spic" was a racist tag that now applied to Cubans. During an interview one Cuban asked a reporter, "Why do Americans call us spics?" He was not alone in his query.[17]

For some Pedro Pans, the new racial designations made it easier to bond with African Americans than with whites. In Victoria, Texas, Roberto Rodriguez Diaz saw lines drawn "between the whites and the Mexicans and the whites and the Blacks." As a Cuban, he remained an outsider but still felt forced to choose a side. "I was not part of any group. I was something else totally," he relayed. To him Cuba was not racist like the United States. There was more integration in the neighborhoods, in public accommodation, and in the schools. Other Pedro Pans report a similar sentiment, but most would not have experienced or even seen racism until they crossed the U.S. border. Cuban children suddenly saw racial lines that had been invisible to them previously. Rodriguez "felt" racism everywhere and was amazed at the segregated water fountains in Florida.[18]

Mario García concurs that he personally did not run into racism but remembers the shock of going to the post office and seeing a separate water fountain for African Americans. Though racism existed in Cuba, it was not legally codified to the degree it was in the United States. It was true that Fidel Castro's government scarcely had any Black functionaries, but García's kindergarten teacher was Afro-Cuban. Nevertheless, his mother would always instruct Mario to "do things the way whites do it." When he looks back, García fails to recall African

American classmates at his high school in Miami but does think about the inflamed racial tension due to the preferential hiring of Cubans over Blacks. "You could get a handyman who had a university degree at the hotels," he said. His mother, along with many women who had been "society ladies" in Cuba, worked as a seamstress making seat covers for Eastern Airlines in a Miami factory.[19]

María de los Angeles Torres remembers her family leaving Cleveland for Dallas. At a gas station in the South, the two water fountains were labeled "whites only" and "colored." "We were not allowed to drink the water—we didn't fit into either category—and we left thirsty," she writes. "For the average white Texan, there was little difference between a 'spic' and a 'nigger.'"[20] Fighting to fit in could be terrifying. Torres alighted in 1961 and remembers a difficult childhood of itinerancy. Though she was reunited with her parents some months later, she characterized the period as "traumatic" with a pervasive sense that she and her siblings were always out of place, the "odd kids out." Living in Midland, Texas, was arduous for the family. "We didn't fit in . . . people didn't want us there. They shot out the windows of our home and told our parents, 'We'll kill your kids.'"[21]

Eloy Cepero recalled Coral Gables High School as segregated at first, consisting of only whites and Hispanics like himself.[22] Mayda Riopedre attended the same school. Her bright green eyes and light skin tone belied her Cuban background. She befriended the dozen other Cuban girls, all of whom identified as white.[23] Though changing, racial divides persisted in Miami, making Carlos Eire wonder why he and other Cuban children attended white schools rather than Black ones when Cubans were not considered fully white.[24] When he arrived at the age of eleven, he was struck that people around him thought of Cubans as indigent. He was forced to answer questions such as: "What was it like to wear shoes for the first time?" and "How was it that you had blond hair and all Cubans big lips?" Weird was the sensation of reading textbooks in Illinois that depicted his homeland as a place of "starving children running amok, half-naked and three-quarters savage."[25]

Sometimes Pedro Pans found white privilege, while at other times they were excluded from it. Such ambiguity perplexed camp personnel tasked with classifying the Cuban children's race. "Mulatto" is a term that often appears in the record. An irked Dorothea Sullivan tried to streamline the options in line with a U.S. racial breakdown of the day: "Please remind your workers that there are only three races—negro, white, and oriental," she admonished case supervisors. That the mostly Cuban staff at the camps would recognize mulatto as an official category made sense, as it was used in Cuba. But in the United States, the category was historically one of ignominy in which one was considered neither white nor Black and thus relegated to an unfortunate life, hence the historical literary archetype "tragic mulatto." Now the children's skin color, which for most had signified privilege in Cuba, could invite degradation. It explained why on one intake form the surveyor recorded that a child "has fine features in spite of his race." The term "mulatto" flummoxed Sullivan, so she concluded that the category "is, of course, a combination of negro and white, but the individual belongs to one or the other depending upon his physical characteristics. If a boy is a negro, the description could say he is very dark or light skinned, etc." Pondering one particular evaluation further, she slipped deeper into the untidiness of racial classification: "Actually, the worker described this child as having a dark olive complexion, and hazel eyes. If his hair is straight, he might be considered white." In the end, all Sullivan could do was fume against the "deprecating remarks" on uneven racial identity.[26]

Sullivan was bedeviled by two racial realities from different nations intersecting at a time when race and rights were under turbulent revision. Father Bryan Walsh was expected to file statistics on how many Cuban children were in group care that also had children of color and on whether these kids were American or Cuban. HEW withheld federal money from segregated institutions of child welfare, and the department required agencies to fill out a confidential questionnaire on segregation that posed questions such as the following:

Have any children in your agency under the Cuban Children's
   Program been placed in a segregated facility?
Have you placed any Cuban Negro children in white foster
   homes?

Have you placed any Cuban white children in Negro foster
homes?
Has your agency experienced any specific problem regarding the
placement of Cuban children who are Negro?[27]

In Monsignor Walsh's papers exist just a few responses to these
inquiries, even though presumably the CWB would have filed them as
part of the paperwork from external agencies. We do not know the
extent to which Cuban children were placed in segregated facilities.
Moreover, when picking through the fastidious records, one cannot
help but wonder about the possible sanitization of evidence. Walsh was
assiduous in his paperwork on everything from billing for building
repairs and dental visits to televisions and milk orders. The priest kept
impeccable records. The government demanded it. But then there are
odd, unexplained absences of documentation. Some of these details
are locked away in the confidential recordkeeping of the children's
files, but we can also suppose that Walsh and Catholic Charities were
cognizant of the program's public face. Perhaps these questionnaires
did not find their way into Walsh's hands. Or they, along with other
files, were excised in the formulation of his archive. Which exclusions
were unintentional and which ones were planned is unknown.[28]

Clearly federal and state agencies were under mandate to abide by
civil rights regulations. From the few filled-out questionnaires that
have survived, we know that one New York agency responded that
all of its placements were integrated, but it encountered difficulty in
finding families who were "willing to accept children of another race."
The agency also advised against "long term placements of children in
families not of their own race."[29] Another disclosed that some Afro-
Cuban children were placed in white foster homes, at least temporarily,
as referenced by the Catholic Charities of the Diocese of Harrisburg.[30]

In a moment of haste, Frank Craft of the Florida Department of
Public Welfare wrote Mildred Arnold of the Children's Bureau as he
tried to track down integrated living situations for the Cuban children. Craft knew that race and racial discrimination in Cuba operated
distinctly from that in the United States, and the problem was that
Cuban children who viewed themselves as white were in actuality

"very dark complected," as he put it. He underscored that not only did the children have to learn English but they also had to adopt a new racial language when crossing the Florida Straits. He observed, "They have been living as though they are white but would not fit into an all-white program. Even some family groups of children vary so much in color that only an integrated school or mixed community could absorb them."[31]

Likewise, Margaret Harnett of Miami's Children's Bureau expressed consternation at trying to find suitable lodging for Black Cuban children and those from a "lower socio-economic group." "Negro" Cubans had been "integrated" in Cuba, but in the United States they were placed in "Negro foster home[s] in the south" in segregated conditions, which added to the trauma of their Americanization and would have cut such homes off from federal funds.[32] Florida's Division of Family Services doubled its efforts to ensure organizations were in compliance with the Civil Rights Act of 1964. Its forms went further than those of the CWB and included the racial categories American Indian, Negro, Oriental, and "Spanish surnamed." It therefore made it difficult to know which box to check if a Cuban child were both Negro *and* Spanish surnamed. This number was low in the Pedro Pan community. In 1974 as the number in care dwindled, only two out of the twenty-two boys at the Cuban Boys' Home were Black.[33]

By 1970 the U.S. government would officially count Cubans in the ranks of "Hispanics," but in the early sixties, this ethnic group had yet to cohere. Furthermore, those girls and boys coming from middle- and upper-class backgrounds also now had to deal with becoming state wards. Walsh gauged few to be from wealthy families, but he could not always be certain of their backgrounds. He did try, though, counting "Chinese, Negro, German, Irish, English, and Spanish" among the children's ancestry.[34] One researcher has estimated that sixteen thousand Chinese Cubans lived in the United States by 1963.[35] At her shelter, Sister María Victoria Ortega let on that at least one child spoke Chinese when calling his parents to avoid eavesdropping by Cuban authorities.[36] In May 1962 the *Houston Chronicle* reported that at the Miami airport George Guarch found "his charges are dark-skinned as well as white (and occasionally there is an Oriental)."[37] It is difficult to contrive the racial breakdown of Pedro Pans because most of the official statistics indicate their ages and sex but not their race.[38]

Outside the camps, Miamians were trying to make sense of it all. Walsh received alarms that Cubans were responsible for an increase in crime. One neighbor in the Matecumbe area complained that her mail was stolen and blamed the boys. The CWB reassured her that "everything possible was being done to properly supervise the boys at the Camp."[39] In one especially heated incident, one of the ten Afro-Cuban children housed at Florida City was cornered by three white men around twenty years of age. Drunk, they jumped the young boy, who was described as a thirteen-year-old "Negro boy," at Bayfront Park pool. Other Florida City boys came to the defense of the child, with one breaking a bottle and going after the assailants, and at that point, the house fathers intervened. Administrators at Florida City let Walsh know that at the shelter, "anti-Negro feeling is very high." In the end, Dorothea Sullivan opted for the path of least resistance by offering to place the children of color elsewhere.[40]

5 | THE "OTHER MIAMI"

Miami is not a microcosm of the American city. It never was. From its very beginnings a century ago, the Biscayne Bay metropolis possessed an air of unreality, a playground divorced from its natural habitat. . . . The thin strip of land between jungle and reef hence became less an American Riviera than a compendium of the nation's foibles.

—PORTES AND STEPICK, *City on the Edge*

Retired psychology professor Marvin Dunn remembers growing up in Florida before the civil rights movement pulsed through the South. His father brought home paychecks as a truck driver, dockworker, and longshoreman. His mother, an African American woman of Cherokee descent, worked in Miami Beach as a maid. Her female employer would drive her home and insist she sit in the back of the Cadillac. That car was a symbol of wealth and prestige. Dunn's father loved Cadillacs, and when he could afford it, he bought a powder blue one in 1959. He avoided parking the car in front of the house for fear that white people—his wife's employer especially—would learn of the family's valued possession. "If a cracker knows that you've got more than he's got," he wagered, "he's going to fire your ass. Don't let them know that you have more than they do."[1]

Dunn attended Morehouse College on a Ford Foundation scholarship at the age of seventeen. When he traveled to college on a bus from Miami to Atlanta, he followed his parents' instructions and sat in the back. He later moved to the middle. As the bus made its way, a white girl in Georgia picked the seat next to him. He had never been that close to a white person in his life. At that point, he says, "You could hear a pin drop." Someone commanded, "Nigger, get up and move." A white Marine in uniform came to the young man's defense. The collective white anger shifted toward the Marine, who was called a "nigger lover." Additional charges rang out: "You must be a Jew." "You must be from the North." "This isn't how we do it down here." The bus driver pulled over and made Dunn get off. He caught the next bus to Atlanta and sat in the back. By the time he graduated, things had changed. He could sit at the front.[2]

Pedro Pans entered an entirely new racial landscape in their new adopted country. That introduction, for most, was in Miami, a "compendium of the nation's foibles," as Alejandro Portes and Alex Stepick refer to it. The city suddenly vaulted into the public's consciousness with the appearance of tens of thousands of anti-communist refugees. The locale imagined as "America's playground" and the "Gateway to the Americas" derived from a European, Caribbean, and Indigenous ecology: Spanish-, French-, Portuguese-, and English-speaking people made their mark, as did a thickset West Indian influence from Jamaicans, Bahamians, Haitians, and Cubans. All gave life to the Magic City.[3]

Six decades after its founding, Miami grew into a contentious test case for racial integration. The brutal violence unbraiding communities throughout the South—something intimately known by Dunn and all African American Floridians—raised the stakes of delivering the nation's postwar promises. The Cold War further pushed the United States to atone for its dismal race record and make good on its commitments to democratic freedom, lest the decolonizing world buy into the Soviet way of life.[4] Cubans complicated the traditional racial divide of Black/white since as "Latin" people, they seemed to fit neither category. They found acceptance in white spaces where Blacks were not permitted, while at the same time their *latinidad* (Latino/a or Latin American heritage and culture) made them not quite white. They fell outside of, or in between, the bifurcated categories of Blackness and whiteness, even as most first-wave refugees could traffic in white spaces. Miamians were divided between welcoming the new anti-communist crusaders and dismissing them as a social nuisance. Cubans were a test of Cold War stamina; they were both an unwanted invasion and a newfound opportunity to combat communism at home. For the first time in its history, the city stood in the nation's center awash with plaudits and under leery scrutiny.

Today Miami stands as a capital of Pan-America, a "Latin city" that invites associations with South Beach diets, salsa clubs, and 1980s drug trafficking. Stanley Crouch called it a "Mafia bastion and a Jewish burial ground."[5] Joan Didion's impression was that "Miami seemed not a city at all but a tale, a romance of the tropics, a kind of waking dream in which any possibility could and would be accommodated."[6] The area landed on European maps in the sixteenth century. Named for a Basque sailor, Biscayne Bay gave harbor to Spanish missionaries proclaiming the land worthy of God and the crown. Ravaging mosquitoes and intractable Native inhabitants cut their time short. But in 1565 Don Pedro Menéndez de Avilés successfully vanquished a competing French settlement and established St. Augustine as a permanent outpost for Spain.[7]

While textbooks often foreground the Spanish in Florida's origin story, the sons and daughters of the African diaspora and the Seminole Indians chiseled the deepest grooves in the state's cultural strata. Florida was a haven for runaway slaves after the Spanish crown made manumission easier for those who converted to Catholicism. Seminoles and African-descended populations lived among one another, with some Natives owning Black slaves, though in a system that offered more flexibility than the American colonial alternative. Fugitive slaves continued to come, with the future existence of "black Seminoles" a by-product of an interracial exchange. Florida remained Spanish until Andrew Jackson won the territory for the United States in 1821. Then the territory's diverse communities waged war against the U.S. Army. One of the most notorious battles involved Dade County's namesake, Maj. Francis Langhorne Dade. In 1835 he and his men were slaughtered while combating the Seminoles and their Black allies.[8]

Florida entered the union as a slaveholding state in 1845 and followed the Confederacy in its secession in 1861. As scholars have it, Florida was "neither Spanish nor southern" and thus evinced a distinct political and social environment.[9] After the Civil War, Black Floridians settled in Lemon City, the northern section of what would become Miami, and in Coconut Grove, the would-be town's southern section. Growing numbers of Bahamian migrants worked on pineapple plantations in the 1890s and built a market that fed the sweet tooth of Bostonians, New Yorkers, and Baltimoreans.[10] On the eve of Miami's founding in 1896 was the disastrous growing season of 1894–95, when freezing temperatures ruined the citrus crops in north Florida. Black workers moved to the southern part of the state, and the agricultural industry followed. The railroad, commercialized by oil magnate Henry Flagler, revolutionized the region's economy and opened opportunities for African-descended people.[11] Flagler was part of the equation, but it was Julia Tuttle, a wealthy widow from Cleveland, who further enticed wealthy northerners to the region's bucolic climate. Flagler's Florida East Coast Railway transported the adventurous to Tuttle's significant land holdings at the mouth of the Miami River. There the town of Miami was born. At the time, 162 out of 400 voters were men of color. Forty percent of the Black population was Bahamian, and families of the African diaspora made their home in the segregated neighborhood of Colored Town. Miami's West Indian population was the second largest after New York City's.[12]

The Spanish-American War installed in the area a company of southern whites who brought with them Jim Crow segregation. Racial violence rose. By 1900 African-descended people numbered 966 in Miami, a quarter of them Bahamian. Colored Town was growing, but its conditions were abysmally inadequate. Poor sanitation led to regular epidemics. The lack of educational and employment opportunities made vice rampant. The city swelled. Homestead was established in 1913 and Florida City in 1914; together they provided new municipal anchors in Dade County and stations along Flagler's railway.[13] Northerners kept coming. Secretary of State William Jennings Bryan and his wife built a house in Biscayne Bay on land they had purchased for $30,000 in 1912. Their "Villa Serena" would survive the Great Miami Hurricane of 1926 that destroyed much of Miami. Not unlike Las Vegas, Miami appeared destined to perpetual reinvention limited only by the American cultural imagination. Bryan, who would give outdoor sermons at Miami's Royal Palm Park, commented that "Miami is the only city in the world where you can tell a lie at breakfast that will come true by evening."[14]

West Indians continued to populate Dade County. In 1920 just over half of Miami's Black population was Bahamian. Residents of color represented one-third of the population but occupied just a fraction of the city's available homes. In the Jazz Age, the Ku Klux Klan rejuvenated across the country and in southern Florida threatened the golden age of Black Miami, its "heyday" as Marvin Dunn has labeled it. Colored

Town residents manufactured their own "Harlem Renaissance." One could watch Count Basie at the Harlem Square Club and Billie Holiday at Miami's Cotton Club. When striding through this Harlem of the South, one could hear the sounds of jazz, see men decked out in zoot suits, and munch on southern and Caribbean delights such as Georgia-style barbecue ribs and hot fish sandwiches.[15]

Colored Town was scouting out a new identity. The population settled on the zone's de facto name "Overtown," as one had to go "over" downtown to get to Colored Town. There was an uptick in white supremacist violence, and Miami was not spared from the Klan's terrorism. What the writer James Weldon Johnson coined as the "Red Summer" of 1919 rolled into the following year in Miami. Bombs went off, and bullets flew into Black homes. The neighborhood's thousands of Black residents armed themselves to counter the terror. Thereafter, segregation became more rigid, with racial zones drawn into plans of city expansion and business proprietorship. Miami continued to grow in the 1920s, but so did racial apartheid. In Miami, Nathan Connolly writes, the "fear of lynching and other acts of racial violence was an integral feature of economic development." In the thick of the Depression, Liberty Square opened. Former Seminole land became the South's first Black housing development in 1936.[16]

Cubans were a small part of Miami's colored community, but they had made a larger impression in Florida more generally. This was the case four hundred miles away in the Black neighborhood of Ybor City in Tampa, where Latinos—Cubans among them—were 25 percent of the population.[17] In 1869 Vicente Martínez Ybor brought his cigar manufacturing trade to the area, where he grew an industry that eventually remade Tampa, Ocala, and Jacksonville into locales defined by Cuban influence.[18] Evelio Grillo grew up in Ybor City and would go on to serve HEW under President Jimmy Carter. Cubans in Tampa did not fit in traditional white/non-white orbits. At that time, the term "Cuban nigger" referred to white Cubans and *tally wop* (Italian without papers) to Black Cubans. Around Clearwater Beach, signs read No Cubans or Dogs Allowed until the civil rights movement brought them down a generation later. When Grillo peered back to this time, he saw white Cubans claiming racial lineage to Spanish origin, while

Black Cubans were associated with Africa. "For all of our sharing of language, culture, and religion with white Cubans," he reminisced, "we black Cubans were black." He went to "colored schools" and, along with his fellow Afro-Cubans, attended a Black Catholic school, where he was called a tally wop by African American children who either could not or refused to distinguish between the Spanish and Italian they heard on the streets.

Grillo more often found himself with Black American schoolmates than with white Cubans. This situation differed from what he would have encountered in Cuba. In segregated Tampa, there were separate churches, recreational activities, and businesses, which Black Tampanians rarely owned. Therefore, African American and Afro-Cuban populations frequently mingled. Still, there was a divide. African Americans had been in the United States longer than the Afro-Cubans and had relatives who had been bought and sold in its slave system. English also hampered interactions, as did the split between Protestant and Catholic fealties. And some Cubans of color feared African Americans the same way whites did and thus avoided certain neighborhoods.[19]

Dramatic changes in south Florida occurred in the genesis of the modern civil rights movement. In Miami the destruction of Jim Crow happened gradually. The city hired its first Black patrol officers in 1944 (though it did not permit them to arrest white people). A landmark issue was access to white-only beaches. In World War II, Dade County allowed the U.S. Navy to use Virginia Key Beach to train Black recruits, and in 1945 African Americans fought for the permanent use of the beach, staging "wade-ins" at white beaches until the county relented and made Virginia Key Beach a "colored beach." Trekking across the Biscayne Bay bridge to Virginia Key still made enjoying the sand and water a laborious affair, however. State troopers stood guard to prevent Blacks from crossing into white Crandon Park's beach unless they were on their way to work.[20] To be Black and enter Miami Beach meant having one's credentials checked before entry. Cubans, however, could use the colored-only Virginia Key Beach and the white beaches. Puerto Ricans fared the same.[21] As Father Walsh was accepting his new assignment, the wade-ins led by the National Association for the

Advancement of Colored People (NAACP) and the Congress of Racial Equality (CORE) successfully integrated Miami's beaches.[22]

Then Miami really grew, doubling in population between 1940 and 1950 and again the following decade to just under a million residents. In 1950 13 percent of Dade County was Black and 4 percent Latino. One study estimated Miami was the most residentially segregated of America's largest hundred cities.[23] Urbanization further squeezed Overtown residents out of opportunities and real estate. Relocating one's family was a constant chore. Liberty City was prime real estate, and Opa-locka transformed into a Black section of the city that was primarily populated by Black veterans. In it sat Bunche Park, named for Ralph Bunche, the first African American to win the Nobel Peace Prize.[24] The police in Opa-locka were all white but heeded the demands of African American residents not to patrol the neighborhood. The veterans enforced order, but such arrangements were temporary. With urbanization and modernization came invasive white surveillance and further racial animosity.[25]

By some measurements, then, Miami was just another southern city. African Americans were domestic servants, manual laborers, and field hands. They had to enter the courthouse through a separate door and were prohibited from using elevators in department stores, where they could not try on clothing or return their purchases. They suffered in segregated housing; could not own businesses on downtown Flagler Street; were barred from admission to Florida's state schools, save Florida A&M; and had to be in Colored Town by dark. Doors to most unions remained closed to them as well.[26]

But by other measurements, the Magic City was ahead of the civil rights curve. Even before the decision in *Brown v. Board of Education of Topeka*, Miami began to desegregate its lavish Miami Beach hotels. There were, after all, affluent Black tourists, too, and Miami business leaders courted their money. In fact, leaders of the Black aspiring class discouraged radical civil rights tactics such as those deployed in Montgomery and Birmingham, Alabama.[27] Marvin Dunn insists that mass demonstrations against Jim Crow occurred earlier in Miami. CORE led training sessions there before the renowned lunch counter sit-ins in Greensboro, North Carolina.[28] Desegregation came slowly, unevenly, and contentiously. After a flawed "gradualist approach" to implementing the provisions of *Brown v. Board*, Dade County in 1959 finally agreed to integrate its schools. When the first elementary school did so, white families disenrolled their children. The University of Miami admitted its first Black students in 1961, yet as late as 1969, HEW reported that Dade County was still not fully in compliance with the Civil Rights Act of 1964. Lawsuits lasted years.[29]

Racial violence threatened not only the colored population but also Miami's Jews. In 1951 bombs tore apart a Black housing complex and a Jewish school, and a failed one unnerved the Coral Gables Jewish Center. Seventy percent of Jews migrating south settled in Miami at this time, which saw the creation of alliances between groups. In the late 1950s, Jewish activists Thalia Stern and Shirley Zoloth were highly active in Miami's CORE chapter.[30] White transplants were different from second- or third-generation southern whites; they were northern liberals who had not grown up with the norms of the Jim Crow South.[31]

By this time, Miami had become Florida's top destination. The war had also necessitated a more dependable infrastructure for business as well as for leisure. There could never be enough air-conditioning and mosquito repellent. As Miami became more Pan-American, the city shifted its racial politics on behalf of economic betterment. Tourists of all stripes needed accommodation and tolerance to spend money.[32]

Miami's renaissance also built a contentious infrastructural feat that would revamp the social and cultural circuitry of the city and surrounding area—namely, Interstate 95 (I-95). This branch of the national highway system promised to revolutionize commerce as the railroad had done in the previous century. The Federal-Aid Highway Act of 1956 envisioned forty-one thousand miles of new construction, with eight thousand of them in urban locations. Like so many of these places, Miami's Black population bore the brunt of the project that yoked Maine to Florida. The goal, according to the Urban Land Institute, was to remove "blighted" neighborhoods and disintegrate the "slums." The blueprint now bisected Overtown, with the uprooted residents looking for alternatives. Liberty City sprouted as the new dominant African American neighborhood.[33]

Many Black professionals supported the 1-95 project as a way to destroy slum life; it was part of uplift, they argued. The African American newspaper *Miami Times* urged its readers to support the endeavor in the name of "progress." In 1957 the Greater Miami Urban League also praised it as "continued progress." But others spoke out against the dislocation of minorities. After all, two-thirds of Miami's Black population had lived in Overtown in 1950. The voices of dissent fell on deaf ears. An estimated 330,000 urban housing units were eliminated and some thirty-seven thousand families displaced yearly due to the national project.[34]

As Cubans were making their way to the Magic City, a new speculative market was afoot. Luther L. Brooks was a white real estate developer from Georgia who pounced on the opportunity to develop rental property in Black neighborhoods. Brooks was, according to one urban historian, "the best-known white man in Overtown." A kingpin of the slum lords, Brooks was a champion of moving Blacks to Liberty City for the purposes of gentrifying downtown.[35] His bread and butter were these poor neighborhoods, so when proposals to build more public housing units arose, he and his variety lobbied against them to maintain their large margins off the slums.[36] Brooks and his ilk, supported by some in the Black middle class, traded in "residential apartheid." While whites in South Florida lived fifteen people to an acre, the central Negro district of Miami crammed six hundred in the same area. But Brooks hired people of color, so even as the press discredited him as a "Slum Baron" or "King of the Tenements," African American voices defended him and elevated his credit. Some of those voices were slumlords themselves. The revered M. Athalie Range, Miami's first Black city commissioner, suffered ridicule as one in some circles.[37]

White Miamians did not want Blacks moving into their neighborhoods. When the entertainer Frank Legree moved into an all-white area, he was met with picketing neighbors and attempted arsonists, four of whom were arrested for attempting to burn a cross at the home in February 1957.[38]

Accordingly, Pedro Pans and their fellow refugees entered a Miami struggling to find its modern identity, a southern city in the growing pains of changing from a predominantly biracial locale to a Pan-

13. Demonstration against Frank Legree moving to an all-white neighborhood in 1957. Courtesy of Bettman via Getty Images.

American metropolis. Critics bemoaned the exiles' presence because, they argued, the refugees strained local resources. There was now competition for jobs and welfare benefits. African American organizations were vexed that Cubans worked for less pay and received more monthly aid than some Black citizens on federal assistance. National welfare expenditures were abysmal. In 1959 Florida ranked thirtieth in per capita income and forty-seventh in welfare funds per resident. Whereas the elderly could receive $66 each month and families with children $81, a single refugee received $73 and a married couple with or without children $100.[39]

When it came to making room for Cubans, those close to Miami's Black community took sides. When Luther Brooks provided testimony to a Senate subcommittee, he asked, "How do you think a colored man feels . . . when he walks down Flagler Street and sees a Cuban with a skin darker than his eating in a restaurant he does not dare enter? Or when he rides by a white school ground and sees children darker than his own, who speak no English. There, gentlemen, are the situations that are creating friction in this colored community."[40]

Labor leader Charles Lockhart and Garth Reeves, the editor of the African American newspaper *Miami Times*, raised a hue and cry over Cubans displacing African Americans in jobs and federal assistance. Officials responded that Cubans came with less and needed more. In 1961 relief agents calculated that the average Cuban family was bringing in $74 per month, but rumors spread that some refugees were receiving more than their share.[41] By the time of the missile crisis, 150,000 Cubans had squeezed into Miami, and two-thirds of them stayed. Florida had no general relief program but did have an aid to dependent children program, which granted a family a maximum of $81 each month. Some managers held that the low number was "designed to punish Negro mothers of illegitimate children" since the amount had not changed since 1951. To keep unemployed Cuban men with their families, they received an additional $19 per month, or a total of $100.[42]

Education was another breaking point. Cubans attended white schools while African Americans awaited integration. The assistant superintendent of Dade County was exasperated by the overcrowding at Miami schools occasioned by the entrance of ten thousand "Latin" students in 1961.[43] But in 1962 the number of refugee children enrolled in Miami-Dade schools jumped to twenty-one thousand, driving the federal government to bump its allocations. Dade County schools used the money to help Cuban kids study English, while African Americans continued to learn in decaying buildings and without classes in Black history.[44] Other secondary beneficiaries of these entitlements were Puerto Rican and Mexican residents, who gained access to spaces that were prohibited for them before the Cubans' arrival.[45] Spanish-speaking school children—Puerto Ricans included—had special earmarked funds for their education. African Americans did not.[46]

Alarm bells went off around cases of suspected fraud. HEW regional representative Wave Perry wrote Frank Craft, wondering if agencies were referring too many refugee cases to the FBI for duping the Cuban Refugee Program. The bureau had dedicated several agents to these files.[47] Congress learned "large numbers of refugees" receiving federal assistance were ineligible because they were earning money elsewhere and under false pretenses. In a random sample, 35 percent of recipients were counting on some financial assistance that would have made them ineligible for the aid they were receiving. Washington dialed up the pressure, but Congress learned that a good deal of the refugees paid back the misdirected funds, spanning anywhere from $100 to $2,000 and greater.[48] A 1962 *New York Times* article found that nearly $300,000 of the federal relief payments had been restored, half of it voluntarily by recipients.[49]

In their pushback, African American organizations sought to curb the preferential hiring of exiles. The Urban League pointed out that too many of the 150,000 Black citizens were unable to move beyond unskilled positions because those opportunities were now awarded to Cubans.[50] As the Black freedom movement pushed forward, African Americans condemned white Miamians for their tolerance of Cubans while continuing their racism toward the city's non-white residents. Signs of refugee favoritism were everywhere. *Miami Herald* journalist Juanita Greene spoke out against unfair support for refugees in contrast to that for African Americans, who were squeezed at the margins of urban development.[51]

That Cubans were supposedly taking jobs from Americans made national headlines. In a letter to President Kennedy, a group of Black ministers resented "those who would cover up the basic issue of the Negro's denial to equal sharing of his country's resources with the cry of Cuban encroachment."[52] President Lyndon Johnson's Office of Emergency Planning found unemployment in Miami to be 5 percent for Cubans but three times higher among Black Miamians. Church relief workers noted growing hostility. Marshall Wise, the director of the Cuban Refugee Center, said the burden was too great to manage it locally. It was now a "national problem." Miami mayor Robert King High remained positive: "I regard this as the greatest opportunity that the United States has had to show that we are what we say we are."[53]

Cubans had a friend in the mayor. High touted the resettlement advances and defended Cubans against the multipronged complaints at a time when other cities chafed at the calling. The city of Cleveland had refused to accept eighty-eight Cuban families because of fears around workers' strife.[54] Of humble origins in Tullahoma, Tennessee, High took an interest in Latin American history. While on his way to becoming a lawyer, he spent part of one summer at the University of Havana learning Spanish. When he ran for mayor in 1957, his slogan was "Take the High Road," and it struck a note among African Americans who supported his campaign to clean up the streets, make headway on civil rights, improve tourism and industry, and embrace the Latino/a population of the city. People affectionately referred to him as the "Mayor of the Americas." A desegregationist, he favored moderate rather than radical civil rights advancement and was slow to crack down on dissent. Lunch counter sit-ins, which occurred in Miami before happening in other Florida cities, proceeded without his interference, and police were instructed to stand down before peaceful demonstrations.[55]

Monsignor Walsh was not impressed. He thought the mayor wanted to have his cake and to eat it too. On the one hand, he accommodated the Cuban population, but on the other, he pushed to resettle them elsewhere. Walsh gauged that High's "popularity with the Cubans has dropped to zero." The aid for refugees was under federal direction, and the city had a poor plan of its own.[56]

There were other murmurs of discontent. Black joblessness caused too many African American men to leave Miami for farm work outside the city. Using the headline "Cuban Refugees Take Jobs from Florida Negroes," *Jet* magazine linked African American joblessness to the presence of Cubans: "The Red-oppressed refugees, persecuted and pitiful, are enjoying the fruits of freedom—especially the right to work—daily denied to black Miamians." One interviewee took umbrage with the hypocrisy: "It makes my heart bleed to know that the only way for . . . Negro families . . . to share the same fruits of American democracy now extended to Cuban refugees would be for them to first renounce American citizenship, go to Castro's Cuba—and then return as Cuban refugees."[57]

While trying to shore up support for an integrated labor bloc, Miami labor representatives also acknowledged rifts. One white real estate agent judged that "the Cuban and the colored stood side by side" when watching local parades, but "colored resentment is nothing more than where the colored man goes down the street and sees a Cuban that is on the dark side who is permitted to eat in the white restaurants." Historically segregated Miami, he opined, had "a little different setup [from] Washington."[58] To top it off, the director of the Cuban Refugee Program was now John Frederick Thomas, a mixed-race Minnesotan. The son of an African American father and Swedish mother, Thomas earned reprehension for caring more for refugees than for the Black community from which he derived.[59]

While exiles benefited from exceptional entitlements, they also suffered the brunt of criticism. They were blamed for higher crime rates and civic unrest. Reports of an increase in "delinquent behavior" and gang violence stoked fears in white Miamians that Cubans would "take over" their community just as Puerto Ricans did New York City. A growing wariness toward Caribbean immigrants lumped Puerto Ricans, Cubans, and Haitians into a regional xenophobia that dispelled any lingering remnants of liberal idealism. Local leaders such as Seymour Samet, the executive director of the Miami chapter of the American Jewish Committee, expressed dismay about the "integration friction" and "juvenile delinquency" that he attributed to an eruption of Miami's racial differences: "American gangs of teenagers and young adults will form to retaliate. Negroes will fight Cubans; Cubans will attack Americans; Fidelistas will step up their incidents against the anti-Fidelistas."[60]

While many shared in Samet's dystopian premonitions, overriding these voices of doom was a steadfast collective feeling that successful absorption of Cubans was a fundamental exigency for U.S. democracy. Even as they themselves faced racism, Cubans were granted access to white spaces. Those coming on the heels of the revolution were middle- and upper-class Cubans whose lighter skin and eventual economic and social clout allowed for an in-between racial identity that made them both outsiders and members of whites-only locations. Some have argued that the Cubans' fierce anti-communism was their ticket to this racial acceptance.[61] Cubans were rarely identified as white, but their anti-communism granted them a kind of political whiteness that translated socially.[62] This occurred at a time when the civil rights politics of African Americans were reviled as communist. Groups such as the NAACP and leaders such as Martin Luther King Jr. earned the attention of the FBI and conservative groups, which levied charges of red-baiting against them.

Into this climate came T. Willard Fair, the president of the Urban League of Greater Miami. Growing up in North Carolina, he had a defiant father who "never gave in" and always "demanded respect for himself and his wife." Fair's mother slept late on weekends due to her nightly work schedule, but against his father's orders, a pesky white insurance man would swing by on Saturday mornings to collect premiums, interrupting his mother's sleep. The man did not listen, so Fair's father opened the door and "smacked him down," an act that was tantamount to "lynching behavior," Fair reflected. He learned from his father "to do whatever he needed to do to demand respect."

While earning a master's degree in social work in Atlanta, Fair stepped up his activity in the civil rights movement, brushing elbows with Stokely Carmichael, H. Rap Brown, Ron Karenga, Ralph Abernathy, and even Martin Luther King Jr. At the age of twenty-four, he wanted to sign up for the army, but an injury prevented his enlistment. So he took a job at the local Urban League in Winston-Salem and in 1963 transferred to Miami. When the position of chief executive officer (CEO) suddenly became vacated, the job landed on him. He began in 1963 with a staff of three people, and in less than a decade he developed the Miami chapter into the largest office of Urban League (UL) affiliates with 476 full-time employees.[63]

Fair was the youngest UL president and CEO. Brash and determined, he departed from traditional boardroom politeness and deference. "I was Muhammad Ali of Black Dade County . . . talking the talk . . . talking back to white folk, sassing white folk," he gloated.[64] As a new resident, Fair thought Black Miamians were "out of touch" and "conciliatory." He aimed to inject a different swagger into the city's political scene. He regularly wore a dashiki, paraded his outspoken and unapologetic viewpoints, and did not kowtow to board members. With delight, Fair quipped, "I got fired every month for three years."[65] With an annual budget of $19,000, he focused on job growth and housing for the Black community. First was obtaining salesclerk positions at the popular department store Burdines. Other firsts followed: flight attendants at Eastern Airlines, pole climbers at Florida Power and Light Company, and phone operators at Southern Bell Telephone Company.

On the Cuban question, Fair says exiles were not an impediment to Black freedom. On the contrary, they were allies. After their arrival, the UL thereupon amended its service population; the organization would serve not just Blacks but "Blacks and other minorities." He says whites fled Hialeah because of Cubans, not African Americans. His constituency, he says, had no hostility, and Fair believed it was better to unite causes. He found greater resistance to integration in Miami than in smaller towns, saying whites were not the problem. Rather, it was scared people of color, or what Fair calls "handkerchief scared head Negroes," in the boardroom who avoided confrontation.

On integration, the UL leader also says that "Miami was ahead of the curve." Initially, the league's greatest allies were Jewish leaders. They and other white ethnic higher-ups at Eastern Airlines and other local businesses and corporations were in search of civil rights credibility because racial equality now made good economic sense. Fair also credits Bishop Carroll and the Catholic Church with playing a vital role in creating a community relations board to talk openly about race and integration to avoid the vivid violence befalling the South. Miami was more progressive than other southern cities, a fact Fair credits to the white northern transplants. While northern whites *did* learn to discriminate in concert with southern white values, ultimately they were outsiders, which made their attitudes more easily changeable. Today all the major power brokers Fair associates with in Miami are Hispanic, but in the 1960s, this was far from the case.[66]

Marvin Dunn also came of political age at this time. His family moved to Miami from central Florida in 1951 and lived in Opa-locka. When rewinding the past, Dunn more often saw Seminole Indians than Latinos, Cubans included. His father was a fruit picker and followed the seasonal migrations north for work. Dunn and his brothers spent three summers on Long Island picking potatoes while attending white elementary schools. They worked mornings, went to school, and returned to the fields until dark. "It was terrible," he confided. But upon returning to Florida, he and his brothers were ahead of their classmates at the Black schools. Education was pivotal. "I wanted to have a job where I didn't have to get up when it was still dark to go to it," he contemplated.

Dunn thinks that the influx of Cubans complicated Miami's racial politics in both troubling and gratifying ways. Unforgettable is the era in which his mother was forced to ride in the back of the bus to her job as a maid. When Cuban women first arrived, they could sit in the front. This, says Dunn, harmed Black-Cuban relations. Discrimination took place "at a deeper level." Just as the freedom movement was delivering gains, Black progress was pushed aside for the needs of Cubans. African Americans were kept out of jobs that required contact with white people. Cubans got these jobs, and the budding bilingual market favored exiles who were quickly learning English. The newcomers took over labor unions when many Blacks were still locked out. Finally, African Americans could not compete with Cuban nepotism, and they were out of luck without knowing Spanish.

Yet Dunn says that when refugees came to Miami-Dade, African Americans saw gradual financial improvement because the whole county's economy changed. Eventually more city and state jobs, as well as municipal representation, became available for African Americans. As noted, Athalie Range served on Miami's city commission in 1966.[67]

Afro-Cubans fell between and betwixt these fault lines. In the national frame, Black Cubans were seldom visible, composing a mere 3 percent of the Cuban population in the United States by 1970. The CRP's newsletter, *Resettlement Re-cap*, only occasionally ran a story about a "Cuban Negro family."[68] The scarcity of Afro-Cubans, in part, was due to the profound racial inequality in both Cuba and the United States. With less money and education, Black Cubans failed to have the necessary connections to leave the island and plant roots in the United States. Cubans of color also likely chose to stay in their country because they had more to gain from the revolution—employment, education, and health care, for instance—than the fleeing whites who had lost much to Castro's socialism. Havana paid a lot of lip service to race relations and repeatedly promised that with equitable economic engineering, racism would disappear.

Pedro Pan Gerardo Simms was part of this group. He eschews the label "Afro-Cuban" and considers himself Black. After a stint at Florida

City, he migrated to Opa-locka, where he lived until 1966. One vivid memory he retains is his first Halloween: "The fact that one could knock on a door, mumble some words and get candy, was a unique experience. . . . 'Trick or treat' was incomprehensible to me."

But Simms also remembers the hatred. Occasionally neighborhood kids would throw rocks at the camp buses or gang up on Pedro Pans when they left the campgrounds. He and some others were barred from whites-only public pools. Simms conjectures that the prejudice he combated was more ethnic than racial; he was a target for being Cuban rather than Black. He calls Cubans a "mixed lot" of Spanish-speaking Blacks and whites. He chooses to identify as Cuban American and racially Black, shies away from the label "Latino," and does not put much stock in Afro and African prefixes because to him they add the same vagaries as "European American."[69]

It seems doubtful, though, that whites in Miami would have spied Black Cubans as Cuban first, Black second. Marvin Dunn thinks Afro-Cubans commonly consider their ethnicity and race in this order: "An African American is more culturally alike to a Mississippi white person than they are a Black Cuban. So there's an alienation of cultures between Black Americans and Black Cubans that is as much of a divide as it is with white Cubans."[70] Cuban life was remaking Dade County. Spanish was everywhere. New restaurants served arroz con pollo, and supermarkets sold yucca, malanga, and plátanos.[71] Writing in the 1980s, Joan Didion observed that unlike other cities where Spanish is spoken widely, Spanish in Miami is omnipresent and crosses socioeconomic lines.[72]

Similar to Marvin Dunn, Monsignor Walsh believed that rather than depressing Miami's economy, the Cubans saved it. "Had it not been for the Cubans, Miami would have been a dead duck," the priest surmised. Stores and banks had new customers, and the refugees were pivotal to U.S.–Latin American markets. Walsh vigorously defended the need to attend to both African Americans and Cubans. He dreamed of a diverse Miami.[73] Other members of Miami's ecclesiastical community were not so sure. One Presbyterian minister weighed in: "I do not hate Cubans." Yet he questioned Walsh's assertion that the "Negroes of Dade County were suffering injustices long before the Cuban problems arose, and that their injustices did not arise from the problem of Cuban Refugees." The minister cited the findings of the American Federation of Labor and the Congress of Industrial Organizations that blamed the rising level of unemployment among Black and white workers on Cubans.[74]

Walsh dug in by casting blame not at exiles but at Miami itself, a city that had failed its Black residents long before the revolution. Besides, he retorted, "who can blame a Cuban for accepting a job at low wages, when his motivation is to get off the welfare rolls? Must we not blame instead the unscrupulous employer? What we need, perhaps, is a reform here—a good state minimum wage law; the repeal of the so-called 'right to work' law." The fault, he concluded, lay with the levels of government for failing "to provide for Americans in need."[75]

Raul Alvaro was a bright-eyed seventeen-year-old when he left Cuba. Originally from Bayamo in the eastern part of the island, the young man was a dedicated Catholic pupil at a Capuchin Franciscan school. With its messages of economic and social equality for all, the revolution had found ample acolytes in the heavily rural region of Oriente. Raul's middle-class family joined the multitudes against Batista. Raul remembers no public high school in Bayamo, only four private ones. Poor people could not matriculate their children past the eighth grade because they could not afford the elite programs. College or decent job prospects were not a reality for most. A wing of Batista's military operation was in the area, so Alvaro witnessed the dictatorial violence up close. His first encounter with dead bodies was on his way to church one Sunday morning.[1]

What motivated Raul's parents to send him to the United States? Why would a mother indefinitely part with her daughter at the airport? What made a father deposit his son on an international flight solo, trusting that everything was in place for his safekeeping? Children carried those moments of separation into adulthood, their last days in Cuba seared into their minds interminably. Virtually all express unremitting thankfulness that their parents made the decision even as they profess that it came with a cost. Few Pedro Pans could imagine sending away their own children under similar conditions. What to make of this disconnect—gratitude for something one would never do?

In the revolution's aftermath, the cascade of events and the fear it inspired made the parents' judgment more reasonable. After his victory, Fidel Castro promised a democratic transformation of Cuba replete with elections. Publicly he eschewed communism. But within months, the world stood agape as the new government ejected U.S. companies, seized land, executed former Batistianos, and made diplomatic overtures to Moscow. As Cuba and the United States drifted apart, many Cubans, a considerable portion of whom originally supported Castro, looked at their country's future with profound uncertainty.

A sizable number of Cubans who had backed Castro—such as the members of Raul Alvaro's family—now had buyer's remorse and sought to rid the island of the dangerous leader. In 1961, when the government closed schools and Catholic religious were fleeing in large numbers, Alvaro joined activists to keep the church vibrant. His father worried about his son's life, so he obtained a visa waiver. The family warily made its way to Havana. Alvaro had less trepidation. He was nearly an adult and already thinking about jetting out on his own. He first stayed at Matecumbe from June to November 1962. "It wasn't a paradise," he scoffed. "The conditions weren't the best. . . . They weren't prepared." He was sent to Helena, Montana, to live in the beautiful stone structure of Brondel Hall, another property of Catholic Charities run by a pleasant young couple with a small child. The first winters there were brutal. Snow was everywhere, and getting to Montana was no small feat. Once at Brondel, he found some thirty adolescent Cubans. Raul went to a Catholic high school and from there to college in Montana. Though he was now too old to be in the care of the CWB, he was able to stay through his freshman year. "I'm very glad that I went to Montana," he said approvingly. "Cuban boys were a novelty," and the locals treated him well. He never lacked invitations to Thanksgiving dinners. "I had a very positive experience," he beamed.[2]

Back in Cuba, Raul's parents must have fretted, as did so many. One fear was that the nation could descend into civil war and put their children in harm's way. Neither was it far-fetched to imagine their cherished sons being forced into military conscription in a battle against the U.S. military should the country decide to invade. Also, all political factions tailored a mind-boggling volume of propaganda. Castro and the new state were making utopian promises while counterrevolutionary cadres—assisted by the CIA—created a great deal of misinformation, which exacerbated the people's anxiety and sparked panic. The most common of such false claims was that the new government would dispossess parents of their children and brainwash them with communism. Reports circulated that authorities would remove the right of *patria potestad* (legal custody), which conferred parental jurisdiction over one's children at home and at school. This news inspired drastic actions. In one instance, fifty mothers in Bay-

14. A Cuban student from Carroll College (*first from left*) and a representative from Montana Catholic Charities, Inc. (*second from left*) greet Cuban
high school students arriving in Helena, Montana, in 1961. Courtesy of the
Diocese of Helena.

amo signed a pact to commit filicide rather than turn their children
over to the state.[3]

Notices of this tall tale were printed and circulated, though their
precise origin and authorship were uncertain.[4] September 1961 saw
authorities confiscate copies of the supposed law in print shops. Someone had tipped off the government. The fake decree said that as of
January 1962 all children over the age of three would be brought into
state care with limited access to their parents. Similar paperwork was
discovered in other printing facilities on the island.[5] These apocryphal
claims falsely legitimized rumors already in circulation. In fact, earlier
the Catholic-backed National Confederation of Parents' Association
had warned that the government was going to assume control of the
nation's children.[6] Communist indoctrination and the elimination of
churches would follow. Father Bryan Walsh believed it credible, say-

ing at one point that young people in Cuba were "picked up off the streets and never seen again."[7] James Baker, however, knew that patria potestad was nothing but a destructive rumor, but it still did irreparable harm.[8] One Pedro Pan's mother could scarcely bear the "pain, anguish, fear, depression" common to all who sent their children to the States. But she was determined not to lose them to a government that might order them to Russia or prison should they not follow the nation's new edicts.[9]

Another major event that pushed parents to send their children away was when the Cuban government christened 1961 the "Year of Education." In doing so, schools were shuttered and scholastic curricula revamped to follow the prescriptions of revolutionary pedagogy. Private institutions, where many Pedro Pan families learned of the ability for children to leave the island, closed indefinitely. Along with closing schools, Cuban officials designed a nationwide literacy campaign. Deborah Shnookal argues that this is what pushed many teetering parents over the edge. The government further elbowed into domestic spaces where ideas about family, education, and religion were the most intimate. The campaign recruited tens of thousands of young people, most of them teenagers, to teach the masses. Not only were children taken out of school but also a significant number of them left home on their new errand. Fearful parents saw their worlds collapsing and the state directing their children away from them. The rumor mill raised alarm at young women making the journey without chaperones; some returned from the *campo* (countryside) pregnant.[10] In a matter of months, communities anchored by now-scrambling institutions—the majority of which were Catholic—saw their ways of life disintegrate.

Lurking in the background of all of this were several precedents of parent-child separation still identifiable in local memory. When many Cubans signed up to fight Francisco Franco and fascism in the Spanish Civil War (1936–39), they were eyewitnesses to Spaniards sending their children to the Soviet Union, France, Mexico, and other countries for safety. In 1937 authorities evacuated twenty thousand Basque children, collectively known as the "Guernica Generation" for the town in northern Spain demolished by the fascists and memorialized in one of Pablo Picasso's most famous paintings.[11] In a macabre ironic turn, few Spanish youngsters came to the United States due to anti-refugee lobbying, most forcefully by the U.S. Catholic Church, which billed the evacuation as a communist conspiracy because the most vocal proponents of the exodus in Europe were fellow travelers of the Left.[12] There were other missed opportunities. During World War II, the *kindertransport* (children's transport) dispensed ten thousand Jewish children throughout England to escape the Holocaust.[13] The United States tragically lagged on this front as well. Anti-Semitism factored into Congress's rejection of the Wagner-Rogers Bill (1939–40) that would have allowed twenty thousand German children—many Jewish—to come to the United States. America's anti-refugee posture would only change after the war when the motivation shifted from saving children from fascism to rescuing them from communism.[14]

Pedro Pan parents remembered such precedents. Elly Chovel and James Baker attested to the heavy impact of this collective memory, as did Carlos Eire.[15] His mother believed that the state would take custody of her children. For both her and Chovel's mother, who was Spanish herself, it sparked associations with the children who were sent to the Soviet Union during the Spanish Civil War.[16] The propaganda worked. The rumor mill took over, and parents were truly frightened. María Vidal de Haymes was sure that the fearmongering led to her brothers' removal. Her brothers were sent to Nebraska and were eventually reunited with Haymes and her family, who arrived via a ship sponsored by the Red Cross.[17]

The chaotic environment and spurious propaganda made the decision to send one's child away rational. Some parents were active in the underground resistance, and a handful worked with the CIA.[18] Terrifying was the proposition that those kids remaining behind could become government collateral used against parents fighting Castro. Others had material holdings they wanted to protect from confiscation. In the end, it was difficult for adults to secure visas, whereas their children could without much difficulty. All believed that in short order families would reunite in the United States or in a post-Castro Cuba.[19]

Later in life, Monsignor Walsh said the matter boiled down to a humanitarian issue. Ultimately nations were chiefly concerned with politics, not human rights. That he was able to shuttle more than fourteen thousand children across national borders was a question of humanity. From his perspective, the church merely stepped in as a beacon of humanitarianism that was absent. Parents, he averred, had the right to raise their children in the manner they chose, even if it meant sending them to the United States. Families of comfort had options.[20]

One of the big questions in Operation Pedro Pan (OPP) lore is, to what degree, if any, did the CIA directly sculpt the program? There is bitter disagreement over this query. Some, including most Cuban historians, hold no doubt that the agency was a key player and possibly the lead orchestrator of what Cubans call "Operación Peter Pan." But it turns out that definitive proof is not easy to come by; incontrovertible documentation is lacking.

What *is* unquestionably true is that the CIA—and other branches of the U.S. government—labored indefatigably to bring down Fidel Castro and his revolution. The best and brightest spanning Washington DC; Langley, Virginia; Miami; Cuba; Guatemala; Nicaragua; Honduras; and elsewhere planned, budgeted, and executed assaults that were economic, military, political, and psychological in skill and strategy. OPP intersected with this capacious patchwork of counterrevolutionary activity. Numerous individuals doctored documents and orchestrated logistics to get children out of Cuba, but they were mere nodes on the much bigger matrix of anti-Castro engineering. Between January and August 1962 alone, the Cuban government counted 5,780 "counterrevolutionary actions." Surely this was an undercount.[21]

President Eisenhower saw Cuba's Fidel Castro as he did Iran's Mohammad Mossadegh in 1953 and Guatemala's Jacobo Árbenz Guzmán the following year. Ike returned to his successful strategy of a hidden hand to remove the dictator. In March 1960 he signed off on the plan to create a paramilitary force of exiles to invade Cuba.[22] John Kennedy inherited the operation but would bungle it in April 1961, with the Cuban army defeating the exile force, accompanied by meek U.S. air support, at the Bay of Pigs. The military strategy necessitated an extensive propaganda initiative headed by David Atlee Phillips, whose cunning had seen success against President Árbenz. The CIA, he later wrote, thought it "unacceptable to have a Commie running Guatemala." Phillips and his family arrived in Havana in 1955, and he, too, was mesmerized by Castro in the early days of the revolution. Of his chance meeting with Ernesto "Che" Guevara, he "admired him" but understood that they would be adversaries. Eisenhower was committed to preventing a "Soviet beachhead" in the hemisphere, and Phillips was to bring about a reprise of Guatemala's regime change in Cuba.[23]

To exert psychological pressure on the Cubans, to destabilize the nation, and to crumble Castro's leadership, Phillips deployed radio transmissions, leaflet drops, and other media and publication outlets to propagate spurious information. The CIA commissioned a fifty-kilowatt radio station located on the Swan Islands off the coast of Honduras. Beginning in May 1960, Radio Swan broadcast claims that Havana would eliminate religious schools and make churches property of the state. Castro would take control of the nation's children and would become "Mother Superior of Cuba." Other transmissions claimed that Castro would make government workers out of priests and nuns, that mothers would lose their children of ages five to eighteen years old, and that Cuban prisoners had been banished to Russia. Cloaked as a commercial station operated by the Gibraltar Steamship Company, Radio Swan was said to be financed and controlled by Cuban refugees without connections to Washington. The New York Times found out about the station sitting four hundred miles from Cuba, another front against "communist propaganda" of which the State Department supposedly knew nothing.[24]

Cuban exiles labored in transnational channels between Miami and Havana to take back their country. The United States funded and groomed some of these undertakings. The Movement of Revolutionary Recovery, headed by Manuel Artime, recruited personnel for the Bay of Pigs and formulated a replacement government.[25] Washington, however, preferred the Cuban Revolutionary Council headed by José Miró Cardona, the revolution's first prime minister until he was forced out. Located at the University Miami, the commercial front was Zenith Technical Enterprises under the code name JM/WAVE and represented the largest CIA facility outside of Langley. Miami was thoroughly outfitted to take down Castro from afar with close to a $150 million annual budget, four hundred American officers, and up to fifteen thousand Cubans on its payroll. In all likelihood, Pedro Pans did not know that from the barracks of Opa-locka airport, hopeful members of the council awaited word of their repatriation during the Bay of Pigs invasion. The plan was for Cardona and the council to erect a new government after the successful invasion and earn diplomatic recognition from the United States and its allies, a plan that did not come to pass.[26]

Certainly this larger apparatus of sabotage enhanced and maybe even enabled Operation Pedro Pan, but it is missing a CIA document trail directly leading to OPP. Pedro Pan and scholar on the subject María de los Angeles Torres has been a vocal critic of the agency's lack of transparency. After conducting Freedom of Information Act requests, she sued the CIA, hoping to find out more, but in the end was unsuccessful. She remains convinced that the complete account of OPP has yet to be divulged.[27] Torres maintains that the agency worked with nongovernment agencies, giving money to groups such as the International Rescue Committee and the National Catholic Welfare Conference, which were instrumental in attaining visa waivers and transporting and resettling Cuban children. Radio Swan was funded by the CIA, as were speaking tours and media publications around the hemisphere by Cubans attesting to the patria potestad rumor. Torres's case is persuasive. She has it that Maj. Gen. Edward Lansdale—a higher-up in strategies to remove Castro—advised that "we should exploit the emotional possibilities of the 8,000 children that were under the protection of the United States."[28]

Cuban researchers Ramón Torreira Crespo and José Buajasán Marrawi cite Operation Pedro Pan as a grand CIA scheme as well. The same agency that planned numerous assassination plots against Fidel Castro and plied voluminous subterfuge against the revolution went after Cuba's children, they insist.[29] That Radio Swan, a CIA operation, focused on parents losing their children is proof of the agency's role in Operation Pedro Pan, they uphold. Another Cuban historian, using newly available Cuban documents, has gone as far as to assert that David Atlee Phillips was present at the early meeting between Father Walsh, the State Department, and the attorney general's office, making him the key link in the CIA-OPP chain.[30]

While official documentation is lacking, there is no shortage of anecdotal allegations by the people involved. Wayne Smith was a young diplomat working in the U.S. Embassy in Havana when it closed in 1961. He believes the CIA was involved and points the finger at Radio Swan and at the collusion between the agency and the Catholic Church that worked together to remove the children. "Irresponsible" and "heartless" were the terms Smith used to describe the mission to separate families just to destabilize Cuba. Marta Núñez, a professor at the University of Havana, was a student at Ruston Academy and had two cousins who left as Pedro Pans. Her aunt and uncle did not join her cousins in the United States until ten or twelve years later because the uncle was found guilty of being a CIA agent. Marta, like many Cubans, believes that the U.S. strategy was to disintegrate the Cuban family to defeat the revolution.[31]

Walsh rendered contradictory positions on the question. He denied the CIA's involvement but then opened up about his own contact with the agency. On another occasion, he reiterated that he lacked "absolute proof"; yet he also conceded, "If the CIA didn't know what we were doing they were negligent." Further, "not to have had the CIA at least watching would be ridiculous."[32] In his review of the U.S. campaign against Fidel Castro, Jon Elliston writes: "The far-reaching methods the United States has used to try to influence public opinion in and about Cuba have included anti-Castro 'goon squads,' rumor campaigns, posters, newspapers, books, comics, newsreels, leaflet drops, and radio and T.V. broadcasts from airplanes, blimps, boats, submarines, secluded islands, and the U.S. mainland."[33] Certainly some of this would have intersected with Operation Pedro Pan. Direct links between the agency and OPP, then, are at best circuitous; the ties are not clearly threaded. The hypothesis of cross-fertilization, even if coincidental, is a likely one.

There were figures who worked on OPP while participating in, or in proximity to, other circles of anti-revolutionary activity. The parents of Gabriel Orozco Figueroa sent their sons to the United States while they remained behind to fight Castro. At age thirteen, Orozco left Cuba on May 20, 1962, along with this brother, five years his junior. They were separated upon arrival at Florida City. While his younger brother remained at Florida City, Gabriel went to Opa-locka. Four of his cousins wound up in Nebraska and made the state their home.

There were difficulties, but Orozco has favorable associations with the program, saying the children lived in nurturing circumstances and received good educations and economic prosperity. But it came with a cost; Orozco would not see his father again until 1978. Tried and sentenced for being a CIA agent, Orozco's father denied the connection but conceded that he ran in groups that did have contact with agents. Father and son also agree that the CIA did not sponsor OPP, but they name Mongo Grau as the principal intermediary between the two.[34]

Ramón Grau Alsina, aka "Mongo," was the nephew of Ramón Grau San Martín, who served as the president of Cuba in 1933 and again from 1944 to 1948. Mongo and his sister, Leopoldina "Polita" Grau Alsina, lived in the heart of the anti-Castro underground. At first the Graus sympathized with the revolution but, as did so many, changed their tune when socialism came into view.[35] From his uncle's house across from Cuba's G-2 intelligence service, Mongo kept visa waivers in his daughter's backpack with alcohol and matches ready to light them if the authorities came.[36] The former president's residency was a stronghold of anti-revolutionary operations. Here visas, waivers, and passports were manufactured and their transportation facilitated.[37] Walsh sent money orders to Mongo to pay for airline tickets as the latter conspired with separatist Catholic leaders in Havana.[38] Juan Carlos Rodríguez has written that Grau worked with the CIA via the Catholic Church, circulating waivers and trafficking lists of children's names for flight.[39]

Mongo published his autobiography in the 1990s after he left prison. Representative Ileana Ros-Lehtinen (R-FL), an important conservative voice for Miami Cubans, wrote a prologue that compared Grau's saving Cuban children from communism to the efforts of Swedish architect Raoul Wallenberg who rescued thousands of Jews from the Holocaust. She even nominated Mongo for the Nobel Peace Prize.[40] Reading his story, we learn about his growing up in his uncle's exclusive circles and taking occasional jaunts to Miami and New York City. The time abroad showed the youngster, whose faith is prominent throughout his memoir, a different face of Catholicism. He was struck that in Cuba a young person never spoke to a priest without first being spoken to, while American priests were much more avuncular and even played basketball with children.

Like others, Mongo thought about the Spanish Civil War when communists sent their children abroad. He thought Cuban leaders aimed to separate families to inculcate young people with Marxist principles. His version of the patria potestad document is that Castro himself dictated the decree, which then floated around government circles. Anti-Castro spies discovered the proclamation, made copies of it, and littered it throughout the island. Panic ensued. After the Bay of Pigs, Grau ramped up his activity by distributing visa waivers and raising money so more children could leave. He wrote the U.S. State Department with alarm, saying that conditions in Cuba were like those in the Spanish Civil War and that children were being sent to Russia. Washington answered by putting him in contact with the Catholic Welfare Bureau. Now at his back were the State Department, the CIA, the Catholic Church, and the extensive support of the embassy. Walsh sent Grau money orders, and Mongo's life transformed into a higher calling: "I had the blessing and cooperation of the Church and I believed the blessing from God." With help from his sister, Polita, his crew counterfeited waivers, which were copied easily from the legitimate ones he possessed signed by Walsh. False passports were reassembled from family members of the recently deceased. Changing a photo and a birth date, and adding a waiver, made them ready for children.[41]

"The key to Operation Pedro Pan's success was the fact that no one took me seriously," he later reflected. A playboy reputation tailed him, making the proposition that a pampered nephew of a Cuban elite family was attempting anything of this magnitude sound absurd. The Grau surname undoubtedly helped. Embassy doors opened. Italy's was especially helpful, as were those of Japan, France, and Mexico. Diplomats and their families and staff could pass names, passport numbers, money, and all that was needed. Grau also relied on Penny Powers, a onetime British intelligence officer who worked closely with James Baker at Ruston Academy. There was also a mishmash of other coconspirators, such as Maria Boissevain, the granddaughter of tsarist Russian mystic Grigori Rasputin. As the wife of the Dutch ambassador, she did not have to pay for travel on KLM. She might have brought up to five hundred visas to Cuba on each trip.[42]

Women played a large role in OPP, perhaps because they could fly more easily under the radar of the Cuban government. They were often the personnel in schools or embassies and influential wives and mothers. Serafina Lastra de Giquel traded in exotic flowers and landscape architecture, yet she and her husband—an orthodontist and a friend of the Bakers—kept lists of names of children and helped deliver documents. Beatriz López Morton, a relative of the Graus who worked part time at a museum, typed children's names on the visa waivers. She was on the CIA's payroll until Cuban authorities detained her, at which point she pursued a life as a double agent for the agency and Cuba's G-2 forces. She would end up in Miami well taken care of for her loyalty to the United States. Hilda Feo and Alicia Thomas also helped Grau. Thomas, a "master forger," was good with a razor blade in the artistry of false identification.

There was also the wealthy socialite Sara del Toro de Odio and Teté Cuervo, a secretary at W. Harry Smith Agency in Havana. Del Toro was an early Castroite until he veered toward socialism. In late 1960 she took five of her children to Miami and met Maurice Ferré, who took her to Walsh. The priest, in turn, gave her waivers to distribute in Havana. She and her husband were eventually caught and imprisoned, and she served six years for her crimes, which did not include Operation Pedro Pan. Instead, she was found guilty of arson, which destroyed a department store, and of participating in assassination conspiracy. After the pair was freed, they rejoined their children in Miami.[43]

Things really unraveled when the black market for waivers and passports exploded. Walsh's name was easily falsifiable, and the priest issued little objection. "Every time we ran out of visa waivers, we made more," Mongo wrote. Airlines ensured that no one could tell the difference. They inserted fake names on the flight manifest; then they replaced them with the names of unaccompanied children at the last minute to avoid their detection by authorities. Heart-wrenching as it was to watch children say goodbye to relatives indefinitely at the Havana airport's pecera, Mongo stayed faithful to the cause.[44]

At the time of his arrest in 1965, he claimed that his troop had stamped forty-seven thousand waivers.[45] Mongo also asserted he had connections to the CIA and the U.S. State Department through the

British consulate, with Penny Powers serving as the go-between. Such a network allowed him to move waivers signed by Walsh and to disperse money orders to parents more easily.[46] The waivers were circulating all over Cuba; many were counterfeit, but still the United States accepted them.[47] At one point, Walsh was asked to authenticate one belonging to a sixty-five-year-old woman. The waiver was dated November 8, 1961, bearing what appeared to be his own valid signature. Whether it was signed by him or forged in Cuba we do not know.[48]

Walsh suggested that Mongo inflated his importance in OPP and that not everything he said about the program was true. Rather, Grau's sister, Polita, with closer ties to Baker's group and the Catholic Church, was more important in the operation.[49] Polita, who sent her own children to the United States, absolved the CIA of direct responsibility but affirmed that her brother worked for the agency. She counted Powers as one of the higher-ups in the operation and was sure that the Ruston employee's proximity to the British Embassy prevented her imprisonment. Polita helped falsify passports and even joined a plan to assassinate Castro.[50] She joined the movement led by Manuel Antonio "Tony" de Varona Loredo—a former Cuban prime minister under the government of Carlos Prío Socorrás—and his group Rescate (Rescue), which, among other things, plotted to bring down the revolutionary government and kill Castro with support of the CIA. Rescate participated in spreading rumors about patria potestad and abetted Radio Swan transmissions by distributing literature that verified its fake news reports over the airways. Polita and the group helped obtain exit papers, airline tickets, and visa waivers. At her uncle's house, she and her brother handed out counterfeit passports and stamped visas in them. Close to figures in the Catholic Church and the Cuban Baptist Church, Polita also claimed that she worked under the direction of the CIA.[51]

James Baker doubted the CIA's direct responsibility for OPP. His school handled waivers and facilitated the carriage of children, though he denied knowing the Graus, having left Cuba by the time they became involved. His career, which began as a teacher at Ruston in 1930, abruptly came to end. Baker had planned to stay in Cuba the rest of his life. When he and his wife packed and left for the United States, he grieved. He always saw himself as an "American Cuban" who was also forced to leave his home.[52]

Not much is known about Penny Powers, yet she was essential to the program. Children were a passion of hers. During World War II, she was a nurse who helped Jewish children escape Germany; then she took a job at the British Embassy in Havana. After Baker left, she undertook the directorship of Ruston and brought Mongo into the operation. Some have said that Powers worked directly with British intelligence. Cuban authorities never apprehended her, and she died in Havana in 1995.[53] There are scant traces of Powers in Walsh's archive. An external audit in 1962 named Walsh as the operation's director; Father John Nevins, the assistant director; George Guarch, the "airport receptionist"; and Penny Powers, the main contact in Havana.[54] Her name also appears in a document from 1963, when Walsh was searching for her whereabouts after the missile crisis. He wrote the British Embassy in Tokyo with a request to contact its counterpart in Havana.[55] He wrote another letter of inquiry trying to locate Powers in 1967, but what became of these queries is unknown.[56]

The OPP underground spread from there. As mentioned, Serafina Lastra and her husband, Sergio Giquel, assisted Baker's group. Serafina sometimes made first contact, visiting families and asking if they wanted to send their children to the United States. They kept the operation up and running after Baker moved to Miami.[57] Ruston teacher Berta de la Portilla; her husband, Francisco (Frank or Pancho) Finlay; and her sister Ester also belonged to this inner circle. The sisters sent their own children to the States while staying behind to back the operation. They collaborated with Catholic school representatives to get kids their documents. The grandson of the famous Cuban physician Carlos Finlay, who had discovered that yellow fever was transmitted by mosquitoes, Frank was the general manager of KLM Airlines in Cuba and arranged flight reservations.

Another important figure was Albertina O'Farrill de la Campa, who was from an Irish Brahmin family in Havana and had been educated in Florida and New York schools. She conspired with different embassies to obtain waivers for the children and even sent her own children so she could wage war against Castro. Her husband had been an ambassador to Portugal, and the couple still bobbed in and out of upper diplomatic echelons. O'Farrill would face prison time. She was dubious of the CIA's participation but estimated the number of children who left to be as high as fifteen thousand. She kept her commitments to Batista until the end and fully believed that parents had lost their rights to the state under Castro. "I am very happy," she later proclaimed, "for helping out with Operation Pedro Pan, and I consider it one of the best operations in the world."[58]

As flights filled, airlines reserved seats for unaccompanied children, but they could not sell tickets without a visa or waiver. Teté Cuervo worked at the W. Harry Smith Agency and verified that Gilbert Smith, the son of the travel agency's founder, would book several seats with fake passenger names that would eventually go to Pedro Pans. Priests in plain clothes would come to the office with children in need of waivers, all arranged by Smith beforehand. Pan Am's Havana office ensured seating priority for the program that could amount to 10 to 20 percent of each flight.[59] Airlines were obligated to provide the Cuban Interior Ministry with the names of passengers, but privately they set aside seats for kids who were listed under different names. Mongo and other individuals would then provide the airlines with a registry of children before the flights, and the airlines would tell the Interior Ministry they had last-minute cancellations.[60]

In the end, Polita and Mongo served fourteen and twenty-one years, respectively, in Cuba's prisons for their activities.[61] Polita was charged with spying and attempting to assassinate Castro and other leaders of the revolution. Torreira and Buajasán write that when she was tried and convicted in 1965, she confessed to having participated in the counterfeiting of 3,500 U.S. visas. She also confirmed having received visa waivers from the CWB via the embassies of Panama, Spain, and Holland, and that this work also benefited from the Liberian consulate's residence.[62] Mongo, who was also arrested in 1965 and imprisoned, was released in 1986, at which point he, too, found sanctuary in Miami. While most likely an exaggeration, Grau estimated that he signed twenty-eight thousand waivers for children. He died in Miami, not far from the stomping grounds of his childhood trips to Miami Beach. His death brought adulation by Pedro Pans far and wide.[63]

The Bay of Pigs failure proved that the revolution would indeed survive. While Cuba was at risk of more violence from within and without, Fidel Castro had staved off the U.S. operation to overthrow him. More parents put their children on planes. Then in October 1962 came the missile crisis, which halted air traffic between the countries and forced Washington to agree not to attempt another invasion. Washington would fail in its mission of regime change. For that reason, John F. Kennedy elicited mixed feelings in the exile community. While he embraced the cause of Cuban refugees, he was also the president who allowed Castro to become stronger.[1] Miami mayoral candidate Raul Masvidal spoke for all exiles when he named Fidel Castro the number 1 hated man in Miami. Number 2, he said, was John Kennedy.[2]

It was true that no event transformed Cold War politics in the Western Hemisphere as much as the Cuban Revolution. In short order, Castro's victory upended long-standing relations between nations bound by what President William McKinley had called "ties of singular intimacy" and President Franklin Roosevelt later touted to be those of "good neighbors." The revolution vowed to correct what it condemned as an unequal and abusive relationship between neighbors. From a Cuban perspective, cementing the revolution meant rewriting Cuba's past and pursuing a successful future that conformed to a Marxist teleology, whereby the working masses overthrew not only a bourgeois dictatorship but a U.S. neocolonial system that had simply replaced Spanish colonialism. Cubans had never been granted the opportunity to be truly free until now.

But the rebirth of Cuban sovereignty was a messy affair. Cubans and foreign onlookers watched with a mix of awe and horror the spectacle of the public executions of Batista officials under dubious due process. Swift legislative acts nationalized key aspects of the economy. Big business and land holdings—foreign and domestic—now belonged to the state. Throughout 1959 Castro assured the people that Cuba was not communist but democratic and that elections were in the offing. But in 1960, Soviet deputy premier Anastas Mikoyan made an official visit and negotiated a trade deal that guaranteed the USSR would purchase 20 percent of Cuba's annual sugar crop for five years. With it came a $100 million credit commitment. After the Bay of Pigs, Castro declared the revolution socialist, and in that same year, the government federalized the educational system. Families with children in parochial schools now had to submit to curricula that focused on José Martí and Karl Marx rather than Jesus and the Virgin Mary. Meanwhile, talk on the street rehashed rumors and misinformation, chief among them the assertion that Fidel would dispossess parents of their children and send them to Moscow for indoctrination.

In its narrowest sense, Operation Pedro Pan was a Cold War invention. When peeling back the deeper layers of U.S.-Cuban history, however, what comes to the fore is an asymmetrical chronicling of relations between the countries, an uneven record of exchange in which the United States for quite some time had exercised disproportionate control over Cuban life. Cuba had operated in the U.S. cultural imagination in a particular way. Presidents and businessmen had long beheld Cuba as the "Pearl of the Antilles," a territory ripe for annexation. Statesmen from Thomas Jefferson onward had envisioned Cuba as a natural appendage to the United States.[3]

After the USS *Maine* exploded under mysterious circumstances in Havana's harbor in 1898, U.S. intervention in Cuba's War of Independence conditioned its break from colonial Spain in one fell swoop. Spain was blamed, and the Americans entered what they would call the Spanish-American War while simultaneously inaugurating the birth of modern American empire. Postwar acquisitions included Guam, Puerto Rico, and the Philippines. The United States did not include Cubans in the armistice talks but instead occupied the island between 1898 and 1902. The Teller Amendment of 1898 made Cuba a nominally sovereign nation thereafter, but in practice Uncle Sam left a heavy economic and cultural imprint in its exit that laid the groundwork for immense commercial and legal control over Cuban affairs. The Platt Amendment of 1903, which began as an appendage to an army appropriations bill that became obligatory for U.S. withdrawal, granted that the United States "may exercise the right to intervene for the preservation of Cuban independence, the maintenance of a government adequate for the protection of life, property, and individual liberty."[4] It gave Washington the ability to govern treaties between Cuba and other countries, to transform the island into a U.S. Navy coaling station and strategic military site, and later to establish a military base at Guantánamo Bay, which is still in U.S. possession today. Legal intervention was affixed to the birth of Cuban sovereignty.

Even before receiving this far-reaching administration, Cuba was thoroughly marked by U.S. modernity. Spain's colony had a functioning railroad in the 1830s and a telegraph system by the early 1850s. Antebellum tourism prompted five thousand American tourists to flock to Cuba annually. During the War of Independence between 1868 and 1898, thousands of Cubans moved to the United States; transnational transit topping one hundred thousand people between the countries was normal by the 1890s. First introduced in the 1860s by Cuban students returning from U.S. schools, baseball gradually displaced bullfighting as the national sport.[5] The back-and-forth traffic built a significant cadre of pro-independence Cubans living and organizing for national freedom in the United States. José Martí was the most salient figure in this group. The patriarch and martyr for independence lived much of his life in the northern hegemon. In addition to New Orleans and New York, nineteenth-century Florida became defined by Cuban influence. Tampa, especially the neighborhood of Ybor City, along with Jacksonville and Key West drew legions of Cuban workers.[6]

Independent Cuba bore U.S. patronage and influence everywhere. Throughout Havana were retail shops and grocery stores that flashed the occupying nation's stamp. There was American Eagle Laundry, and everything from American beauty products to musical instruments was standard fare on customs ledgers.[7] Efforts to resist the Yankee hypnosis arose, however. During the occupation, Habaneros, it turned out, did not necessarily want to celebrate George Washington's birthday, as the U.S. military government wished, and when U.S. authorities and Cuban elites abolished the time-honored practice of cockfighting, Cubans from other social strata complained.[8] But when Cuba won independence from Spain, it was the U.S. flag that flew over the iconic

El Morro fortress in Havana. English replaced Spanish in government officialdom. U.S. goods flooded the market, and signs proclaiming English Spoken Here were prominently displayed in store windows. Thus went the anglicization of everyday life: upscale Cubans now drank *tea* at *garden parties*.

American capitalism and customs strove to modernize Cuba through the progress-oriented, benevolent empire. It was a pressing preoccupation among the urbane to renounce "backwardness" and all things "primitive." Electric lights, typewriters, bicycles, telephones, and American-made toilets now graced Cuban homes. Modernity further redesigned the circuitry of the nation. Cars replaced horses and carriages; contemporary sewage and waste disposal were the benchmarks of U.S. cosmopolitanism. The desire was to live, in Marial Iglesias Utset's phrase, *a la americana* (in the American way).[9] North American economic control solidified this dependency. Sugar was king. U.S. industrialists went from owning 21 percent of sugar production in Cuba in 1905 to 63 percent in 1926.[10] By 1920 a whopping 73 percent of Cuban imports came from the United States, and by mid-decade U.S. investment in Cuba was well over $1 billion.[11] By the 1950s U.S. culture was everywhere in print and on screen. Cubans knew *Lassie*, read O. Henry, and absorbed world events from the U.S. Information Service. They enjoyed the feats of Superman and the foibles of Mickey Mouse, and they aped home spaces, such as the decor of *el living-room*, after those of their North American counterparts.[12]

But more vitally, the 1898 intervention solidified certain depictions and assumptions about Cuba and Cubans that gained saliency in U.S. imperial discourse. The "truth" about Cuba, as many American spokespeople held it, was that the country could not exist without Uncle Sam's authority. In the northern cultural imagination, Cuba was largely a land of Black and mixed-race people whose lack of civilization hampered its path to progress. This logic was merely a rewriting of prior colonialist assertions that marked non-white populations as inferior and thus needing European uplift. Just as paternalism was etched in the rationale of colonialism's civilizing mission (*mission civilisatrice*), it was also adopted in U.S. imperial or neocolonial logic. In the longer history of intimate ties, Cuba became another Haiti. These parallels were made often, with one fin de siècle *New York Times* writer warning, "We cannot afford to have another Haiti." Military governor of Cuba Leonard Wood expressed his concurring concern that "the establishment of another Haitian republic in the West Indies would be a serious mistake."[13]

The perceived racial inferiority of Cubans made for a kind of political childhood. Throughout U.S. government memorandums, speeches by the cultural elite, and in everyday popular culture were images of Cubans as unkempt and infantile. This "knowledge" of Cuba legitimated the assertion that the country was not fully fit for sovereignty. When Cubans rose up against their government in 1906, the United States again intervened militarily, and Governor-General Charles Magoon viewed the typical Cuban as "raising and training his children from birth to manhood to know not discipline."[14] Similarly in the 1930s, Undersecretary of State Sumner Welles lamented that Cuba had long depended on U.S. leverage. He said such dependency hampered its development and used infantilizing imagery to draw the point: "You cannot keep a child in braces until it reaches the age of maturity and expect it to walk successfully alone."[15]

The view that Cubans could not be trusted with full autonomy due to their poor biological and developmental fitness was affirmed by R. Henry Norweb, who served as the U.S. ambassador to Cuba in 1945–48. He communicated in 1946: "Many of them possess the superficial charm of clever children, spoiled by nature and geography—but under the surface they combine the worst characteristics of the unfortunate admixture and interpenetration of Spanish and Negro cultures—laziness, cruelty, inconstancy, irresponsibility, and inbred dishonesty."[16]

The persistence of such claims was as expansive as it was reductive. When Fidel Castro assumed leadership, the U.S. press often caricatured him as childlike or dwarflike. In one instance, *Time* magazine likened Castro to "a college radical" and later published a cover cartooning the *camandante* (commander) as a little person dressed in a baseball uniform following the team captain, Soviet premier Nikita Khrushchev.[17] Upon meeting Castro, acting secretary of state Christian Herter relayed that the leader was "very much like a child in many ways" and "quite immature regarding the problems of government."[18] And CIA director

Allen Dulles advised, "The new Cuban officials had to be treated more or less like children."[19]

This historical likening of Cubans to children made up the backdrop of Operation Pedro Pan. If by the 1960s, U.S. residents were bent on caring for Cuban children, that task could not be separated from the historical habit of seeing all Cubans as childlike. The call to rescue the world's youth from communism was itself an altruistic outgrowth of empire.

8 | A NATIONAL TEST

Mario García counts the day he arrived in the United States as his second birthday, a day indelible in his memory. The day he left Cuba, his father prodded him, "It is time to go." His mom sat silently. The boy snatched some fur from his cat Simon to bring with him, along with three changes of clothing as stipulated by the Cuban government. He wore a blue pinstripe suit with an ironed shirt and tie. His mother advised him to dress dapperly: "People treat you according to the way you look." After twenty-eight days, his trip would be final; that was the grace period the Cuban government allowed for emigrants who had second thoughts. "On the 29th day, I cried, because I realized that I had to become an American," he said. Going back was no longer an option.[1]

Openly displayed before the world was the ability—and willingness—of Americans to absorb and accept Cubans of all ages. As the numbers overwhelmed Florida's resources, federal officials looked to accelerate the speed and expanse of their resettlement. In 1962 Arthur Lazell, the director of the Cuban Refugee Center, spiffed up the public relations campaign to move more Cubans out of Miami. Dubbed "Operation '62—Tell One, Help One," the campaign was to remind Americans that the Cuban refugees were a "national responsibility."[2]

The hospitality and hope that Kennedy inspired was not so easily implementable. It tested the limits of the country's willingness to make good on racial inclusivity. The topic made its way to the Senate Subcommittee to Investigate Problems Connected with Refugees and Escapees. Chairman Philip A. Hart (D-MI) invoked language reiterative of Presidents McKinley and Roosevelt when he described Cuba as "our near neighbor, a nation with whom we have had most intimate relations." Bemoaning that the neighbor had fallen to communism, he and the committee heard testimony from José Miró Cardona, Cuba's prime minister who was muscled to resign just thirty-nine days after the revolutionary victory. He thanked Washington leaders on behalf

of "Cubans who have been forced to flee the communist hell of persecution" and called the United States "a great nation for the Christian."[3]

Washington had made a covenant with the anti-communist Cubans.
But hostility toward the exiles grew more clamorous. President Lyndon
Johnson had to contend with letter upon letter from voters lambasting
the open door to refugees. "Miami Already Has Too Many Refugees"
and "Miami Fears Effects of New Influx" were headlines from the *Miami
Herald*, which spoke for a growing chorus of detractors.

Angry missives landed on the president's desk, snapping that an
"American feels unpleasantly like a foreigner" from Flagler Street to
Biscayne Boulevard in Miami. Another grumbled, "I used to make
75 dollars a week, now some Cuban has my job and is being paid 55
dollars a week." Some fretted that exiles posed a security threat. After
the Bay of Pigs, the Department of Defense more strongly lobbied for
resettlement out of Miami while still supporting centralized exiles'
power in the Magic City with chosen representatives ready to retake
the island upon Castro's downfall. Cubans, it was thought, should
avoid assimilating too much lest it impair their ability to return and
rebuild their country.[4]

Miami-Dade County became a national vortex of Cold War anxiety
and a laboratory for the changing demographics. Mayor Robert King
High beamed that his city was a natural place for Cubans. Little Havana
was growing and the refugee center bulging.[5] Roger W. Jones, the assistant secretary of the State Department, seconded that the integration of
Cubans was crucial to U.S. strategic interests because other countries
were looking to Washington for leadership as they faced down their
own communist threats.[6] As chairman of the Senate Subcommittee on
Refugees and Escapees, Senator Ted Kennedy (D-MA) took a road trip
to Miami and posed in photographs with Director John F. Thomas of
the Cuban Refugee Program and mingled on a bus with refugees who
had recently come ashore. The photo op showed the United States was
still fully invested in the Cuban exodus.[7]

Resettlement not only challenged local communities everywhere but
also gave them the opportunity to show off their hospitality. Seeking a
cosmopolitanism that avoided provinciality and isolationism, Americans could feel confident that opening their doors to global integration

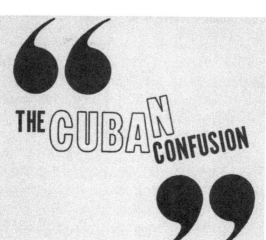

"THE CUBAN CONFUSION"

Refugees from Cuba are pouring into South Florida at a rate of more than 1,000 per week. To date, more than 80,000 of them have arrived. Their presence is breeding some trouble and a great deal of disagreement, centering mainly on two points: what kind of effect are the refugees having on Miami . . . and what should be done with them? "PROJECT 4" reports on the changes being wrought in Florida and the nation by "The Cuban Confusion."

JANUARY 11 AT 10:30 P.M.

INDEPENDENT LIFE
And Accident Insurance Co.
HERALD LIFE INSURANCE CO.

 WJXT
at Broadcast House

15. Card advertising *The Cuban Confusion* television program on WJXT (Jacksonville FL), circa 1961. Courtesy of the State Archives of Florida.

kept communism in check. When after the Bay of Pigs debacle *Life* magazine derided Uncle Sam in the article "A Failure That We Must Recoup: 'Hell of a Beating' in Cuba," readers could still be proud that they were extending their hands to Cubans from sea to shining sea.[8] Civilians could redress governmental shortcomings by rallying around homegrown initiatives. For instance, in Key West in April 1961, a Christian group promoted anti-communism and the absorption of Cubans into the community by sporting signs that read Liberty and Democracy, America for the Americans, and Yankees Yes, Russians No.[9] *Reader's Digest* published an International Rescue Committee solicitation for Cuban refugee aid: "Thousands of refugees in our country—families, friends and compatriots of the ill-fated Cuban freedom fighters— deserve our friendship and compassion as they mourn their dead and pray for loved ones still deprived of liberty." Now "victims of communism" had "a chance to become self-supporting."[10]

The CRP's newsletter, *Resettlement Re-cap*, serialized the progress on a monthly basis. Americans could keep tabs on the influx of exiles in stories such as the one borrowed from the Catholic publication *Family Digest* that told the story of Oscar and Lucila Pérez. Readers learned the couple "had the fear and the steady strangulation of freedom which had come with Castro and communism to Cuba" and that "escaping communistic tyranny had been their only aim, and faith in God and the U.S. their only hope." Thanks to St. Dennis Parish and the people of Royal Oak, Michigan, the Pérez family had transformed into "typical American suburbanites."[11]

Locals scrambled to cordon Pedro Pans further from Moscow's magnetism. The president of the Beaverdam Baptist Association in South Carolina wrote Secretary Ribicoff on behalf of women from nearby churches who were willing to house children to "prevent their forced indoctrination in communism." Martha H. Hynning, the acting director of the Children's Bureau's Division of Social Services, replied that the women could petition Frances Davis's Child Welfare Division of Florida Public Welfare. In the National Archives is an astounding number of similar entreaties. People from all over the country, wishing to foster and adopt children they had never met, wrote offices in Miami and Washington.[12] Many of these letters landed on the desks of Flor-

| SPONSOR CUBAN REFUGEES |
| Fulfill Their Faith in Freedom |
| JUNE 1963 |

RESETTLEMENT RE-CAP

A PERIODIC REPORT FROM THE CUBAN REFUGEE CENTER — FREEDOM TOWER, MIAMI 32, FLORIDA
U. S. DEPARTMENT OF HEALTH, EDUCATION, AND WELFARE — WELFARE ADMINISTRATION

U. S. CUBAN REFUGEE PROGRAM   JOHN FREDERICK THOMAS, Director, Washington, D. C.
J. ARTHUR LAZELL, Director, Refugee Center   HARRY B. LYFORD, Editor

FREE WORLD FRIEND First friend in the free world for Carmen Luisa Santiago is Andy, Boxer pup mascot of a U.S. Coast Guard cutter. Six-year-old Carmen Luisa, her parents and eight other Cuban refugees were picked up by the cutter from British Cay Lobos and brought to Miami. The group had escaped their home-land by small boat and were spotted on the cay by Coast Guard Air patrol. In a total of 4,500 Cuban escapes to free-dom by small, open boats the Coast Guard has played rescue roles in 3,850. (Photo Courtesy U.S. Coast Guard.)

THE SCORE

REGISTERED
Week ending May 31 496
Since January 1961 165,210
Weekly average, last 8 weeks 363

RESETTLED
Week ending May 31 293
Since January 1961 60,430
Weekly average, last 8 weeks 358

By Agencies since January 1961:

	Registered	Resettled
CRS	112,105	34,798
IRC	36,201	13,126
CWS	13,575	10,581
HIAS	3,329	1,925

(See Page 4—"Need For Resettlement?")

CATHOLIC-PROTESTANT COOPERATION IN RESETTLEMENT ANNOUNCED

Catholic-Protestant cooperation to facilitate resettlement of Cuban refugees is being undertaken at the U.S. Cuban Refugee Center, Miami, under an agreement by Catholic Relief Services and Church World Service. Successful working out of the plan will mean that the Catholic resettlement agency -- which has more registrations of refugees than all three of the other agencies coordinated by the government -- can take advantage of a Church World Service backlog of home and job placement opportunities. Church World Service, which represents 27 Protestant denominations in resettlement, explains the coopera-tion as follows:

"We now have very few resettleable Protestant Cubans who have not been given a home and job opportunity, following a two-and-a-half year period during which thousands were screened and flown to many parts of the country, where Protestant churches found a haven and employment for them. In view of the fact that CWS has a large backlog of home and job placement opportunities in various parts of the country, we would like to make these op-portunities available to refugees registered in Miami with the Catholic Relief Services. (Concluded on Page 2)

J. ARTHUR LAZELL NAMED DIRECTOR OF THE CUBAN REFUGEE CENTER

J. Arthur Lazell is the Cuban Refugee Center's new Director. The an-nouncement was made by John F. Thomas, Washington, D.C., Director of the Refugee Program, on a visit to Miami May 27. Mr. Lazell had been Acting Director since May 13 when Marshall Wise returned to his permanent posi-tion as district manager of Miami's Social Security Office. As Director and Deputy Mr. Wise and Mr. Lazell had been the Center's executive team since early 1961. Mr. Lazell is a graduate of Maryville College, Tennes-see, and Princeton Theological Seminary, New Jersey. As an ordained Presbyterian minister he served churches in New York and Pennsylvania. During resettlement of Hungarian refugees in 1956-1958 he had charge of the Presbyterian program. He has also been a newspaper reporter and cor-respondent, radio-television news editor and commentator, magazine writ-er, and author.

MR. LAZELL

16. Front page of the June 1963 edition of the Cuban Refugee Center's *Reset-tlement Re-cap*. Courtesy of the State Archives of Florida.

ida Social Services. As the director of the Cuban Refugee Assistance Program in Florida's Department of Public Welfare, Fern Pence was inundated with such queries as well as notes of gratitude. "Through persons like you," one refugee wrote, "we learn to understand and love the people of this country."[13] Before leaving her position in relief efforts, Mirtha Sierra passed a note to Pence: "You can be proud of your Department, as it is an example of brotherhood and friendship, because here we all feel like we were members of the same big family, as you and all my superiors have treated me with great affection."[14] Another Cuban worker promised, "I know that someday in the near future we will return to our country with the help of the Americans, and may I say to you that the friendship between our countries that was sealed with American and Cuban blood in San Juan Hill in 1898 cannot be destroyed by the hate of a demagogue who is only a toy-puppet handled by the communists."[15]

Pedro Pans dispatched their own letters as well. Seventeen-year-old Gerardo Ameijeiras wrote President Kennedy on August 30, 1962, asking him to assist with a boarding school scholarship and finding a suitable foster home. The letter came in Spanish but was translated and found its way to Director of Social Services at the Children's Bureau Mildred Arnold, who composed a reply some weeks later.[16] Jacqueline Kennedy may have laid eyes on a missive from José L. Hernandez, though the cool response drafted by Arnold just days before the missile crisis directed the boy to a Catholic agency near him. In Arnold's division, sometimes the responsibilities of writing replies fell to Lucille Batson, who often scripted generic responses using recycled boilerplate language.[17]

But some from upper officialdom did respond. Attorney General Robert Kennedy corresponded with Aurelio Pineiro of Wayne, New Jersey, who sent a letter and a dollar to help fund the Red Cross's initiative to get Cubans safely to the United States. Kennedy promised to pass along the boy's letter to the State Department and help him reconnect with his parents on U.S. soil. The thirteen-year-old wrote Kennedy again, explaining that his uncle and aunt wanted Aurelio to live with them in Illinois, in concert with his parents' choice, but the CCP had become more restrictive in who could claim the children. Kennedy pledged to prod HEW on the matter.[18]

Mining the trove of personal letters that were sent to authorities illumes some of the hidden facets of the program that public documents do not divulge. There is a hefty paper trail between legislators and federal and state offices from people wanting to help children as well as complaints about government subventions. The occasional irate constituent griped about the exorbitant costs to care for unaccompanied children and other refugees. How exactly was Washington using taxpayer money? Others wondered why assistance came from Social Security coffers when citizens had to work and wait for their entitlements. Finally, others expressed grievances around religious institutions receiving federal money.[19] Monsignor Walsh's CWB also fielded negative reviews of its work because the funding it received besmirched the country's commitment to the separation of church and state.[20]

Then there were the grouses around Cuban behavior. One woman took her frustration all the way to President Kennedy, alleging that Cuban teenage boys were "molesting the young girls in the neighborhood." Mothers were forced to keep their daughters under lock and key, she complained.[21] A former air force officer who had lived in Cuba for many years wrote Secretary Ribicoff detailing a horrific visit he made to Camp Matecumbe, where he saw four hundred boys housed in "wooden shacks and tents" with only six toilets and twelve showers to share. Why, he wondered, were so many young men from "upper economic classes" continually ill at the shelter? Mildred Arnold answered that while overcrowding was a problem, expansion was underway. She pointed out that teenage boys such as the ones at Matecumbe were hard to resettle since the foster families' preference was always for younger children.[22]

Overcrowding was rigorously harped on throughout the commentary. Colorado had several institutions that breached their maximum occupancies.[23] Worse was when children wound up in facilities lacking official childcare credentials. Charles Rovin of the Bureau of Indian Affairs urgently wrote Frances Davis about one child in foster care at Ganado Mission on the Navajo reservation in Arizona. The mission did not have proper licensure, and the government lacked jurisdiction on Native American land.[24] Walsh was well aware of the objections and disorders.

Parents in Cuba were also incredulous at some of the information they were receiving. Their children, for the most part, were cut off from them. Calls to Cuba were restricted and often not permitted.[25] Yet communication with parents was crucial to maintaining a young person's emotional well-being and facilitating their reunion later. Camp administrators encouraged and sometimes mandated letter composition, doling out special meals to those who wrote home.[26]

Just before the Bay of Pigs invasion, a frustrated Penny Powers in Cuba contacted former U.S. ambassador Philip Bonsal, alarmed that six hundred children had left the island in the preceding weeks and still another seven hundred were ready and waiting. She was flabbergasted to learn that unaccompanied children were not met at the airport. Word had also gotten back to their parents. One father who had sent his four children learned that his two daughters ended up at St. Joseph's Home in Brooklyn and his two sons at Saint John's Home of Rockaway Park, New York. Phone calls were prohibited, but one of the boys wrote the father, who gave the letter to Powers. The son said things had been "horrible" and that were he to stay he would soon become sick. Boys snuck tipples and ate without dinnerware "as if they were animals." Desperate, the father went to Miami to see Walsh.[27]

Powers went up the chain of command and wrote Commissioner of Social Security William Mitchell. She exclaimed that the "orphanage atmosphere" was odious and did not do "anything to further the future Cuban American relationship" or give "the children an idea of a democratic way of life." The differences between a child's home in Cuba and their new environs in the United States were just too extreme. That siblings had been separated was also unfathomable. Families thought their kids would remain in Miami until their reunification. Why hadn't all children been sent to large boarding schools, such as those in Cuba modeled after American institutions? The optics left much to be desired: "As the children are mostly in orphanages spread all over the United States, it gives the parents a feeling of complete hopelessness and also makes them feel it is a foregone conclusion that the children are thought of as orphans."

Powers also went after Walsh, contending that the CCP should no longer be a "Catholic enterprise." Instead, HEW or another government department should receive and screen the children and send them to appropriate shelters or homes.[28]

Walsh pushed back, clarifying that while a few children were in orphanages, for the most part his group relied on foster homes and boarding schools. When homes were substandard, such as one in

Philadelphia and one in Brooklyn, the children were removed. The program did separate siblings on occasion, but the CWB worked to minimize this. Not all correspondence was bad; the priest had a bevy of letters expressing gratefulness for the program. He argued that no children were resettled outside of Miami "who were unwilling to go." This, however, is a questionable claim. Children actually had little say in the matter. Many young refugees were afraid that leaving Miami would mean a delay in rejoining their parents, and a slice who left anxiously requested to return to Florida as soon as possible.

A furious Walsh further corrected Powers and charged that she did not have the facts straight but was instead relying on "rumors." His version was that the father had two, not four, children in the United States, along with two nephews and one niece. He agreed to have his children sent to Brooklyn but had seen them prior to that in Miami. After hearing his complaint, the CWB sent the group to Buffalo, and that appeared to settle the matter. Moreover, the CWB staff had indeed met the children at the airport. This imbroglio points to the untidiness of the program as well as a persistent fight for control. The priest read Powers's assertions as an attack on religious childcare more generally. Yet Powers was under no obligation to send minors to the CWB. In the end, he argued, Cuban families preferred their children's placement with Catholic families.[29] If it ever was good, the relationship between Powers and Walsh had soured.

Clearly the program needed better public relations, but where would the money come from for it? Dorothy McCrary, a supervisor of the Child Welfare Division's Cuban Unit, wrote to her colleagues in the Children's Bureau, the United Hebrew Immigrant Aid Society, and the Jewish Family and Children's Service in search of better press on children who left Miami. Resettlement had earned a terrible reputation, and now young refugees were reluctant to leave the Magic City. Desperately needed were tales of triumph from children who had been placed elsewhere.[30] But these more favorable anecdotes were in short supply. As Pedro Pans aged into adulthood, a considerable number still had not seen their parents. In June 1965 Walsh opened his mail to find a letter from a boy who had written Lucille Batson, who in turn suggested he write the monsignor. The boy and his sister, ages fifteen and thirteen, respectively, had seen the quarters of Kendall, Matecumbe, and Florida City before their transfer to Indiana. Four years had passed, and they still had no word on their parents. The boy pleaded for the priest to do something.[31]

From her law office on Northwest Second Avenue in Miami, Pury Lopez settles into her Pedro Pan tale with a mix of contemplation and flair. After the government closed the schools, she left Cuba on January 15, 1962. She wore a tag marking her as a lone minor. Her new home would be Florida City. Unlike others, Pury had no family in Miami. Her father was a high-ranking member of Cuba's sugar industry and worked closely with Julio Lobo, the island's richest man, whose mills cultivated half the country's sugar. As a young girl, she lived on the property of the Tinguaro mill in Matanzas Province, spending kindergarten and first grade at a French-Canadian music school in Colón. Then in 1958 her family relocated to Havana, where she entered the Catholic school Colegio del Apostolado. After Castro's victory, her father was put under house arrest. Considering both Miami and Spain for his daughter, he created a false dossier that included an ailment requiring treatment in the United States. The underground helped Pury's family, and she suspects that her parents may have been a part of the clandestine resistance. Her mother sent Monsignor Walsh a letter requesting a waiver.[1]

At age ten, Pury joined the thousands of children making their way to Miami. Though she and her young compatriots did not know it, they were joining a new generation unto itself in a nation where kids were becoming an obsession for the first time. "For its first hundred years of existence," writes Kriste Lindenmeyer, "the United States was a young nation with about half its population seventeen or younger." By 1940, however, the proportion of children fell to a quarter of the population.[2] What had changed? Birth rates, death rates, immigration flows, science, and medicine that lengthened longevity, certainly. But the very conception of childhood itself had altered. With the World War II baby boom came widespread enthusiasm for children. The population exploded: from 1946 to 1960, the country birthed 60 million new citizens.[3] Many—Pedro Pans among them—would need institutional care, social services, and new child-rearing approaches that were taking shape in the postwar era.

No organized child protection service existed until the New York Society for the Prevention of Cruelty to Children popped up in 1875. Childhood was not recognized as an academic-worthy period of development until the twentieth century.[4] At the dawn of the republic, colonial New England granted adoption-like arrangements such as apprenticeships and indentured servitude, and if children had no reliable family member or master, they might have earned the charity of almshouses or an occasional orphanage. Otherwise, an abandoned waif could only hope for a family willing to house her. Ursuline nuns set up the first orphanage in French New Orleans in 1727, but these homes did not grow appreciably until the nineteenth century. The number of orphanages skyrocketed after the Civil War when thousands of children were bereft of one or both parents. Escalating immigration and epidemics of cholera and yellow fever made the number of parentless children swell. In 1851 Massachusetts passed the nation's first adoption law. In the West, the United States stood alone. France did not have adoption laws until 1923, England until 1926.[5]

Accompanying the spike in urban populations—New York City's was 515,000 by 1850—was a growing underclass of homeless children. Disease and death among those under five years of age reached unfathomable proportions. In 1852 New York City police estimated that three thousand children lived on the streets. In response, Charles Loring Brace, the director of the New York Children's Aid Society, organized "orphan trains" beginning in 1853. Following an education in religion and philosophy at Yale University, Brace attended Union Theological Seminary in New York City, where he discovered his mission to help the urban poor. After witnessing the depravity and destitution of the Five Points district, he threw himself into the hardscrabble elements of society by directing his energies to the "evils and dangers threatened from the class of deserted youths."[6] Christian charity fueled these ventures westward with the belief that relocation backed by ecclesiastical virtue would enable foundlings to thrive far from the ills of urbanity. Boston reported six thousand indigent children, and New York's number soon ballooned to thirty thousand. We will never know how many were taken without parental consent. More important for middle- and upper-class urban reformers was that the nation would prosper by saving poor young people from deviance while supplying much-needed labor. City paupers could become western farmers. The move to agrarian life—the bedrock of American democratic virtue since the revolution—promised to transform children into productive citizens. Between 1853 and 1929, as many as 250,000 kids were shuttled across the rolling plains.[7]

Eventually, asserts Paula Fass, "scientists, doctors, and educators . . . gradually replaced amateur child savers." Children were now research subjects with measurable dimensions of imaginative play and emotional development.[8] Fin de siècle thinkers studied early stages of human development by looking at the environments that structured childhood. They became the subjects of social reform and early documentary photography, such as that of Jacob Riis and Lewis Hine, whose work helped pattern the country's first child labor laws. By 1910 over 123,000 children lived in orphanages. The Progressive Era spawned greater interest in foster care. Experts were divided as to whether orphans thrived better in state institutions, such as orphanages, or with actual families. The era conferred more respectability to sociology, psychology, pediatrics, and the budding social work profession in matters of juvenile health that diminished the role of religious and charitable rubrics for childrearing. Policy makers took note. The first juvenile court was created in 1899, and ten years later President Theodore Roosevelt convened the White House Conference on the Care of Dependent Children with two hundred participants. Family care now took precedence over the institutionalization of needy children.[9]

Congress established the Children's Bureau in 1912, and the nongovernmental Child Welfare League of America was founded in 1921. Childhood now would be more rigorously observed and regulated by the state.[10] As childhood turned more academic, a plurality of voices started to rise against the prevailing theories of eugenicists who supposed that the biological and social "fitness" of children depended on parentage, or their "stock." The counterforce against this racial paradigm founded new anthropological and sociological models that made children into something other than simply laboratory progeny.

Minors needed proper guidance, and this could be arrived at systematically and socially.[11]

This sea change of academic and government activity led to new cultural projections of America's youth. The 1930s manifested an urgency to document the plights of Depression era abjection, which helped sell New Deal programs. One of the hallmark pieces of legislation was the Social Security Act of 1935. Under it fell the Aid to Dependent Children Program that issued assistance to families for childrearing. It also fastened the federal Children's Bureau to state public welfare agencies.[12] A record 144,000 boys and girls lived in orphanages by the middle of the Depression. Foster care systems advanced, and more government subsistence entreated parents to refrain from giving up their children.[13] Perhaps the most iconographic image of this period was Dorothea Lange's *Migrant Mother*, which joined thousands of stock images of suffering everywhere with a second world war in the offing.[14]

After World War II, young people of the 1950s were the inheritors of a culture of abundance and consumption that lavished the middle-class family home.[15] The number of fostered children surpassed those in group homes and orphanages.[16] There was pressure to match cultural and ethnic backgrounds. Race, nationality, language, and especially religion were important traits for child resettlement.[17] Parenting had also changed. Appearing in 1926 was a new kind of magazine, *Children, the Magazine for Parents* (later *Parents*), which published tips on proper childrearing. Expert advice was everywhere in popular outlets. Dr. Benjamin Spock's *Common Sense Book of Baby and Child Care* was first published in 1946 and to date has sold more than 50 million copies. Where Spock focused on babies, Erik Erikson waxed philosophically on adolescence in his 1950 landmark book *Childhood and Society*.[18] Postwar liberalism stimulated deep changes to the family structure. After reeling in the Depression and surviving world war, more Americans had access to economic stability and upward mobility, which meant a new suburban idyll for the nuclear family. But with postwar modernity came points of instability in the family unit. Adolescents drove with more frequency, listened to antiestablishment rock 'n' roll, and were now consumers in their own right. They had become, to the horror of their parents, "teenagers."[19]

As baby boomers, Pedro Pans came of age in an era that was placing a high premium on the world's children. The United Nations issued its first Declaration of the Rights of the Child in 1959, and the next year President Eisenhower convened a White House Conference on Children and Youth, where delinquency was discussed as a "worldwide problem." Cities were in the spotlight, as were the topics of race, youth, and crime. Delinquency had become a national obsession and was racially charged. In 1954 HEW and the Children's Bureau organized a conference titled "Moving Ahead to Curb Juvenile Delinquency."[20] Films such as Blackboard Jungle (1955) and West Side Story (1961) foregrounded young people run amok, with the latter lyricizing the perceived Puerto Rican threat in New York City in song and dance. Young people were to be saved, but they were also to be feared.

Raising a fit family was a foremost assignment in the Cold War. As the two nations were cutting diplomatic relations, Cuba and the United States issued competing claims of social betterment that centered on life at home.[21] In starkly different ways, Havana and Washington each argued that its model of organization—socialist or capitalist—was exceptional in its ability to provide for the family. Pedro Pans entered the United States as sanctified members of the Cold War family unit. In Cuba Castro and other leaders equally made the revolution a moral imperative, adopting one of its many sacrosanct expressions, "The Revolution is for the Children."[22] They were the future of the reengineered socialist nation, inheritors of the great political experiment in the Western Hemisphere.

Across both nations, then, the period's confrontational language was inscribed on the bodies of their youth. In the United States, salvaging Cuba's children meant rescuing the island itself. As with the Vietnamese or Chinese people, they were communist people in need of saving, as they had been since the days of the U.S. intervention in Cuba's War of Independence in 1898. While in Cuba, it is unsurprising that much of the revolution's triumphalism focused on rejecting U.S. paternalism. Rather, the narrative said socialism granted true autonomy to Cubans while improving daily life for their children.

The American household was the prized unit of society, an essential thread in its fabric. It could prevent a reprise of fascism and totalitarianism, and be a lodestar to the Third World. U.S. prestige meant watching over the world's families. Accordingly, more Americans consulted international adoption agencies as a way to save legions of non-white children from "second-world" communism and impoverishment in the "third world." The number of orphans in the country also dropped from 16 percent of the child population in 1920 to 5 percent by 1954.[23] With more domestic children being placed with families, Iowans, Kentuckians, and Texans now looked abroad to Germany, Japan, and Korea to acquire their young. American greatness could be displayed through its parental prowess.

Harry Holt and his wife, Bertha, were a rural couple from Oregon, who, after receiving special permission from Congress, proceeded to adopt eight war orphans from Korea and create their own adoption agency.[24] Similarly, author Pearl S. Buck, who won both the Pulitzer and Nobel Peace Prizes, founded Welcome House after adopting seven Chinese children.[25] In droves, Americans signed up to adopt and sponsor children. Sponsorship allowed one to care for a child in absentia. The Christian Children's Fund (CCF) was one such trailblazing organization. Established in 1938 to help Chinese victims of the Japanese invasion, its founder, J. Calvitt Clarke, was convinced that "the hungry children of the world are more dangerous to us than the atomic bomb."[26] By 1961 the organization was supporting thirty-six thousand children in forty-eight countries. "Virtual" rather than "legal" adoption meant that Americans could send financial support, communicate with their dependents though letters, and in some cases even visit them overseas. Towns adopted other towns and sent food, letters, money, and everyday staples in these transnational routes of U.S. goodwill.[27]

The reason for this massive buttressing of child welfare was that by most measurements it was still woefully substandard in the United States. Study upon study marked the country's protective services as inadequate. In 1960 the Child Welfare League of America issued its *Standards for Child Protective Services* and found far too many cases of abused, neglected, and exploited children. Modern guidelines were needed, and finally Congress started taking child abuse and neglect more seriously. Child abuse made headlines, with victims of "battered child syndrome" appearing in *Newsweek, Time,* and *Life* magazines.

Shocking revelations of rampant abuse disclosed how undercounted and underreported the violence had been. Sixty thousand cases in 1974 skyrocketed to 2 million a decade and a half later.[28]

With more federal and state assistance available to families, fewer children went to orphanages. The institutions were costly and their outcomes questionable, and their use declined by the 1960s. Foster care held steady, tipping toward three hundred thousand children, or just less than 2 percent of the child population, by 1965.[29] But racial biases were in the fabric of institutional care. In-country transracial adoption was rarely an option, and there were few resources for African American orphans and young Black mothers in need of assistance. In 1951 Black children made up only 4 percent of adoptions. A decade later, 5 percent of non-white babies eligible for adoption found a permanent home, while 70 percent of white infants were placed. Only when there was a "shortage of white babies" did agencies put up African American infants and toddlers. Not until the civil rights movement reinvented the child welfare bureaucracy could the National Association of Black Social Workers in 1972 demand more same-race placements of African American children.[30]

When Americans made room in their homes for Pedro Pans, they already had been looking overseas for children for some time. Between 1953 and 1962, fifteen thousand children came under custody of American parents. With international laws easing, mixed-race adoption rose with a preference for the offspring of servicemen and Korean, Chinese, and, later, Vietnamese women. But state rules could prove burdensome to hopeful parents. Regulations might oblige couples to be of the same religion as the child. There were age limits too. In New Jersey one had to be younger than forty years old to adopt a child.[31] Even with more flexibility, adoption still invited stigma. In a controversial but famous study published in 1960, Marshall Schechter claimed that adopted children were a hundred times more likely to have serious emotional problems than non-adoptees.[32]

Pedro Pans were not adopted, but they became part of the Cold War's drawing of battle lines across the world's young. When the USSR bandied the motto "Thank You, Comrade Stalin, for Our Happy Childhood!" throughout its state discourse, the United States answered with suburban schlock that placed a high premium on the American way.[33] "For both superpowers," Margaret Peacock has revealed, "the need to defend kids . . . and mobilize youth for national defense opened the private lives of individuals and their families to increased regulation and surveillance."[34] Both countries moved to protect its children: in the United States, from communist tyranny and conformity; in the Soviet Union, from capitalist profligacy and inequality. The intent of each was to bolster the nation's reputation as the leader in childhood greatness.[35]

U.S. publications showed the waywardness of socialist societies. They were places hobbled by beleaguered family structures and suboptimal motherhood. Tales of state-run nurseries and schools in China, the Soviet Union, and Cuba horrified readers. The opinion was that these countries limited mothers' access to their children in care. In contrast was the visual and textual onslaught of vignettes on Americans leading the way in family health and success. Capitalist kinship was victorious.[36] It turned out that national defense needed management in private spaces as well as public, religious life as well as secular. Elaine Tyler May has shown that Americans' interest in the nuclear family grew in the nuclear age. The idea of home "seemed to offer a secure private nest removed from the dangers of the outside world." It provided a space for material abundance and familial fulfillment that could effectively protect against communism. "Domestic containment" safeguarded the home and family. American women reportedly outdid their Soviet counterparts in maternal responsibility. In 1959 the "kitchen debate" between Vice President Richard Nixon and Soviet premier Khrushchev in Moscow displayed the theatrics of technological superiority and material abundance in the home. Soviet women were shown as working too hard and without the luxuries of modern conveniences, unlike American homemakers. Cold War modernity entered domestic spaces, creating a link between missiles and mothers in the bifurcated world.[37]

This feminine ideal depended on masculine leadership that could protect against the dangers of the atomic age. The projection of an able patriarch floated in and out of the 1960 presidential debates. Richard Nixon suggested that the president needed to be a role model for children, a father figure for the country:

One thing I've noted as I've traveled around the country are the tremendous number [sic] of children who come out to see the presidential candidates. I see mothers holding their babies up, so that they can see a man who might be president of the United States. . . . It makes you realize that whoever is president is going to be a man that all the children of America will either look up to, or will look down to. . . . And I only hope that, should I win this election, that I could approach President Eisenhower in maintaining the dignity of the office; in seeing to it that whenever any mother or father talks to his child, he can look at the man in the White House and, whatever he may think of his policies, he will say: "Well, there is a man who maintains the kind of standards personally that I would want my child to follow."[38]

Nixon's patriarchal moralism would turn out ironic in the 1970s, but in 1960, presidential manhood required not only a combative spirit to keep enemies at bay but also one that could look after the country's children and ensure domestic stability. Child well-being was a flash point in the U.S.-Cuban confrontation, part of the paternalistic line of sight that clashed over which country—that is, which model of social organization, communist or capitalist—could adequately nourish future generations. It effectively centered on the question of which male leader could successfully raise the nation's children and secure its mothers and wives.

As the country turned to domesticity, U.S. citizens were now in charge of saving the children of the "undeveloped" world. The charge was to save them from communism while expanding the girth of the U.S. sphere of influence.[39] Cuban children were designated as part of the global population that needed saving. They belonged to populations in jeopardy but whose very status was also a function of U.S. statecraft. Assuming responsibility of Korean, Chinese, or Vietnamese children, for example, both eclipsed and justified U.S. military engagement in East Asia. The other side of rescuing the world's children were acts of American empire that made their saving necessary in the first place. Cuban children, torn from their national origin and biological parents, remained living symbols of the purpose to defeat communism and reaffirmed the vision of American benevolence.[40] Moving to the middle-class suburbs, entering Uncle Sam's school systems, and eating apple pie would help secure those children against the dangers of the world. The American dream was posted as both regal and real, and it was bestowed upon the privileged few, such as the Cuban young people who stood as victims of wayward development.

Americans learned from Cuban parents that "the Castro regime [was] bending every effort to capture the minds of youth."[41] Such news from the daily press spurred everyday residents to take action and embrace the cause of Cuban freedom against the ravages of communism. It prompted the Cuban Women's Anti-Communist Organization to start a campaign to collect Christmas toys for refugee children. María Alba of Miami felt shock and pity when at Christmas Fidel Castro denounced Santa Claus in Cuba. Castro reportedly proclaimed, "Santa Claus was an American, a very cold American who would not bother to pay any Christmas Eve visits to Cuban refugee children."[42]

For its part, the Cuban government did not hesitate to turn the revolution into a referendum on gender and family. Women, Fidel Castro proclaimed repeatedly, were freer in the new Cuba, with their emancipation a "revolution within the revolution," as Michelle Chase points out. Women had actively fought the Batista dictatorship in all-women civic groups, and a portion, perhaps 10–20 percent, marched in the urban wing of the resistance.[43] After 1959, bureaucrats constantly reminded the public that the revolution was also "for the children," a sentiment that stemmed from the early days of independence and floated among the maxims of the founding patriarch of the Cuban nation, José Martí.[44] When glancing back at Martí's day, one sees the language of infantilism was written in the texts of U.S. empire, when the United States intervened in the war that Cubans waged to free themselves from Spanish colonialism in 1898. Like other imperial or colonial subjects of the day, Cubans were often cast as political children unable to govern themselves. This catalog of images and assertions also depicted Cubans as a non-white people devoid of order who were irrational and unpredictable, childlike in their worldview. Generations of U.S. leaders and politicians maintained this line as they drifted into the Cold War.

Countering these long-held images were the ultra-masculine *barbu-dos* (bearded ones) of the July 26th Movement with its chief leader, the virile Castro, as the corporal antidote to the effeminate bourgeois nation. Cuban nationalism now incorporated the repeated argument that U.S. imperialism was the chief enemy of the family.[45] Castro announced that Cuba would never "make any law that separates children from their families." Rather, the revolution provided conditions for bountiful creation. In one of his characteristic thunderous speeches, he cajoled his auditors to be fruitful and multiply. "Those who have fewer children," he expounded, "are those who belong to the aristocracy. They have one or two, but those who have many children are the real revolutionary class, the class that is with the revolution: the workers and the farmers."[46] The government exerted daunting pressure to ebb the tide of outgoing exiles. The revolution needed a fecund body politic to maintain an ample number of workers and soldiers. Having too few children risked economic impoverishment. Prenatal care and state-run nurseries got a lot of coverage. Cuba's stated goal was a classless society that, unlike capitalist countries, prioritized familial health over individual financial interests.[47]

But the government also needed to counter charges that it was dispossessing parents of their children and religious fealties. The magazine *Bohemia* showed priests baptizing "not children of privilege but those who did not inherit fortune from yesterday's Cuba, a Cuba which will soon disappear." The new state gave a full-throated denial that the government was abducting and brainwashing children by tendering feelings of belonging for Cuban citizens of all ages. They could feel part of the *patria* (homeland), unlike the counterrevolutionary *gusanos* (worms) who were fleeing north.[48] Castro dismissed the patria potestad rumor as the "most absurd invention" and a "shameless tale." Its worst victims were mothers, he exclaimed, and he argued the revolution "never perpetrated a single act that violates the sacred rights of parents."[49]

Castro combated CIA propaganda with this own. He insisted the revolution favored not the "children of multimillionaires," the "*malcriados*" (spoiled brats) who wanted to live "pretty"; rather, it fought for the "workers and the children of workers." Modernity under colonial

Spain and the neocolonial United States had bequeathed to Cuba an "exploitative capitalist society . . . the enemy of motherhood, enemy of children." The lack of health care, education, and social services, and the evidence of poverty, malnourishment, childhood prostitution, and disease, particularly in rural areas—all were the result of a Cuban bourgeoisie that catered to U.S. desires. Castro went as far as to accuse U.S. neocolonialism of fostering sexual improprieties, colluding with Cubans of influence who "sold our children of humble families to the tourist who would come for alcohol and entertainment, selling the little girls of workers, the little girls of workers and farmers to the marines who came to entertain themselves. That is what they did: prostitute the little girls from modest families."[50]

Thus, liberation from capitalism and neocolonialism helped free Cuban women from Yankee men. Castro now asserted a revolutionary masculinity—a "paternal duty"—that safely secured families against foreign aggression and disempowerment.[51]

Evidence of familial haleness bubbled up across the island. Havana quickly legalized perhaps as many as hundreds of thousands of couples living in extramarital arrangements in Operation Matrimony, a further sign that families were made stronger and more wholesome under the revolution.[52] There was now better prenatal care, state-run nurseries, literacy campaigns, and new schools educating the masses.[53] Some Cuban students were sent on educational opportunities to places such as Prague or Moscow and with parental consent. The government flooded society with images of socialists caring for their young more effectively than capitalist nations did.[54]

The Year of Education stirred up a massive campaign. Minister of Education Armando Hart provided the whopping statistic that 79 percent more kids attended elementary school between 1958 and 1961, and he praised adult education and new schools in rural settings.[55] State media found parents to disavow salacious rumors. In one interview, a parent dismissed the patria potestad hearsay as mere "ridiculousness." Those children who did go to the Soviet Union went with parental consent.[56] Upon visiting Cuba in the early 1960s, Chicana activist Elizabeth Sutherland Martínez saw government schools and daycares as an effective way to debunk the "enemy propaganda [that] painted pictures of babes snatched from the hearth forever, or daughters losing their virginity in the absence of parental control."[57]

But the counterrevolutionary propaganda was everywhere. News came from Cienfuegos that police had interrupted a print operation disseminating false news on patria potestad.[58] *Time* magazine printed a version of the apocryphal law adding that children between the ages of three and ten years old would live in government housing with visitation rights strictly controlled.[59] What for Monsignor Walsh and Pedro Pan executors was a humanitarian rescue of children became part of the anti-Castro violence for pro-revolution Cubans. They saw Operation Pedro Pan as simply another underhanded attempt to destroy the socialist government.[60]

With all the focus on families, and if it knew it was happening, why did the Cuban government not do more to stop the exodus of children? Operation Pedro Pan took place in a tornado of activity when the revolution was in the throes of consolidation. On the one hand, the government did not want to give credence to the rumors by taking away parents' rights to send their children to the United States if they so desired. This is the view of Eusebio Leal Spengler, Havana's onetime city historian, who conjectured that preventing parents from remitting their children would have verified the notion that the government was taking away patria potestad.[61] Castro regretted those parents' decision but stated that the government would not impede them from determining what was best for their children.[62] For the government to demonstrate its commitment to parental rights, Cuba let mothers and fathers send their kids.

On the other hand, the Ministry of the Interior in Havana stood firm that it did know about Operation Pedro Pan.[63] Deborah Shnookal's research shows that the government was mindful of the exodus but simply did not have the personnel to shut it down. Havana had to confront higher priorities: sabotage, assassination attempts, and economic survival.[64] The more sinister explanation is that parents who transported their children were more tractable for the Cuban government. The kids could be bargaining chips when dealing with parents wanting to see their offspring again. Mothers and fathers became much more accommodating in their desperation.[65]

Of course, authorities knew. Evidence of the massive child exodus was everywhere. Monsignor Walsh was at best naive and at worst disingenuous with his guarantee that absolute secrecy was realizable. The random copy of the unaccompanied child passenger manifest from Mercedes Diaz Dash's flight on January 25, 1962, lists twenty-five children, ages four to seventeen, along with their destinations in Miami. With this many kids on a single flight, the cloak-and-dagger operation was just too big. Next to the children's names were the names of those relatives—"uncle," "cousin," or simply "friend"—planning to collect them. Those who did not have a family member—two out of the twenty-five listed—went to a camp, in this case Kendall. Also, caregiver names may have been listed that either were invented or were of people who did not, in the end, retrieve their wards. Those children also would have wound up in the shelters.

Hundreds, if not thousands, of Americans wrote Father Walsh and other representatives of the program, wanting to know how they could acquire a Cuban child they had never met. These inquiries landed in Secretary Ribicoff's office and from there often wound up on the desk of Frances Davis at the Florida Department of Public Welfare. One from Altoona, Alabama, announced: "I would like to respond to any way that I could help in the Cuban Refugee Center. I would also like to say I could keep a small Cuban child in my home, and would like to adopt one if there were any chance of this, if you are interested please write me."[66] Other searching souls from different denominations, such as those from the Methodist Children's Home in Alabama, sought to house Cuban children.[67] Similar charitable notes were mailed by the staff of the Baptist Children's Home in Phoenix and by one woman from Lime Springs, Iowa, who had learned about the Cuban juveniles in magazines. She and her husband had two preschool children of their own and were looking to boost their clan with a Protestant Cuban youth while helping to serving the nation's defense. She wrote, "We would like to help those who must flee Communism in any way we can, and we feel that our community and family would be greatly inriched [sic] by having children from a different country in our midst."[68] Though many letter writers did not know it, adoption was not an option in the CCP, and childcare could only be handled through licensed institutions.[69] The presence of Cubans reinforced Americans' dedication to anti-communism while bolstering their own sense of cosmopolitanism. One no longer needed to leave Iowa to experience Havana. Havana could come to Iowa.

In promoting the American way, communities across the country bragged about acclimating the young newcomers. *The Observer*, the newspaper of the Catholic Diocese of Rockford, Illinois, scripted a headline fit for a Norman Rockwell painting: "Cuban Children Meet Snow, Peanut Butter, English Language—and Come through Fine." In the face of escalating nuclear arsenals and accreting world instability, Americans could insulate and inoculate themselves with homemade sentimentalism.[70] Locals in Pueblo, Colorado, were abuzz with news that forty-three children ages five to twelve were living in Sacred Heart Home. A human-interest story portrayed one girl praying, another studying, and others eyeing themselves in the mirror while boys played basketball. Cuban children, it turned out, could enjoy a typical life a la americana.[71]

As nationwide disbelief spread over Washington's ineffectiveness at defeating the threat that lay ninety miles south of Florida, civil society took it upon itself to lift the national mood by hosting Cuban exiles. Their little bodies furnished testaments to the evils of the Red menace. A Miami news story published one child's astounding claim: "Fidel kills children."[72] On December 23, 1965, Florida's Department of Public Welfare put on a White Christmas Snow program at the Dade County Auditorium to raise money for unaccompanied Cuban children in exile. Audience members proudly absorbed the Cuban and U.S. national anthems followed by Christmas caroling, ballet, and seasonal sketches.[73]

Children were the focus, because, it was feared, they were ripest for socialist conscription. Monsignor Walsh rejected this claim and assured, "Only a few of the children arriving here have shown effects of the Communist indoctrination."[74] Catholics mobilized even further. In Michigan interested families were screened by Catholic Social Services of Wayne County for child placement.[75] The image of white, middle-class families saving needy Cuban children helped re-create the Cold War American home. But with such charitable acts came a racial anxiety deeply rooted in the American grain. Common understandings of the day held that ties to cultural markers such as diet, language, and religion would hasten assimilation. Racial identity, however, remained a retardant factor in the route to adaptation, a potent variable of difference that was seen to hamper acclimation. Agency officials, for example, found the creation of interracial foster families problematic.[76] Some of these host families nagged about "gregarines, noisiness, [and] volubility" in the young refugees, a burden that diminished when "the children took on American ways and became more relaxed in their new mode of life." Things went smoother when "foster parents learned how to appreciate the spontaneity and charm of the Cuban children."[77]

Following Catholic counsel, Walsh lobbied for the greater use of foster families.[78] Some of the households were interracial and intercultural. The record mentions a "Chinese-American couple" as well as a "Protestant" one.[79] Some families required special facilities for children deemed "educationally disadvantaged." The term "disadvantaged" could refer to special needs or underperforming children, as well as kids with superior scholastic skills who were underachieving due to their environment.[80] One encounters language such as "special" or "neurotic" to describe the behavior of some kids. While a "normal" home life was the goal, with parental abandonment came psychological issues that racked unaccompanied children. Some families inappropriately took advantage of the situation or were ill-equipped to care for minors. One representative of the Jewish Family and Children's Services observed, "A lot of disturbed people feel that they need children for their own satisfaction."[81]

To put a more positive spin on the Cuban Children's Program, the U.S. Information Agency commissioned David Susskind for a documentary titled *The Lost Apple* (1962). Named for a Latin American nursery rhyme, *The Lost Apple* depicts Pedro Pans adjusting to their new lives in shelters. Still imagined to be temporary residents, they are portrayed as lucky escapees of communism who are also fated to lose their childhood innocence in the process.[82] Carlos Montalban narrates the film, which opens with Roberto, a forlorn boy on his way to the Florida City camp. With narration in the second person, the intended audience is children. "You are alone. You don't know why you're here." It is abundantly clear who bears the blame for Roberto's harrowing journey—Fidel Castro. We see children making their way through a caring ambience of religious and government design. They call and write their parents, pray before meals, and learn appropriate Bible verses. A priest from the camp pledges that the children now in the "sheltering skies of the United States" are destined to build the "Cuba of tomorrow." The film has the secondary function of orienting its viewers toward their new reality. It dispels the false information many parents told their children, such as they were on temporary leave to study in the United States. One Pedro Pan, Gladys, wishes to transfer to Washington State because she has friends in Yakima, at which point she is bluntly told this is not a scholastic journey. The film concludes that children will rejoin their parents, but "sometimes you have to wait a long time to find the lost apple." In the end, Gladys is able to go to Washington, but Roberto must continue to wait. He is resigned but accepts that one day he will recover his apple.[83] Monsignor Walsh and the CWB approved of *The Lost Apple*. The film's producers were pleasantly impressed by the "remarkable spirit" of the Florida City camp, and the U.S. Information Agency looked to distribute the film throughout the Americas.[84]

Child exiles appeared elsewhere on the screen. "The Plight of Pepito: Cuba's Lost Generation" was a special report by Florida's first television station, Miami's WTVJ–Channel 4. The host of the segment was Ralph Renick, one of south Florida's most beloved newscasters, whose impressive list of interviewees had included Harry Truman, Martin Luther King Jr., Fidel Castro, and even Soviet premier Nikita Khrushchev.[85] It opens with a boy, Pepito López, watching a baseball game. Floridians learn that Pepito is "a political problem," a "symbol" and an "image" of a world that he did not create. Unlike Pedro Pans, he arrived with his family in tow, and public health officials greeted them at the airport. On display are U.S. charity and professional services for the world's refugees. On top of vaccinations, Pepito and his family receive the beneficence of random Americans who readily open their homes to them.

The segment gave a starring role to the Cuban Refugee Emergency Center. We see government representatives dutifully chaperoning

Cubans through an orderly system of refuge. Cuba is sure to be fit for return within weeks or months, Renick wagers. Meanwhile, the United States has saved Pepito from mandatory military service in Cuba. "Pepito prefers to play with a wooden bat than with a wooden rifle," the newscaster chimes. Florida governor Farris Bryant and Secretary Abraham Ribicoff make an appearance, assuring viewers that American officials are fully committed to the refugees. The spot acknowledges the inconvenient nature of the exile problem but in the end prods Miamians to keep up the country's tradition of sanctuary. Besides, Cubans were assimilable, the piece confirms, proving so with a concluding shot of Pepito in center frame reciting the Pledge of Allegiance.[86]

10 | FOR GOD AND COUNTRY

Eloy Cepero found his Americanization sojourn unimaginably fortuitous. Like so many, he and his brothers were brought up in a Catholic family; their father was an attorney and their mother a school principal. When Eloy began to stray from discipline, his parents sent him to Havana's exclusive Candler College, a Methodist school founded in 1898 by Bishop Warren Akin Candler, brother of the founder of Coca-Cola, a big purchaser of Cuban sugar. The head of the school took a liking to fifteen-year-old Eloy and told his parents about the visa waivers, then contacted a Methodist church in Coral Gables, Florida. Church congregants learned that Cuban children were on their way and needed care. Heeding the call were McGregor Smith—one of the most well-known businessmen in Florida and the chairman of the board of Florida Power and Light—and his wife, a Tennessean who traced her lineage to Andrew Jackson. Mrs. Smith convinced her husband that they should foster Eloy and his brothers, despite the couple's reservations concerning their possible racial type. The way Eloy tells it, Mr. Smith became a loving, fully dedicated surrogate father to the three boys. Clearly, Eloy loved him and is indebted to his compassion.[1]

More than not, Pedro Pans found their way to the United States through churches and parochial schools. It made sense. The Cold War was as much a referendum on faith as it was on which country would lead the world's children and families. Americans have long understood their country as one invented out of the co-freedoms of religion and commerce. The Puritans structured their communities in terms of a divine errand into the wilderness. In their jeremiad, they told of seeking a kingdom on Earth through trial by fire with the hopeful reward of heavenly delights in the afterlife. After World War II, a different trial appeared in the showdown between capitalism and communism, freedom and enslavement, and—for a majority of Americans—God and godlessness. Christianity wasn't new in U.S. political discourse; it had long substantiated the nation's exceptional standing and justification for expansion, from the notion of manifest destiny to the Spanish-American War. But the Cold War rehashed this logic while firmly connecting it to global markets. The fight against communism was the cornerstone of the U.S. crusade of deified economic power. The consumerist ethos was not antithetical to this line of Christianity; rather, it redoubled it in the name of freedom. The Soviet Union represented the opposite, an atheistic anti-consumerism.[2]

To understand Americans, then, one needed to understand their churches. So thought Soviet premier Joseph Stalin, who advised his ambassador to the United States, Andrei Gromyko, to witness the sermons of American preachers so he could grasp the "American mindset and value system." Americans held the unwavering belief that the Soviet plan for the world was one of spiritual vapidity. President Harry Truman saw the Cold War in precisely these terms when he insisted that the "international Communist movement is based on a fierce and terrible fanaticism. It denies the existence of God, and wherever it can it stamps out the worship of God." American religiosity was more relevant than ever because the fate of humanity—with the risk of nuclear war ever present—was at stake. Even the tight-lipped military man Dwight D. Eisenhower took notice of the religious zeitgeist when he became the first sitting president to undergo baptism. Under his tenure, the country emblazoned the new national motto "In God We Trust" on its currency and added "one nation under God" to its pledge of allegiance. This was the dawning, as William Inboden writes, "of a new American civil religion."[3]

Civil it may have been, but immutable it was not, as great folds of U.S. theology creased along postwar life. The Catholic Church found itself in a unique position of ascendancy. With the inauguration of John F. Kennedy, the first Catholic president in the White House, Catholics were more adroit in their politics. Monsignor Bryan Walsh was a product of this evolution. He evoked the expanding commitment to Cuban children as fulfilling the double duties of God and nation: "I was more than willing to accept the consequences of my act if I could save 200 children from communism . . . and I told the State Department of the United States: Let them come. Some months later hundreds of priests and religious followers began coming to Miami and then I saw all of this in the context of the Marxist war against religion."[4]

Operation Pedro Pan crystallized amid profound changes in Catholic and Protestant ecumenicism, but this history was fashioned over the longer course of intimate ties between Cuba and the United States.

In Cuba Catholicism never enjoyed the prestige it had in other Latin American republics. On the cusp of the revolution, 90 percent of Cubans professed a Catholic faith, but only 10 percent regularly practiced.[5] Back in the mid-nineteenth century, visitors to the island commented on the church's lax system, with prelates exerting weak influence and clerics indulging in delights that bordered on sacrilege. The War of Independence pushed clergy to choose between their Spanish employers and their nationalist parishioners. When Cubans rose up against the Spanish crown, a fraction also did so against the church, which for the most part supported the monarchy in line with the Vatican. The Catholic hierarchy still held sway, particularly in parochial education, but it was tenuous. Rural areas were rife with spiritual neglect. After Cubans broke free from the yoke of Spain, Catholicism was marred by its associations between the church and erstwhile colonialism. A fresh wave of Spanish—and thus Catholic—immigration blanketed the island, but many Cubans had distanced themselves from the church. As independence neared, American Protestantism slowly found a way to fill the void.[6]

The U.S. occupation enshrined the church-state separation in the Cuban Constitution of 1901. America's civilizing mission also expanded parochial education for the island's elite. After 1898, Methodists, Presbyterians, Baptists, Episcopalians, and Congregationalists sprouted in greater numbers. Protestant missionaries were bolder in their evangelism, but they, too, received a cool welcome. While Catholicism was paired with Spanish colonialism, U.S. religious emissaries were suspiciously eyed as agents of the occupation.[7] But Protestantism did make headway. Cuban expats returning from the United States carried with them their Episcopalian, Baptist, and Methodist credos. Methodists quickly set up schools across the island. Cuba beckoned evangelicals bent on civilizing the underprivileged as part of the moral frame of empire, but the Protestant turn was driven by something more. The postindependence capitalist economy was catalyzed by U.S. coffers and counsel. Protestantism was pragmatic in that it put the market and liturgy in a sensible package. Moreover, religious schools were instrumental in Americanizing young Cubans and ensuring that they embrace this packaging as both moral and practical. This influence should not be underestimated. Though numbering only 150,000 out of a total population of 6 million, Protestants had dug deep roots in Cuban soil by the time of the revolution.[8]

As more from the comfortable classes opted for private school and study abroad, Cuba's public education system deteriorated into another sign of the widening gap between rich and poor. The 1950s was a fertile time for private schools; 35 percent of primary schoolchildren attended them, and the quantities of middle and secondary school pupils, many Catholic, were on the rise. In 1953 only a little more than half of Cuban children attended school.[9] Private education made headway with the middle class as well. Here students found U.S.-inspired curricula and classes in English, and read textbooks from the north, sometimes under the guidance of American teachers. Priests from Philadelphia's Villanova University helped create a sister institution in Havana in 1946. James Baker's Ruston Academy broke ground in this milieu, as did the Methodist Candler College, which advertised its program as one that prepared students for study in the United States. One Ruston student later remembered that the school placed a heavy emphasis on U.S. civic and democratic virtues, and classes included English and U.S. history, geography, and literature.[10]

After 1959, educational inequality was a focal point of the revolution. The Year of Education (1961) signaled an overhaul of the bourgeois system that included the elimination of private schools. In fact, many Pedro Pan parents learned about the Cuban Children's Program during these closures. Cuban education needed calibrating to the new state ideology, for the island's youth were more important than ever. Forty percent of the population was ten to twenty-five years old. When re-creating the school system, the government upped its private data collection. Some parents took it as a sign that it was identifying children destined for the Soviet Union. The revolution increasingly wedged itself into their intimate lives, leading to a breaking point for those thinking about leaving.[11]

Catholics especially were untrusting. After 1898, Jesuits, LaSalle Brothers, Dominicans, and Ursuline Sisters redesigned the church to be compatible with postcolonial Cuba. In 1926 the Jesuits founded the Catholic University Association, and Pope Pius XII appointed Archbishop Manuel Arteaga to be Cuba's first cardinal in 1946. The church appreciated under his stewardship while spurred by competition with Protestant churches. When Batista surged to power once again in 1952, the church, for the most part, backed the coup. There were exceptions, however. Archbishop Enrique Pérez Serantes of Santiago de Cuba disapproved. An outspoken Galician who knew the Castro family, Pérez helped broker leniency for Castro and his fellow rebels who were imprisoned after their failed attack on the Moncada Barracks on July 26, 1953.[12]

Once Castro was freed, the revolution proceeded at a time when the church was woefully understaffed for a Catholic laity of possibly millions. Few, however, observed on a regular basis. In a 1957 survey by the Catholic University Association, 52 percent of rural workers identified as Catholic, and 42 percent indicated no religious affiliation. Rural Cuba suffered from a scarcity of priests, with over half of respondents saying they had never seen one. Church life was mostly tied to urban spaces, mainly in Havana. Eventually large numbers of Catholics revolted against Batista. Monsignor (later Bishop) Eduardo Boza Masvidal preached to revolutionaries inspired by one of the leaders of the urban wing and early martyr of the cause, the fiery Catholic José Antonio Echeverría, who was killed in 1957. More Catholics stepped up in his place. But Catholic support for the revolution thinned out, with Cardinal Arteaga standing idly by as Castro rolled into Havana. The church decided on a wait-and-see approach. Castro commended Catholics who had given themselves "to the cause of freedom"; he was, after all, one of their own, a student at the Jesuit preparatory school Belén. Archbishop Pérez gave Castro a shot by extolling him as a fighter against corruption and a pursuer of social justice in line with the Gospel. Any efforts at making an alliance between Castro and the church, however, would rapidly fall apart.[13]

Some have argued that Fidel's victory depended more on a stagnant secularism than on ringleading the faithful. Revolutionary Marxism fared with greater ease in the countryside because of the paucity of religious centers in agrarian districts. When Castro enlisted the church in consolidating his government, at first many believers followed. More than a million people attended the National Catholic Congress in November 1959, including Castro himself. Melding a sense of Christian charity with the revolution meant floating the military moniker "Operation Christian Humanism." One group tried the motto "Either Christ or Wall Street" to rally Catholics to the anti-American position of Castro. This variant of humanism was an overlooked focus in the comandante's revolutionary discourse. As historian Lillian Guerra has written: "Fidel explicitly rooted the grand narrative of redemption in the teachings of Jesus Christ and the rituals of Catholic Christianity as never before. Fidel's appeals to Christian-inspired notions of justice, millenarian impulses, and divine mission intensified as citizens responded to them, merging the vision of militarized democracy in which all citizens were foot soldiers in the 'trenches' of their homes, schools, workplaces, and daily lives with the millenarian future that only the state could reveal."[14]

Castro's columns wanted to exude moral rigor, which meant sexual chastity and Catholic wholesomeness.[15] But the church and the revolution would part ways. After Castro's executions of Batista supporters and the visits by Soviet dignitaries, the charges of communism grew cacophonic. The church had to take a stand. When Anastas Mikoyan visited and placed a wreath at the statue of José Martí, students from the Catholic Villanueva University and their allies removed it as an anti-communist protest. A violent confrontation ensued between the police and the students with threatening pro-revolution taunts from onlookers and neighbors. When the government did away with private schools, sixty-five thousand students in Catholic classrooms had to search for alternatives.[16] The church was not able to rid itself of associations with aristocratic, colonial Cuba. Nearly 80 percent of the Catholic elite were still Spanish, and 85 percent of the church's personnel and activities were centered in Havana.[17]

The Vatican sided with the anti-communists, as it had for some time. Pius XI's encyclical *Divini redemptoris* in 1937 officially pronounced communism an enemy of Catholicism. The rector of Villanueva, Auxiliary Bishop Boza Masvidal, was a champion of Rome's stand, and his personality pumped through the veins of his students who confronted Mikoyan. Boza used the pulpit to attack the government and stoke rebellion.[18] Archbishop Pérez, who had helped free Castro from prison, also stepped up his criticism. Even as Castro further attempted to mollify the church with superficial comparisons between revolutionary ethics and Christianity, socialism was just too big a pill to swallow. Faith leaders issued a joint declaration in favor of social justice and free speech while underscoring the church's rejection of Marxism.[19]

With more gusto, Castro and other functionaries equated anti-communism with counterrevolution because it divided the nation. But curiously Fidel also took the position that to be anti-Catholic or anti-Protestant was equally destructive of Cuban unity and thus out of step with the new order.[20] Ultimately he could not have it both ways. He and President Osvaldo Dorticós Torrado now went on the offensive against the church hierarchy, and more services were interrupted with protests. The Vatican counseled Cuban bishops not to inflame the conflict further.[21] The showdowns between nationalists and anti-communist clergy mounted, exploding in majestic cathedrals such as the one in Santiago de Cuba. The government accused Catholic leaders of espionage and treason. In November 1960 readers of *Time* magazine learned from Archbishop Pérez that Cubans were forced to choose: "Rome or Moscow." CIA propaganda pressed these fear buttons and conscripted Cuban Catholics into the anti-communist fight. Director Allen Dulles confirmed that Catholics were irreplaceable assets in Cuba.[22]

The fault line between the church and the revolution hemorrhaged after the Bay of Pigs, when Castro proclaimed the nation officially socialist. Leaders repeatedly ripped "Falangist Clergy" as a nod to Spain's influence on the church. It was not long until bishops and priests were put under house arrest, making exile their only option. A bewildered Cardinal Arteaga sought asylum at the Argentine Embassy.[23] Castro only intensified his volley of attacks. September 1961 saw the government clearing the Catholic house, and soon Havana expelled 130 priests and other religious to Spain. Some church leaders were even put in Military Units to Aid Production, the state's internment centers for social and political outcasts where internees underwent revolutionary "reeducation."[24] Because so many religious were Spanish, Castro could defend the decision to eject them as a coup de grâce to the remnants of colonialism.[25] In Miami Monsignor Walsh was apoplectic and raised the alarm to Bishop Coleman Carroll.[26]

Father Walsh upheld that the Cuban Catholic Church was never involved formally with Operation Pedro Pan, though some of its representatives did fish for and secure visa waivers.[27] Cuban researchers argue the opposite: the church helped make Pedro Pan a success. Radio Swan transmissions warned the government would take over the church, and Bishop Boza was close to anti-Castro groups.[28] Based on her interviews with Cuban parishioners, Margaret Crahan writes: "Increasingly there was a sense among the Catholic faithful that it was their moral responsibility to be counterrevolutionary. . . . The ideological struggle became more marked and there was growing fear expressed of children being 'lost' to Marxist indoctrination."[29]

The dilemma of "Rome or Moscow" folded into the larger one of "Washington or Moscow."[30] In August 1960 Cuba's eight bishops signed a letter endorsing the right for Catholics to oppose communism.[31] Boza stepped up as a leader of anti-Castro rage, with Catholic students chanting, "Long live Boza! Down with Fidel!"[32] A portion of these protestors would become Pedro Pans.[33] The revolution, however, drowned out or purged their voices. Bishop Boza was deported to Spain in September 1961.[34] Commander of the Armed Forces Raúl Castro railed against the action and labeled prelates "war criminals in priests' robes" who were "trying to poison the minds of our children against the revolution." They and their lackeys were "instruments of Yankee imperialism." Clearly Fidelismo (Fidel's doctrine) was replacing Christianity as Cuba's dominant religion.[35]

As most schools closed by April 1961, many young people ventured to the countryside to lead a literacy campaign. In July Castro announced that a thousand agricultural workers were on their way to study in the USSR.[36] Minister of Education Armando Hart vilified exclusive pedagogy, claiming to have been personally visited by a father who exclaimed, "They are making a counter-revolutionist out of my son in the private school he is attending."[37] The number of shuttered private institutions reached 1,245. Meanwhile, the exodus of Catholic workers continued. In May of the same year, 182 Marist Brothers packed their bags for Miami. Jesuits, Dominicans, Franciscans, Capuchins, Piarists, and Augustinians followed. In another wave, six hundred nuns chose Florida after refusing to teach Marxism and wear secular clothing. The effect was consummate: "Of the 2,000 religious women who had staffed more than 350 Catholic institutions on the island, only 100 remained," writes Michael McNally. There were an equal number of priests who stayed in the country.[38] One Catholic publication reports that by 1962, 70 percent of priests and 90 percent of nuns had fled Cuba by choice or under obligation.[39] The church's presence was eviscerated.

If taking the temperature of the Catholic Church outside of Cuba, however, one would have seen Rome rising. In the United States, a different sort of insurgency was brewing against Protestantism, the insuperable religious identity of the country since its founding. The storied past of the Anglo-Saxon Protestant nation assailing the Catholic Church was tapering. The descendants of the millions of Catholic immigrants who had poured into the country now achieved a different social status and posed an opportunity for Rome to strengthen its influence in the Western Hemisphere.[40] The beginning of this ascendance was when Catholics found their celebrity voice in the 1930s with the enormously popular Father Charles Coughlin. In his weekly radio rants, the Michigan priest was the moral voice of many and at one time ranked "the most useful citizen of the United States," according to the majority of respondents in a 1933 poll.[41] Coughlin was untouchable until his support for President Franklin Roosevelt drifted, and the timber of his addresses squeaked with anti-Semitism. Meanwhile, more radical forms of stewardship, most notably in the work of Dorothy Day and the Catholic Worker Movement, attacked economic inequality and racism during the Depression.[42]

After World War II, American Catholicism moved, in the words of David J. O'Brien, from a "church of immigrants and workers" to a preferred religion of the bourgeoning middle class. Catholics were now more accepted in American life than they had been historically. The virulent anti-Catholicism manifested in nativist groups such as the Know Nothing Party of the mid-1800s and the Ku Klux Klan a half century later was largely relegated to history. The church fell in line with anti-communist fundamentalism when Pope Pius XII threatened excommunication for anyone supporting Red politics. The Vatican was comfortably aligned with America's Cold War. The dawning of the atomic age was a boon to religious affiliation and attendance. Postwar suburban sprawl consisted of communities anchored by churches and synagogues that saw their attendance rise 30 percent. The number of people reporting a religious identity climbed to 65 percent of the population. The rate of conversion to Catholicism accelerated, with Catholicity doubling between 1940 and 1960. The nation needed priests. In these years, enrollment in Catholic schools rose 129 percent, far outpacing public school enrollment. The Archdiocese of New York City alone built two hundred new elementary schools in the 1950s. In the Big Apple, one in three schoolchildren was enrolled in a Catholic school. Across the nation, it was one in eight.[43]

In the Cold War, Protestant and Catholic divisions eased. Religious descendants of the Reformation joined their fellow papists in seeing the defeat of godless heathens as a spiritual call extending back to colonial days, when Indian "savages" were considered uncivilized because they lacked Christianity. Communism was a rewriting of that age-old savagery, and Cuban children escaping religious intolerance rehashed the Puritan errand that had long underwritten the doctrine of American exceptionalism. It was ensconced in the origin narrative in which Europeans seeking religious freedom (rather than commercial enterprise) populated the budding colonies and flourished according to Biblical design.

Katherine Oettinger, chief of the Children's Bureau, thought in precisely these terms when she wrote: "The right of people to freedom of thought and religious belief has reverberated throughout our society from the days when the early settlers came to our shores to escape a tyranny that was intolerable. The refugees now coming to the United States from Cuba are, in many respects, following this tradition."[44]

Their plight resonated with the faithful who aimed their Bible verses at communism while answering the Christian calling of hospitality and service. Writers for *Christian Century* heralded the Church World Service for relocating Cubans and encouraged U.S. citizens to open their homes to the exiles.[45] Not only did the publication warn that "religion was on the wane" in Cuba but it also lamented that the place Christopher Columbus happened upon—"the most beautiful island eyes have seen"—was now spiritually dead. After a rich religious history of Catholicism, Protestantism, and syncretic religions such as Santería, Marxist secularism had tragically transformed the island into a "beautiful but violent" land.[46]

All of this came to pass as the Vatican itself was undergoing a tectonic shift. In the fall of 1962, the Second Vatican Council convened, sparking a four-year meditation over the future of the church. Vatican II moved Mass from Latin to vernacular languages, eased rules governing dietary restrictions on Fridays, and gave greater weight to a new ecumenical movement. Catholicism was becoming more mainstream. Kennedy was inaugurated in 1961, and *Time* magazine named Pope John XXIII "Man of the Year" in 1962. Together, writes David O'Brien, Pope John and President Kennedy "brought an end to the isolation and aloofness long characteristic of American Catholic life."[47]

In the middle of this spiritual reckoning came tens of thousands of Cubans who would forever alter the Catholicism of South Florida, where, it may be said, American Catholicism began. The region's oldest European settlement is St. Augustine, which was founded by Spanish Catholics when Don Pedro Menéndez de Avilés laid claim to it in 1565. U.S.-Cuban channels of exchange developed in part through the church, when south Florida and Havana established a priestly corridor of back-and-forth travel. Menéndez made Biscayne Bay in Miami the blessed center of his operation in 1567. However, the inhospitable climate and lack of cohesion among Jesuit priests, Spanish soldiers, and Florida Indians made a permanent settlement impossible. The Jesuits would return years later along with Franciscans. In 1870 the Diocese of St. Augustine served all of Florida's ten thousand Catholics. In 1931 the Catholic Welfare Bureau was born, and the St. Augustine Diocese made strides under the episcopacy of Archbishop Joseph Hurley beginning in 1940. Hurley spearheaded the creation of eighteen new parishes and took a more aggressive approach to fundraising and real estate acquisition. A shrewd speculator, he helped broker purchases that would benefit his parishes for years. One prime property was the 150 acres on which would rest Camp Matecumbe, where many Pedro Pans would spend their first months in the United States. The state's population growth accelerated between 1940 and 1960. Florida climbed from the twenty-seventh most populous state to tenth, and its Catholic population billowed nearly 200 percent.[48]

In 1947 Miami's Catholic Welfare Bureau was folded into the diocese and its larger organization, Catholic Charities. In 1958 Pope Pius XII splintered the St. Augustine Diocese to establish the new Diocese of Miami and placed it under the direction of its first bishop, Coleman F. Carroll, who had been the auxiliary bishop of Pittsburgh. The new diocese had fifty-one parishes and eighty-six priests to shepherd 165,000 laypeople across sixteen counties. Father Walsh arrived in Miami at this time of momentous change, and there he found familiar company. Ireland had supplied Florida with an ample share of seminarians. Almost instantly, Walsh was appointed the director of the Catholic Welfare Bureau, and he threw his energy into his calling. But there was friction. The diocese was created against Archbishop Hurley's wishes. Hurley felt snubbed by the church's expansion, and Carroll did little to bring his predecessor into the transition or to give him sufficient credit for his previous work. Tension between the prelates climbed higher. Questions of personnel and real estate filled the fissure, to the point that an apostolic delegate and episcopal commission had to step in to facilitate communication between the bishops that had dwindled to silence. In 1960 the Holy See weighed in. Hurley's land deals were now needed by Carroll's new bishopric. Carroll traveled to Rome in 1961 to request an injunction against Hurley, a petition that was met. The property matter was not settled until 1965, and bad blood between the two bishops remained, cleaving Florida Catholics. Under Bishop Carroll's direction, however, the number of parishes blossomed from fifty-one to ninety-four, and the number of priests went from 86 to 305. In May 1968 Miami became its own archdiocese, serving a community of four hundred thousand.[49]

Exiles waded in during this transformative period. Although some religious knew Spanish, the young diocese was woefully unprepared for the mass influx of Catholic Cubans crossing the shore. In 1959

17. Residents of St. Joseph's Home, Pedro Pans among them, in Helena, Montana, 1962. Courtesy of the Diocese of Helena.

Carroll created the Centro Hispano Católico for Cuban and other Latin American refugees. It was a locus of medical services, English classes, childcare, food distribution, and other areas of assistance. The Diocese of Miami initially allocated $1.5 million to the enterprise.[50] As a young eager priest, Walsh undoubtedly felt pressure to cultivate the Catholic presence in Miami. The influx of tens of thousands of Catholic Cubans—including unaccompanied children—presented the perfect opportunity. Writing a colleague in 1962, Walsh radiated, "God has been very good to us in our program." He was thankful that "some 11,000 Cuban boys and girls" had been saved "from communistic indoctrination in their homeland."[51] The Cuban crisis was of biblical significance, so believed Bishop Carroll, who exhorted: "The recent arrival to this area of nearly one hundred thousand Catholic refugees from Communist oppression in Cuba has given the Diocese of Miami an opportunity to take to heart the admonition of Saint Paul, 'Bear one another's burdens, and so you will fulfill the law of Christ.'"[52]

A new crusade was afoot. Carroll sounded Gabriel's horn against the "Church of Silence in the lands held in the death grip of communism, especially in Cuba."[53]

Catholic Charities mobilized across the nation. In Montana the Diocese of Helena asked its fifty thousand congregants to host unaccompanied children. More than 130 children would land in the state between 1961 and 1967. St. Joseph's Home and Brondel Hall housed children waiting for foster placement. Director of Montana Catholic Charities Monsignor Daniel Harrington petitioned parishioners in his state: "To hearken to the need of these Cuban youths at this critical time is not only a real act of charity, but true patriotism at its best."[54]

Walsh could be proud of his work. He received a litany of letters of gratitude. Pilar Caballero Arnaiz of Weehawken, New Jersey, was grateful that her niece had come to possess a visa waiver from the CWB. She could now leave Cuba, thanks to Walsh and "the benevolence of Our Lord Jesus Christ."[55] In the summer of 1963, Bishop Carroll appointed Monsignor Walsh as the secretary of the Diocesan Board of Catholic Charities and the director of the Cuban Children's Program.[56]

In March of that year, after some of the dust had settled, Monsignor Walsh and Bishop Carroll traveled to Havana to attend the funeral of Cardinal Arteaga. There Walsh found seminarians in the company of Archbishop Pérez, who, unlike so many of his subordinates and parishioners, had stayed. The church's relationship with the government had improved somewhat, although the funeral was fraught with political speculation.[57] Afterward, Walsh sent a letter to Pérez, asking for his blessings and prayers for the Cuban children.[58] The archbishop died in 1968 but evidently maintained a workable relationship with the Castros through it all. His funeral at the grand cathedral in Santiago was adorned with wreaths sent by many mourners, including one from Fidel and his brother Raúl.[59]

11 | ABUSE

> But, when nothing subsists of an old past, after the death of people, after the destruction of things, alone, frailer but more enduring, more immaterial, more persistent, more faithful, smell and taste still remain for a long time, like souls, remembering, waiting, hoping, upon the ruins of all the rest, bearing without giving way, on their almost impalpable droplet, the immense edifice of memory.
>
> —MARCEL PROUST, *Swann's Way*

Alex López was scuttled away on Pan Am flight 422 in June 1962 after his mother became convinced the new government would send her son to Russia. His parents had submitted his name to the parish in Matanzas, and it arranged for his departure. Rather than Moscow, López went to Matecumbe, then to an orphanage in Cincinnati, and finally to a foster home until his parents came in 1966. As a twelve-year-old, López should have gone to Florida City, but it was full; so he ended up in Matecumbe, where the older boys stayed. It was a yearlong nightmare. He and five hundred adolescents were packed in the camp like sardines with six bathrooms and a shortage of running water. The solution was outdoor latrines in the heart of swampland. It was a place, he admitted, where "terrible things happened." López alleges that he was sexually abused by a priest. When he complained, the program moved him to Opa-locka in an attempt, he says, to silence him. There, things only became worse. He harbors tremendous anger for Monsignor Walsh, believing the priest knew about the abuse.[1]

The dreadful circumstances of Pedro Pan children were not confined to awkward instances of maladjustment. The trauma could reach the most intimate places: shelters, orphanages, foster homes. Some testimonies point to abusive interactions, recollections that linger, as they do for Proust's narrator, in the "immense edifice of memory." Much of the Pedro Pans' accounting has minimized or even erased these moments in the public exchange of common experience. But for a portion of these children, beyond the taxing ordeal of leaving home alone were episodes of emotional, physical, and sexual abuse.

Other Pedro Pans share similar stories. One living in a Catholic orphanage in New Orleans was overwhelmed by the sight of "rough people and sexual predators."[2] Sometimes the abuse was perpetrated by other children.[3] A counselor at Matecumbe recorded unwanted sexual advances among the boys in what he called "homosexual problems." Beyond shelters, foster homes shifted from nurturing spaces to incubators of abuse. Upon clearance to house children, couples received manuals that prescribed the day-to-day running of a household. Yet these spaces took a dynamic life of their own and could be disastrous for children.[4] Singer Candi Sosa left Cuba when she was ten years old along with her older sister and younger brother. She arrived as Dulce María Sosa and demonstrated a precocity for performance by appearing in David Susskind's *The Lost Apple*. After six months at Florida City, she and her siblings were placed with a Spanish-speaking foster family in Long Beach, California, for two and a half years. During this time, her foster father sexually molested her during rides to her music lessons. The family had a Cuban uncle who lived in California, but given that he was unmarried, the law prevented him from taking custody of her and her siblings. Her sister reported the abuse to the school's nuns, who accused Candi of lying. They gave her a choice: go to an out-of-state home by herself or stay with her siblings. She chose the latter. Sosa withstood the assaults for two and a half years, at which point the family was reunited.[5]

Another who has been vocal in exposing this history of abuse is Roberto Rodriguez Diaz, who arrived at his new home in the United States on December 30, 1961, at the age of eleven. While at a Marist Brothers school in Cuba, a priest had approached his parents and warned them about patria potestad, prompting them to send him north. It was a familiar trip for the family. His grandfather had worked for a U.S. auto parts company, and in 1957 the family went on vacation in Miami. After obtaining a visa waiver, the boy was scurried to Miami on a KLM flight.

Rodriguez was thankful for his Florida City assignment because he understood Kendall and Matecumbe were "in the jungle." A few months later, a Florida family took custody of him, and from that moment on, he witnessed physical abuse toward the other five children. "I saw the worst abuse in my life in that house," he shuddered. From there, he went to Opa-locka for several months, where he claims he suffered sexual abuse. After notifying the administration, things got worse. He was transferred to the Devereux School in Victoria, Texas, where he was joined by five other Pedro Pans. Rodriguez says that over his two-year stay he saw children put on regimens of pills and shock treatment. He himself was drugged four times a day, which made him lose "total recall" to the extent that he could not read a book properly due to short-term memory loss. His mother and sister arrived in 1965, and his father came the following year. Eventually the family made New Orleans their new home.[6]

Rodriguez later learned, after reading through letters in his file, that his godparents in New Orleans had tried to get custody of him but the CWB rebuffed them. He decided to sue the Catholic Church. He brought a case against the Miami Archdiocese to force its admission of wrongdoing and irreparable harm.[7] His accusation arose at a time when more people around the world were bringing to light the rampant sexual assaults within the church and the Vatican's veil of secrecy behind it. In a complaint filed in 2006, Rodriguez sued Archbishop John C. Favarola and the Miami Archdiocese for concealing "the sexual exploitation of children by its clergy." The case also blamed shelters for lacking proper personnel and measures to protect children against sexually abusive staff and older boys who were sexually aggressive toward younger ones. It alleges that Rodriguez and others were abused at Opa-locka by older inhabitants, adult supervisors, and priests, and that they were taken to downtown Miami, where they were "sexually molested" by "child molesters and other predators." The case also contends that Rodriguez faced sexual violence by employees of the Devereux School in Texas. Most glaring in the complaint is the only named perpetrator, Monsignor Bryan Walsh, who Rodriguez alleged sexually abused him in his office repeatedly.[8]

His case was dismissed two years later by a Miami-Dade circuit judge because the statute of limitations had expired, a decision that was upheld by Florida's Third District Court of Appeal in 2009.[9] The court found that the statute of limitations did not apply, nor was there cause to invoke the "doctrine of delayed discovery," which says that adults who suffered trauma earlier in life but are not cognizant of it until later may sue for damages. In a two-to-one ruling, the appellate court upheld the dismissal. When Rodriguez attempted to draw media attention around his protest of the dismissal, an archdiocese spokeswoman clapped back and charged that the Pedro Pan was "defaming a widely respected priest who saved the lives of 14,000 children."[10]

Rodriguez is not the only Pedro Pan to file a grievance against the church. Director of Catholic Charities in Helena monsignor Daniel Harrington was named in a wide-ranging abuse case against the Diocese of Helena in 2015.[11] María de los Angeles Torres's research discloses that boys in Helena complained of physical abuse while in the church's care and hinted at sexual impropriety against the monsignor.[12] In another instance, the *Miami Herald* reported a lawsuit against Father Joaquín Guerrero and the Archdiocese of Miami in 2002. While living at Kendall Camp at age fourteen, a man alleged that he was repeatedly abused for several months. In 2004 the church settled.[13] Alex López also identified Guerrero as the abusive priest at Matecumbe.[14]

Another clergyman, Reverend Ernesto García-Rubio, was defrocked for the sexual abuse of minors in the children's program in the 1960s and 1980s. The Miami Archdiocese knew of allegations against García-Rubio as early as 1968. In that year, Archbishop Carroll received a warning that the man of the cloth was forced to leave Cuba because of "serious difficulties of a moral nature." Church language of the day was vague. Such a phrase could connote homosexuality, pedophilia, or child abuse. Sex abuse allegations against the same man again arose in the 1980s by Nicaraguan and Salvadoran teenage refugees. In 1988 the Miami Archdiocese sent García-Rubio to Saint Luke Institute in Maryland for what the *Miami Herald* termed a "pedophilia evaluation," but in the end the institute could not confirm the diagnosis.[15]

Some months after his failed appeal, Rodriguez publicized his story, which he says freed him up to be more open with people. He harbors no anger at his parents because he believes they tried to be truthful. However, unlike many Pedro Pans, "grateful" is not one of the words he uses to describe the program. He returned to Cuba in 2011 for the first time in fifty years, looking to relive the fond memories he had repressed. It was a step toward the unrealizable wish many of us fantasize from time to time—the return to childhood. The visit was "very, very emotional." As with other Cuban exiles who have returned, he yearned to see his old house. The current owner gave him a few minutes to sit in it alone, as Proust's narrator does, to relive some of the images locked away in the immense edifice of memory. That initial return has sparked several more trips in the time since.[16]

Undoubtedly what is palpitating thus, deep inside me, must be the image,
the visual memory which is attached to this taste and is trying to follow it to
me. But it is struggling too far away, too confusedly . . .

—MARCEL PROUST, *Swann's Way*

Mayda Riopedre looks back at her childhood with adoration until the
traumatic days of Pedro Pan. "Tragic" is the adjective she uses repeatedly, but through it all, she is convinced her parents "made the right
decision." She was lucky and could speak to them by phone during
their separation. When they arrived a few years later, she met them
in Miami and thought her life would be the same. It wasn't. "It was
very tough," she sighed. Her mother took a job in a factory, her first
outside of the family's home, and her father resorted to waiting tables.
Exceedingly grateful that she was with them again, Riopedre accepted
the total overhaul of what she had known and loved.[1]

What is it to have trauma at the basis of collective memory? Though
most Pedro Pans did not suffer sexual or physical abuse, the very
separation from one's parents inflicted some level of psychological or
emotional harm, even if brief. Upon tasting the familiarity of the past,
Proust's narrator is thrown into the maelstrom of memory that is at
once uncontrollable, uncertain, and formless. Such is remembrance's
joy and pain: it comes when we least expect it in both mediated and
unmediated fashion. Proust reminds us that we are the creators and
the victims of memory. It is something irrevocable yet pliant, wholly
subjective yet costly in its proposed incontrovertibility. It underwrites
the essence of our identities, and we scorn alternative truths that seek
to correct it.

What Proust did not probe were the ways memory is also communal
and political. The marrow of Cuban America is memory, the sinew that
holds the exile identity together. In Cristina García's novel *Dreaming
in Cuban*, the character Celia calls memory a "skilled seducer."[2] The

novel traces the lives of a family living on both sides of the revolution in a lyrical narrative of exile, memory, and multigenerational womanhood. In one poignant scene, Felicia's niece Pilar lashes out at the frustration of being told how to be Cuban American, with her own choices secondary to the political events that have shaped her existence: "I resent the hell out of the politicians and the generals who force events on us that structure our lives, that dictate the memories we'll have when we're old. Every day Cuba fades a little more inside me, my grandmother fades a little more inside me. And there's only my imagination where our history should be."[3]

As the revolution endured, Cuban America solidified; refugees turned into permanent residents. Americanizing a la cubana meant recalibrating one's sense of cubanidad, which necessitated a kind of splitting of personalities—navigating between Pedro and Peter. Such a reality points to a question raised by Bharati Mukherjee: "What does it mean to invent rather than inherit one's homeland?"[4]

Inventing one's newfound nation is at the core of the American immigrant experience, but these journeys differ tremendously. In the 1960s Cubans entered a community that had been represented in an assortment of ways in the longer history between nations. Popular culture made for a particular Cuban likeness. *I Love Lucy* star Desi Arnaz is what Gustavo Pérez Firmat has called the "exemplary Cuban-American subject" and *I Love Lucy* the "great Cuban-American love story." Arnaz was from Santiago de Cuba, where his father was the mayor and a supporter of Gen. Gerardo Machado, the eventual dictator of the republic in the early 1930s. After Machado fell from power, the Arnaz family moved to the United States in 1934. As an entertainer, Arnaz breathed life into a Cuban American archetype— some would say stereotype—in the 1950s that informed how Americans viewed newly arriving refugees. That type may have had little in common with the reality of Pedro Pans and their fellow exiles, save their national origin, but it became figurative of what it was to be Cuban in the United States.[5] Yet if Arnaz embodied a comedic and flirtatious Cuban type fit for cultural consumption, Cuban American identity also came to signify dislocation, a state of in-between that never fully settles.

Pedro Pans belong to the "1.5 generation," or those who left their country as children and grew up in the United States. The very 0.5 in the 1.5 category suggests a status of belonging neither here nor there. Politically, the children often do not share the same level of contempt for communist Cuba that their parents harbor and are more open to the land they scarcely knew. Oftentimes they are unable to express this curiosity because of the political volatility Castro's Cuba historically invites in the exile community. Questions lie unutterable, self-censorship a necessary feature of family gatherings. Pedro Pan memory is unique in its association with abandonment, with a Cuban identity reconstituted through an adult lens looking back at a childhood pained by separation.

In the Pedro Pan past are rich anecdotes rife with pleasure and pain, joy and loss. There are stories of personal transformations and arduous acclimation. As a collective, Pedro Pans overwhelmingly have favorable associations with the program. Yvonne Conde's research from the 1990s unveiled that only 7.5 percent out of her 442 respondents reported negative experiences. In contrast, nearly 70 percent viewed their experience as a positive one, using words such as "stronger," "tougher," "independent," "hard-working," "self-reliance," "discipline," and "survivor" to describe the attributes they gained living in the United States.[6] While there are also tales of weighty difficulty and even abuse, they too often get suppressed or overlooked in public discussions of the program. More frequent are the laudatory memories that uphold the narrative of Cuban American sacrifice and anti-communist heroism by those thankful for America's many opportunities. Such is the Pedro Pan double helix. Tasting the madeleine opens up a torrent of sadness and elation, nostalgia and anger.

Exile is often envisioned as a kind of death and rebirth. Carlos Eire has written that exile memory loses itself in a "vault of oblivion" where traumatic experiences are stored. "Refugee ethics," he theorizes, are different from those of the "fully settled."[7] Forgetting is part of survival. Joyce Carol Oates has ruminated over the condition further: "To survive, for the refugee, is to be buffeted between the grief-suffused admonition to remember the losses of the homeland and the self-protective counter-admonition to 'forget,' the effort of which will be enormous and lifelong."[8]

What does the group remember, and what does it forget? Paul Ricoeur advanced the idea that there are uses and abuses of memory but also a "duty of memory."[9] What is the "duty" of Pedro Pan memory, and how is it formed?

Trauma nestles firmly in the heart of the Pedro Pan experience, a stone in the edifice of exile. Pury Lopez says her "traumatic moment" was at the pecera, where she sat with her parents outside the fishbowl until she made the lone journey to the plane. She wore no jewelry and held no possessions, save a doll from China. As was custom, and to the young girl's horror, authorities dismembered it to look for contraband. On her KLM flight, flight attendants pinned a luggage tag on her that read "unescorted child." Today she hazards that it was a "trust in institutions" that allowed OPP to occur, something that probably would not happen today.[10]

Though she harbors no feelings of anger, the word "trauma" manifests itself multiple times in her story. A recurrent word in many Pedro Pan testimonies, trauma is the foundation of their collective identity, something cemented into the new nationalism the children inhabited. The severity of the trauma may hinge on their lack of choice. Pedro Pans were forced to live through something not of their own making. Added to this is the quandary of how to reconcile feelings of abandonment with those of gratitude. Nearly all on record say their parents made the right decision, yet none has said they could send their own children if faced with a similar predicament.

In the months it was unfolding, Operation Pedro Pan was discussed in terms of trauma. Social workers at the CWB attended presentations such as "The Separation Trauma of Cuban Children."[11] After World War II, trauma—including that found in children—was something more adequately researched and written about in social science fields. But as a modern concept, trauma was first acknowledged in the nineteenth century and conceived as a condition of distress or shock entrenched in the spines of victims of railway accidents. What were thought to be microlesions on the spinal cord eventually wounded the psyche, and neurologist Paul Oppenheim established "traumatic neurosis" as the effect of undetectable physiological changes in the brain.[12] Ultimately the wounding of the body and brain led to harm incurred by the mind. Trauma was then seen as a psychological phenomenon.

Sigmund Freud took the concept in a new direction. In *Beyond the Pleasure Principle*, he expounded that people relive catastrophic events not of their own choosing during traumatic neurosis.[13] World War I greatly impacted the field of psychiatry, including Freud's own thinking, for then legions of veterans were suffering from combat-related trauma in otherwise healthy bodies. Psychoanalysis gained currency after the war because of its effective treatment of soldiers afflicted with shell shock. Freud posited that the trigger experience itself was not traumatic; rather, the oscillation between the original event and the later repressed memory of the event was harmful.

The history of war, it turns out, greatly coincides with the history of trauma studies, especially in the United States. Following the Vietnam War, the third edition of the *Diagnostic and Statistical Manual of Mental Disorders*, or DSM III, in 1980 made post-traumatic stress disorder (PTSD) an official psychological malady. Today trauma may be diagnosed in a victim, witness, or deliverer of violence, such as a soldier. It can be accompanied by scenes of jarring circumstances that repeatedly surface in the consciousness as hallucinations or as invasive, cognitive associations. Trauma—and specifically PTSD—is defined in part by the failure of memory. The victim is unable to unearth or assemble the events that caused the wounding. What is said to be a traumatic event is reconfigured later as flashbacks, nightmares, or inexplicable behaviors or movements.[14]

Trauma may "involve a betrayal of trust," as Jenny Edkins has written, "when the very powers that we are convinced will protect us and give us security become our tormentors: when the community of which we considered ourselves members turns against us or when our family is no longer a source of refuge but a site of danger."[15] At some level, Pedro Pans register a betrayal by their parents but then feel unmitigated gratitude for their decision, making for a difficult double bind. They remain dutiful children but may repress the sadness or even anger that resides at some level for not having a choice in the separation.

But this collective trauma also makes up their contemporary community identity. Different theorists have ruminated over what has been referred to as collective consciousness or generational memory. Jeffrey Alexander has formulated "cultural trauma" as a phenomenon "when members of a collectivity feel they have been subjected to a horrendous event that leaves indelible marks on their group consciousness." Trauma is social. "Events are not inherently traumatic," he argues, nor is trauma "the result of a group experiencing pain." Rather, it is the "acute discomfort entering into the core of the collectivity's sense of its own identity." It is the establishment of a "master narrative."[16]

There is a master narrative that holds Pedro Pans together and from there the general Cuban American collective more broadly. Of course, not all Pedro Pans say they were traumatized by their crossings. For those who do invoke the term, there are distinctions in the intensity of their wounds. Those who experienced abuse in shelters or foster homes can differ in their processing of trauma from those who were reconnected with their parents after a brief time apart. Many render barely any hardship in their stories, while others are still gravely affected by the incidents they endured. But the larger narrative relies on the trauma for the community to thrive, socially and politically.

Many credit it with the origins of ambition, which ultimately led to their success. Commonly recited lines are "we were just children" and "our parents did the right thing." With these sentiments is the children's duty to never go back to Cuba, for it would betray their parents' honor. Displacing the painful variables of their childhood was their newfound status as anti-communist heroes, celebrants in the new nation. The feeling of trauma is a basis of this collective memory but is then firmly linked to anti-communist nobility. How to confront trauma when one is championed as a hero in the new nation?

When delving into Mercedes Diaz Dash's vault of memory, we find a childhood filled with the sounds of horseracing from the nearby hippodrome in the upscale neighborhood of Marianao. Americans frequented the area; English was spoken everywhere. She attended the prestigious Colegio del Apostolado. The days leading up to her departure bustled with family members and endless packing. Her parents maintained the unwavering belief that the government was going to take their daughters and brainwash them. Mercedes was kept in the dark. A couple of days later, she was at the airport saying goodbye to her parents, who told her, "We'll see you soon." At first, the journey seemed promising. She and her sister ended up with a well-to-do foster family in northwest Miami. The foster mother was the daughter of a neighbor who lived across the street from the girls in Cuba, though their papers falsely stated that they were relatives. This living arrangement proved miserable, and Mercedes now wishes that the pair had spent more time at a camp. The foster father was a professional jockey, and his wife was distant and negligent. At one point, the girls' aunt and uncle came to the United States. After reclaiming their son at another foster home, they went to check on the sisters at their home. They found them profoundly unhappy and worrisomely skinny.

Her Miami was one of No Vacancy signs directed at Cubans in apartment complexes and the sounds of people chanting, "Cubans go home." Mercedes and her sister were the only Spanish-speaking children at the first elementary school they attended. English came slowly because her foster family spoke Spanish. There were no English as a second language programs in those days. Her sister cried a lot, and the pair fought constantly. They were made to eat different food from the family, and her sister was forced to wash the girls' own undergarments. Though in an upscale abode, they were laughed at and not permitted to sit on the furniture but on the floor. They ate food doled out by the refugee center. "We were weird. We were rare," she huffed. "We were treated terribly." When their aunt and uncle retrieved them in Miami, the siblings moved into a more modest one-room house. They slept with the lights on for fear of cockroaches. "We were dirt poor, but we loved it," Mercedes remembered gleefully.

After the family moved to Arlington, Virginia, the young Cubans began to feel more American. Some Hispanics were at their new school, but Mercedes decided to make friends with the white Americans by roller skating and joining their adolescent escapades. Her sister, meanwhile, clung to her Cuban roots. She sought Latino/a kids at school. To this day, Mercedes claims that her English accent is less noticeable than her sister's.[17] Language is a persistent theme in the 1.5 generation. How good is her English? Does he still have a Cuban accent? These questions measure assimilation and success.

JAN 1963

18. Mercedes Diaz Dash (*right*) and her sister, Rosario Diaz Juliano (*left*), ages ten and twelve, respectively, lived with a foster family in Miami before moving in with relatives. Courtesy of Mercedes Diaz Dash.

Language is always on José Azel's mind when the former Pedro Pan writes poetry. The words come out in Spanish, though most of his personal and professional life is governed in English. He is unsure of his written Spanish, and he still prefers having it translated from English by others because he is afraid of making errors. "The only thing I write in Spanish is poetry," he acknowledged. "I don't understand poetry in English at all."[18]

At his uncle's house in Miami, Mario García's cousins spoke English all the time. But he credits the poet Emily Dickinson with opening up a literary world in which he could "feel American." After Dickinson, he conquered his first novel, *You Can't Go Home Again* by Thomas Wolfe. Reading the book cover to cover was García's further gateway to American sentimentality. Nineteenth-century literature, it turned out, would become a sustaining passion. In 1976 he completed a PhD in comparative literature at the University of Miami. Fluency in English gave him the confidence and ability to excel in the United States. It also shaped his politics of self-reliance and why he questions the merits of bilingual education today: "The Pedro Pans didn't have any teddy bears. . . . We had to find our own teddy bears. . . . That's why we all succeeded." On weekends he would cut grass for "old ladies in the neighborhood" who made him lemonade and talked to him. "Those were my English teachers," he gushed.[19] He also experienced the "sweet little victory" of vividly dreaming in his second language.[20]

Embracing the nation meant Pedro Pans acquired new traditions, holidays, and periods of national mourning. Mario remembers the day John F. Kennedy was assassinated. He was in algebra class when the principal issued the news over the speaker system. Mario's teacher was an Irish American Catholic, and Mario was the first child she hugged. Grieving one's adopted nation signals one's belonging in it, and even today Mario tears up while telling this story. The sadness is in part for the teacher and the slain president, but it is also a seminal moment in his crossing over. A part of him pushed Cuba further away in mourning the death of his new nation's leader.[21]

As distant as Cuba may seem for the 1.5 generation, it persists in the vaults of memory and demands a place in the present. In his house in Miami, José Azel is surrounded by Cuban art, and every now and again he uses Google Maps to locate his boyhood home in Cuba. He remembers Lebanese food as a staple on the table, for his paternal grandparents had emigrated from Lebanon around the time of World War I. His father was an influential lawyer, and his connections enabled him to obtain a visa for his son. Once in the United States, José and his brothers rented rooms in a large home of mostly Cubans. He started delivering newspapers. In Miami some banks made special allowances for Cubans, so-called character loans to help refugees get on their feet. Loans could be granted based on one's family name or a relative, and again his father's reputation made the credit available. The young boy also faced racism and remembered the signs: No Blacks, No Dogs, No Cubans. He was in gangs as a kid, something he likened to a *West Side Story* kind of lifestyle. At dances, American kids would be in one place, Cubans in another.[22]

Though permeating throughout many a Pedro Pan memory is the fulfillment of success, not all were so lucky. Mario García had a cousin who could never conquer the mental health problems suffered stemming from parental separation. For Mario, Operation Pedro Pan lay "dormant" for many years, but as he ages, it has become important to him. Now he thinks about that time "nostalgically." He, too, is forever thankful for his parents' decision, calling them heroic. He keeps in daily contact with another cousin in Camaguey who is a psychology professor. He often wonders what would have happened had her parents sent her to the United States. In the end, he can only speculate: "She would have gone to Harvard."[23]

13 | BITTERSWEET REUNIONS

In 1964 the parents of Mercedes Diaz Dash found themselves in Spain, still trying to get to the United States to see their daughters. Someone with their father's name had been a member of the Communist Party in Cuba, so the U.S. Consulate in Madrid withheld the coveted visa. To get clearance, her father had to rummage through his American contacts to find reputable people to vouch for him. In 1965 the family was whole again. Not wanting to stay in Miami, because the only jobs he could find were manual labor in the shipyards or the Everglades, Mercedes's father took the clan elsewhere. The separation had been rough. After the girls left Cuba, he had a nervous breakdown. They landed in Arlington, Virginia, where Mercedes began attending junior high that same year. "We were big celebrities," she chimed. The local newspaper tailed the family with regularity and touted the local Cubans in their daily routines. Operation Pedro Pan was never a part of this public identity. She and her family were simply "Cuban."

Mercedes says that both parents repressed their memories of Cuba. Nostalgia was meant to be kept internal, and they "pushed it to the side." One could only utter how bad Cuba had turned out under Castro. Her relatives held out hope that they would soon return. One of her aunts did not unpack her suitcase for a year. She would wash her clothes, fold them, and put them back in the suitcase and use the clothes as she needed them, convinced that she might have to return to Cuba at any moment.[1]

Brave were the children making the journey, but even thicker skin was needed for the parents who sent them. The act unfathomable to most was unbearable to those who did it. Cuban filmmaker Marina Ochoa remembers when her parents dispatched her brother. Shortly afterward, letters appeared with "Mami, ven" (Mommy, come) scribbled all over the paper.[2] The torment must have been unimaginable. Family reunification was always the principal goal, but the enterprise brought unforeseen difficulties. Parents faced mind-numbing obstacles when trying to reclaim their children. Even after obtaining an exit visa, one could be denied departure at the airport due to any bureaucratic glitch. It could take several attempts before one could successfully board a flight. Periods of separation increased after the missile crisis. When air travel between nations ceased, parents were required to travel through a third country such as Spain or Mexico. Those nations had their own rules and waiting periods. One often needed an affidavit of support from someone in the United States promising to host the applicant lest he or she become a public charge. For those schlepping through a third country, securing refugee assistance in the United States became more difficult because the money was initially reserved for those arriving directly from Cuba.[3]

In Cuba authorities closely reviewed petitions before signing off on the exit visas. Pending charges against applicants or the possession of special skills or knowledge—such as with doctors or scientists—could delay or preclude the issuing of a passport.[4] Some mothers and fathers were unimaginably lucky. Lobbying by Attorney General Robert Kennedy yielded a Christmas exchange of $53 million in food and medicine for prisoners of the Bay of Pigs invasion. Planes and cargo ships carrying supplies to Cuba would return with Cuban family members. This deal ended on July 3, 1963, but not before nearly ten thousand people had squeezed through. These contrivances were not without their risks. One mother attempted to procure a small vessel to join her son and was sentenced to a year in jail for doing so.[5]

The missile crisis forced the U.S. government to become more cautious about Cuban spies and agents. Not all Cuban exiles were anticommunist, after all. The first ones fleeing the revolution were among Batista's upper echelon, who were followed by elites who were losing their properties and holdings. But in the subsequent wave were some communists and socialists who fought with the July 26th Movement. More binding in the exile population than anti-communism was antiCastroism.[6] As of July 31, 1963, the general visa waiver program for Cubans had surged to over 617,000 applications, of which 479,000 had been granted. More members of the U.S. government and everyday Americans now were wanting to limit the flow of refugees. The open-door policy had reached the point of saturation, and the waiver program was canceled that year.[7]

The children's program was aging. With parents cut off from their kids indefinitely, more minors would reach the age of nineteen without familial support. New procedures permitted agencies to file an extension of financial assistance with HEW.[8] This matter provoked Beth Thompson of the Dade County Children's Bureau to write Senator George Smathers (D-FL), a member of the Senate Finance Committee. She wrote that too many children were hitting the cutoff age and simply needed more time to become self-dependent. Also, a few special circumstances justified extending the benefits. Thompson mentions "mental retardation" and "emotionally disturbed" young people who required extensive care.[9]

By 1963 nineteen-year-olds without parental assistance could apply for financial support directly through the Cuban Refugee Program. Such a move would also authorize Pedro Pan families relief even if the parents did not register in Miami to permit a quicker reunion. Thus, children could be the signatories of federal entitlements on behalf of their parents.[10] Crossing the U.S. border did not guarantee a parent instant reclamation of his or her child, however. Before releasing minors, authorities conducted a home study that examined household earnings and determined a general impression of the family. The process could stall.[11] In some cases, one or both parents had landed but reunification with the children was delayed because the CWB did not know they were in the country.

The four sons of the Villaverde Rodríguez family went to the Kendall and Florida City camps, and from there to a family in San Antonio. They were able to rejoin their parents, who had entered through Mexico, in Union City, New Jersey.[12] Ed Canler considers himself fortunate because he only spent a year without his parents, who were able to come just before the missile crisis.[13] Not so for former Miami mayor Tomás Regalado, who was thirteen years old when he disembarked in Miami. His father stayed and fought against the revolution, was later imprisoned for this activity, and would have to wait until 1980 to see his son—then a grown man—again.[14]

Though in the end, the vast majority of Pedro Pans did reconnect with one or both parents, the process could be bittersweet. Children now faced a yawning chasm in the family dynamic. Exile ages one, and the children grew up quickly and unpredictably under new exigencies. Roles between children and parents reversed. Pedro Pans were the ones conducting the business of the house because they knew English and the adopted country's cultural machinations. Some lost their fluency in Spanish, making it difficult to communicate with the very people who first gave them language. Others vacillated in rejoining their guardians. Rejecting one's family could be a psychological defense against the fear of losing one's parents again. This made for a horrific sensation when parents lost their children twice—once in Cuba and again in the United States.

When his mother and father arrived, Mario García assumed the role of the man of the house. They had to consult the sixteen-year-old for nearly everything, from answering the door to communicating with the electrician to telling them to close the windows if playing music too loudly. They had sent a child but rediscovered a man. He located an apartment for his family and had saved money by bussing tables at Suzanne's Restaurant in downtown Miami. The subject of politics, though, was a conversation stopper. The older generation had the most anger. The changes his parents witnessed were "traumatic," and they "were never the same again."[15] These changes made for an awkward dynamic:

> WE were the ones who had already worked in the US and made enough money to welcome our parents with cash available to pay for rental of that first apartment, plus the basic necessities: beds, towels, cooking utensils, and, in the case of Cuban families—a pressure cooker, a coffee maker and, for my musician father, a saxophone. Then, we would be the ones speaking for the family, as mom and dad could not speak a word of English. We would deal with banks, door salesmen, school principals and anybody else that the parents needed to communicate with to become official in a new country. It was a fast track into adulthood.[16]

Families were reconstituted in a different context altogether. They came, they toiled. Cubans who had been professionals—lawyers, doctors, business owners—became baggage handlers and janitors. Here was the novel experience of downward economic and social mobility.[17] The music performer Willy Chirino took on a newspaper route to help his family get by.[18]

María de los Angeles Torres has written on the rifts between the 1.5 generation and their parents by centering on the question of how to be Cuban outside of Cuba. Cuban parents, she says, were "also caught in a contradiction: on the one hand, parents wanted their children to follow 'Cuban ways,' while on the other hand they opposed their children's desire to return to Cuba."[19] Mari Vilano was sent to Buffalo where she changed her name to Billie. She hesitated to see her parents when they came almost four years later. Her subsequent transition from Buffalo to Miami was equally difficult; even though Vilano was again immersed in the familiar capital of Cuban America, she found more racism in Miami than in Buffalo. She was even spat on in school.[20]

For a long time, Silvia Wilhelm resented her parents for sending her to the States at the age of fourteen. Traveling by way of Jamaica, the passports and visas for her and her cousin originated from the British Embassy. She also wound up at an orphanage in Buffalo not long after landing in Miami. Wilhelm understood that she would have to persevere for only four months. It seemed reasonable. She knew some English, having studied in the United States for a brief time. But Buffalo was the opposite of Cuba in climate and temperament. "I remember that I would look at the sky day after day and see all the snow and I would begin to cry and cry and cry, without knowing what was going to happen." When she became a parent, the resentment stretched: "When my children were growing up, I would look at them and would think that I could never part with them or send them to another country with the possibility of never seeing them again, based on a possible rumor. So I judged my family for a long time and resented their decision."

She eventually came to terms with their choice, and her first return to Cuba in 1994 enabled that healing. She accepted that her parents sent her out of love and is now relieved that they did.[21]

Reunification demanded emotional fortitude and bureaucratic persistence. After five years of separation, Roberto Rodriguez resumed life with his parents, but it was a trying affair. The longing had been too devastating.[22] Even after pocketing an exit visa several times, the mother of Carlos Eire was continually rebuffed for three and a half years until finally arriving through Mexico.[23] Sometimes a breakdown in communication delayed reunions because, as noted previously, the CWB did not always know when the parents were in-country.[24] Parents had to find their own bearings. Some requested that the bureau continue tending to their children until they could forge a stable living situation.[25]

Other times parents transferred guardian rights to family friends and made preparations for formal adoption. This happed to thirteen-year-old Francisco Méndez. Fears of communism and the prospect of more violence in Cuba prompted his family to send him to the States. His own family wavered with divided loyalties. On his father's side were farmers from Oriente who sympathized with the revolution. From Matecumbe, he went to an orphanage in New Jersey, where he faced the racism and physical reprimands of the nuns. His mother completed the paperwork to transfer custody to a family friend so that he could legally be adopted. Francisco ruefully points out that his mother did not lose patria potestad in Cuba; she lost it in the United States.[26]

On extremely rare occasions in the archive, one encounters evidence of parents summoning their children to return to Cuba. The CWB had a policy: should a parent request the child's return, the child was to contact Monsignor Walsh. Both parents had to sign an affidavit stating the reason, to agree to resume full responsibility of the child, to prepare the necessary paperwork with Cuban authorities, and to send a cable authorizing their kid's return.[27]

Some Cuban parents did regret sending their little ones, and in at least one case, a mother sued for their return. By phone, she threatened legal action to regain custody of her children, who were living with their aunt in Miami. But U.S. law held that unaccompanied children were wards of the juvenile court and thus presented a formidable legal challenge to summoning one's child back to Cuba.[28] Both the State Department and the CCP needed to sign off any such recommendations made by Walsh. By April 1964 the CWB had received at least three cases in which parents demanded their children's return. What happened with these cases is unknown.[29]

The legality of OPP was nebulous. Nothing similar to the program had ever existed, and protocols were always changing. Walsh was uncomfortable legally labeling children as refugees. Following definitions of the Children's Bureau and the Children's Division of the Florida State Department of Public Welfare, the priest mandated: "Children who arrive from Cuba with no immediate place to go are to be considered a special and privileged group, and that the agency providing the care must not jeopardize the child's immigration status." The question involved the jurisdiction. Who had the final word in maneuvering a lone Cuban child through the system—the courts or the parents? Before repossessing their offspring, parents were subject to scrutiny. The young refugees were now protected by child welfare laws. Walsh believed parents should retain a lot of discretion. It was their right to choose if their kids would receive care from the CWB as well as who could take custody of their children in their stead. He wrote, "Whenever notification is received from parents in Cuba stating their choice is a relative or friend, we have an obligation to discharge the child to the indicated person."[30]

Children still remained under their parents' legal custody. Childcare agencies, the language went, "have only physical custody of the child unless there is court action modifying parental responsibility." But what would occur, for example, should a child need surgery? What about emergency cases? The CWB developed consent forms to mail to Cuba for the parents' signatures. Some children flew to Miami with signed forms, and in at least one case, a power of attorney was obtained from parents over the telephone.[31] There are also findings of children discharged from the program and readmitted anew. Joining a relative or parent did not always work out. Parents, too, had aged, even if in only a matter of months or years. Some faced illness upon arrival or suffered psychologically themselves. Exile was a condition in which not everyone thrived. Sometimes children were released to an environment that was later deemed hazardous for minors, so they reentered the program. In 1962, with minimal investigation into the situation, the program could release Pedro Pans to relatives or friends with a letter from their parents in Cuba. But as its vetting procedures became more stringent, more children lingered longer in shelters or had to return to them after an unsuccessful leave.[32]

Walsh estimated that 90 percent of those under care were able to reconnect with one or more parents by June 1966. Still, delays were ongoing given regulations set by the Cuban government. Certain professionals had to stay behind, as did young men between the ages of fifteen and twenty-six because of obligatory military service. Some children did not see both parents due to a death or illness, or a father or mother stayed behind to take care of aging family members.[33] Walsh was proud that the CWB never received a request from Cuba to find a misplaced child in the United States, nor did a Pedro Pan contact the bureau to help find a lost parent.[34]

José Arenas had to wait until 1968 to see his mother and father again, at which point they never discussed politics. Living in a lower-class neighborhood in Habana Vieja, Arenas remembers no refrigerator, television, or telephone in the home, only a radio. Among his occasional indulgences was a sweet ice cream cone on a hot day. "We were a happy family," he says, but today money is still a constant preoccupation. Arenas has worked as a mid-level manager for a paper company for over fifty years, first in New York, then in Miami. It is a profession for which he was groomed, his father having labored in a paper factory in Havana that made purchases from Perez Trading Company, the very place that now employs his son.

Arenas's paternal grandfather was Spanish and his maternal grandfather Argentine. He attended the Catholic school Escuela Pías with money from his godmother. At age sixteen, he and his brother went to the United States, trailed by their sister three months later. He remembers liking the prospect of leaving Cuba and in fact had a visa to enter Spain, but he had cousins in Miami. "You're going to study," his parents told him. The brothers went to Matecumbe, an area that was "all jungle," he remembered, and full of adolescents sleeping under army tents. At night, the sound of kids crying because they missed their families pierced the air. Arenas had family on Calle Ocho, not far from signs that read No Pets and No Cubans Allowed. After a stint at the shelter from May to December 1962, the brothers were transferred to the Mission of the Immaculate Virgin in Staten Island at Mount Loretto.[35]

One of the largest orphanages in the country, Mount Loretto had earned a mixed reputation. Originally founded in 1871, the orphanage moved to Staten Island in 1883 as a sanctuary for abandoned children, whose numbers were surging with each new immigrant wave to the area. The building's design followed innovations in urban planning hatched by social reformers such as Jacob Riis and Frederick Law Olmsted. The intent was to maximize light and fresh air for the residents to reduce the risk of infection, which was plaguing Manhattan's Lower East Side. Staten Island was still quite rural, an Edenic elixir for the destitute.[36]

When the Arenas brothers arrived there, ten inches of snow blanketed the grounds. Six young men were lodged in a suite. Every two to three hours there was roll call, which was like an alarm in the night. Arenas winces while chronicling the pungent foot odor he lived with there. At night, he would apply rubbing alcohol on a cloth and tie it around his neck to avoid the stench. So troubling and vivid is the memory that even today he remains very sensitive to smell. He routinely lights aromatic candles in his office for comfort. Mount Loretto was a terrifying place. Most of the other kids had survived troubled home environments, and many had violent criminal records. Racial violence flared, and fights were common. After being accused of instigating such a fight, the brothers were put in a small room and made to stand with their noses touching the wall and their arms extended outward for three hours.

Arenas and his brother were allowed to go to nearby Tottenville High School, where they were stigmatized. When they went to the store, employees surveilled them, suspicious that they were Latino ne'er-do-wells from Loretto. They stomached the new daily occurrence of racism. One day they were invited to a barbecue at a white girl's house. Upon answering the door, the girl's mother told the boys to leave. After the friend vouched for them, Arenas remembers telling his brother to be on his best behavior. They refrained from drinking beer or eating much food. They now were representing all Latinos, not just Cubans. After leaving Loretto, the brothers moved to 136th Street in Manhattan, a place they rented from a Dominican woman who also provided meals.

Arenas then obtained his job with Perez Trading. When the business moved to Miami, he followed.[37]

Arenas had to wait a long time to see his parents, but there were children whose parents never came. Justo Rodríguez waited and waited but could not hug his folks until he visited them in Cuba twenty-one years later. Antonio Prieto did not see his family for sixteen years. He had been told he was going to the United States for a week. Finally in 1978, he saw his mother in Hialeah, and by his account, it was not an ideal reunion. Insurmountable distance lingered, filling him with regret. "I'm still paying for some of the memories I have," he admitted.[38]

After flights between the United States and Cuba were grounded, the next major opportunity for parents to rejoin their children came in 1965. In the fall Castro made the surprise announcement that the port of Camarioca would open for those wanting to head to Florida. Boats ferried some three thousand people over the course of a month. In December President Johnson and Castro made further agreements. Twice a day, five days a week, and at a cost of $50 million to the U.S. government, the air transport "Freedom Flights" began. After more than three thousand trips, close to three hundred thousand Cubans had left by 1973 when the program terminated. In their inaugural month, the planes carried parents who had previously sent 128 unaccompanied children.[1] Monsignor Walsh was relieved. The airlifts were a "Godsend for reuniting families."[2]

The year 1966 was a momentous one for exiles. Upon arriving in the United States, Cubans traditionally had received a "parole" status that granted automatic asylum and refugee benefits.[3] In 1966 President Johnson signed the Cuban Adjustment Act that made for a clearer path to citizenship. The temporary fix became permanent; exiles were here to stay.[4]

Walsh boosted his efforts to supply the Cuban government with lists of parents to prioritize them on the Freedom Flights.[5] With rolling delays, more parents pursued the third-country route of Mexico or Spain, making the parent-child reconnections horribly arduous.[6] As the years lumbered on, the children's program shrank. Fewer children were showing up, and not as many required services. But again the accounting is inconsistent. In March 1966 the Florida Department of Public Welfare counted 1,500 Cuban minors in the foster care systems of forty states.[7] Around the same time, the Catholic *Our Sunday Visitor* cited a lower estimate of 1,204 still in the program.[8] Walsh provided a much smaller number of 262 children in homes outside of Florida: 242 in CWB care, 12 under the Children's Bureau, 2 warded by United

Hebrew Immigrant Aid Society, and 6 in other welfare programs.[9] From the archive, the reasons for these discrepancies is not clear. With the airlifts towing an average monthly cargo of four thousand passengers to Miami from Havana, the numbers were falling. Families were increasingly whole again.[10] In the fall of 1968, thirty Catholic agencies were on the books, caring for 144 children, 67 of whom were in Miami.[11]

As the numbers dropped, agencies cut their ties to the program. Des Moines put up children until July 1967; Tucson did not renew its contract that August.[12] When the Atlanta Catholic Family Services opted out, Father Walsh wrote a letter of gratitude for its work: "The effort of the Federal government and the voluntary agencies has been a notable success in the history of social welfare in the United States and in American Catholic Charities services."[13] "Never before," he wrote in a letter to Atlanta's archbishop Paul Hallinan, "have so many Diocesan Catholic Charities been asked to participate in a federally financed program."[14] As the 1960s crossed into the 1970s, the Catholic Welfare Bureau reinvented itself as the Catholic Service Bureau. In January 1971 Walsh's operation was responsible for 165 children. One was a seventeen-year-old boy who Walsh said swam across Guantánamo Bay to the U.S. naval base to seek asylum.[15] By 1974 the Cuban Refugee Program had resettled 300,000 of 461,000 registrants and distributed $957 million in assistance.[16]

In the weeks leading up to Richard Nixon's 1972 reelection, HEW drew up a five-year phaseout of the program. The decision would move federal financial responsibilities to state coffers. Governmental support for the refugees was losing steam. The Senate Appropriations Committee mulled over discontinuing reimbursements to the states. HEW promoted a measure that after July 1, 1972, Cubans who had been in the United States over five years would no longer be eligible for financial and medical assistance through the CRP, and after June 30, 1977, the program would cease its funding entirely.[17] This was a remarkable drawdown considering that after fifteen years, and starting with a budget of $4 million, the CRP had spent over $1.1 billion on six hundred thousand refugees. Its annual price tag was $90 million, but demand was shrinking.[18] It was the end of an era. After July 1, 1977, money from the Migration and Refugee Assistance Act would end.[19]

Entitlements lasted three more years, and the center in Miami closed in 1981.[20]

Politics played a part, but so did reshuffling the president's cabinet. HEW split in 1979 into the Department of Education and the Department of Health and Human Services. Monsignor Walsh fretted over the future burden on Florida taxpayers and the toxicity the subject posed once again locally.[21] What would happen to the kids when the money dried up? One child in the program was only five years old. All Walsh could do was lobby his case.[22]

Toward the middle of the decade, the Cuban Children's Program underwent a name change. Going forward it would be called the Cuban Children's Services, with Dorothy McCrary as its director. McCrary had worked her way up since her days as the director of Child Welfare Services at the Florida Department of Public Welfare. As the country was celebrating its bicentennial, Pete O'Connor, the coordinator at the Cuban Boys' Home, reported that still under his watch were seven "true unaccompanied children including full orphans." O'Connor was also troubled that beyond his lot were thirty-one juveniles under care who had at least one parent in the United States and eighteen others in shelters who had both parents in-country. The Catholic Service Bureau was the legal custodian of eleven of them.[23]

And in a flash, the first phase of the program terminated. In February 1978, with fourteen boys in care, Walsh was honored for his sustained work.[24] He had overseen the flourishing of Miami's Catholic Charities, having started with a staff of 11 people and expanding it to 421, and with a base budget of $100,000 but reaching $60 million that served twenty thousand people yearly. What a journey it had been since he first took a job in the brand-new Diocese of Miami in 1958.[25]

Then Fidel Castro rocked the Florida Straits once again. On April 1, 1980, six Cuban citizens rammed a bus into the Peruvian Embassy's fence in Havana and requested asylum. Within a few days, the mob grew to over ten thousand dissidents. Castro responded with an announcement that the Mariel port was open to people wanting to leave. Over the next several months, 125,000 people took up the offer and drifted to U.S. shores. President Jimmy Carter initially indicated an "open arms" approach to the new wave of refugees but was conflicted about taking them in. It was an election year, and the president was still suffering from America's "crisis of confidence" in his faulty leadership. He declared a state of emergency in Florida, signed a $10 million allocation for the new refugee wave, and with the help of the U.S. Navy and Coast Guard, threatened boat seizures and fines for vessels returning to Cuba for additional exiles.[26] Just as the refugee program was drawing to a close, another Cuban crisis befell south Florida.

The Marielitos (the emigrants who left from the Mariel port) were unlike those who had arrived in prior waves. They were more often from underprivileged neighborhoods, and approximately one-third of them were not white. The Cuban government billed the moment as another successful ejection of anti-revolutionary *escoria* (scum). Castro took the opportunity to discharge some prisoners, criminals, and people in rehabilitative institutions. Negative images have stuck to this generation, and Marielitos have never quite shed the characterization "undesirable." Of this group, Miami mayor Maurice Ferré carped that "there was no way to control the criminal element. These people who were not mentally stable were out on the street right away. . . . [T]hey went out and started to commit crimes and to become vagrants." But as historian Victor Triay shows, most were ordinary Cubans wanting to rejoin their families. With their frayed clothes and bruised bodies, they were the updated spokespeople of a Cuba suffering from the revolution.[27]

The Marielitos broke land as truthtellers who dispelled the myth of social equality under the revolution. "They say racism doesn't exist in Cuba," scoffed one arrival. "That is a lie. A black person is always black and that makes a difference. . . . Here I may be alone but I am free."[28] Marvin Dunn speculates that because Black Cubans came from the "lower strata," the Mariel generation and onward have suffered marginalization, as its members were presumed to be criminals or mentally ill. In general, the view toward Black Cubans was negative, with many believing that Castro foisted on the United States the "bad Cubans."[29]

"Bad Cubans" is an epithet Marielitos and subsequent exiles share. But chroniclers of this history point out the pejorative association does not meet reality: most actually worked hard and became productive citizens.[30] Yet many older Cuban refugees—Pedro Pans among them—

speak poorly of their later compatriots. "Unfortunately, the new Cuban generation is different," José Arenas intimated. He finds younger Cuban Americans off-putting, especially those peddling modern slang from the island. When Arenas moved to Miami in 1979, Cubans of the earlier era still reigned. Within a couple of years, however, older Cubans grew leery of their compatriots. The newcomers' reputations sullied those of the first wave who had worked hard to succeed in the United States and now held significant political clout.[31] Mario García reports something similar, saying his generation thinks the more recently transplanted—*los Cubanos castristas* (the Castro Cubans)—are lazy.[32]

The Mariel crisis was unfolding as the United States was reformulating its policies on refugees. Following a decade doddered by U.S. foreign relations quagmires from Vietnam to Central America that yielded a string of impromptu refugee laws, Washington needed something more consistent, durable, and comprehensive. The outcome was the Refugee Act of 1980, which better systematized refugee admissions into the country. The act was brand new when the Marielitos disembarked, but it only applied to Cubans for a short time when it became evident that thousands more were on their way. Fearing exorbitant federal costs, President Carter saddled states and volunteer agencies with the financial responsibility while reverting to the old system that had granted the group special status as parolees.[33]

Interspersed in this large wave of refugees were perhaps as many as two thousand unaccompanied children.[34] Once again, Monsignor Walsh looked to house them in local parish shelters that could volunteer their beds.[35] The Pedro Pan archive refers to this effort as the Cuban Children's Program, Phase II. It now had a different process. The Cuban government obliged parents to formally authorize their children to leave alone, and every child had a passport.[36] Yet once again, the children went to group or foster homes. The state of Florida kicked in the funds.[37] The federal government was again cajoled to find reimbursement money. Victor Palmieri, the State Department's coordinator for refugee affairs, worked with Father Walsh to ensure the process went smoothly.

Within Walsh's line of sight were 188 unaccompanied kids, the majority being boys, by August 1980. The Catholic Service Bureau lodged

63 of them.[38] Some stayed at Bethany Residence, located at 2400 sw Third Avenue, which held a contract with the bureau until June 30, 1981. It received $380 a month per child.[39] Others stayed at Boystown or the Catholic Home for Children during the 1980–81 fiscal year.[40] Opa-locka once again unlocked its doors. But tolerance for refugees had dropped, especially for the new crop. In a letter to Archbishop Edward A. McCarthy, Walsh moaned that Miami was again "oversaturated" with refugees. Resettlement needed to accelerate. The Irish priest was older, more venerable, and brazenly uncensored. He let the archbishop know that "many if not most of those in the camps have been so traumatized that they may be permanently damaged by the ineptness of the government handling of their cases." In July alone, unaccompanied minors suffered 175 rapes, 5 suicides, and 186 stress fractures. He did not hide his bleak assessment: "Very few of the Catholic Agencies throughout the country have the capacity to care for these adolescents who, by the way, should not be described as children."[41]

Now Walsh was dealing with criminals. Licensed professionals were in greater demand, and some, such as a group of professors from the University of Miami working for the Spanish Family Guidance Center, seconded the monsignor's alarm in their letters to the archbishop. The kids were winding up in federal detention centers: Fort McCoy, Wisconsin; Fort Chaffee, Arkansas; and Fort Indiantown Gap, Pennsylvania, among others. Nevertheless, the guidance center found 500 out of the 750 boys to be "normal," psychologically speaking, and so why they were not suited for conventional church offerings was a mystery. The professors urgently counseled: "These youngsters are eager for a new 'humanizing' experience."[42] Fort McCoy was particularly bad. Some of the Mariel children had already lived in some form of detention in Cuba, but in the United States, many were mixed in with adult refugees and exposed to sexual violence and horrendous forms of discipline.[43]

In phase 2 of the children's program, the federal government collaborated with the reconfigured Florida Department of Health and Rehabilitative Services.[44] Some of the children disembarked from small boats in Key West with other refugees and from there pushed on to Miami after processing. Courts appointed legal guardians in certain cases, but until that happened, the new dependents had to rely on rectories and parishes. Men and women who came through the program in the 1960s signed up to rescue the Marielito children. Reverend Ernesto García-Rubio, the priest who would later be defrocked for sexual misconduct, had served the children's program in 1961 and renewed his commitment in 1980 at Our Lady of Divine Providence Parish, which listed seventy-five children from various countries in the rectory.[45]

Americans and their media had decidedly cooled toward the calling to comfort the huddled Cuban masses. Sixty percent of the country harbored negative impressions of the new refugees, while only 19 percent viewed the boatlift as a positive event.[46] The Unaccompanied Minors Program lasted a fleeting moment and ended as quickly as it began in June 1981.[47] The remaining occupants of the Cuban Boys' Home, the first shelter Walsh opened for young men in December 1960, were transferred. He estimated that the boatlift brought nine hundred unaccompanied children, fewer than other approximations. If true, then most were reunited with family members and vetted caregivers in short order. After June 30, 1981, the program was no more. Incoming cases would be channeled through willing child welfare agencies.[48]

It was an auspicious ending. Catholic Charities had just celebrated its fiftieth anniversary. Walsh was proud of the project that came to define his life's work. The boy from a remote corner in Ireland had matured into one of Miami's finest public luminaries. Beloved by most Pedro Pans, he could retire tremendously satisfied and later fill his archive with letters of praise.[49] In 2001, as festivities geared up for the fortieth-anniversary celebration of the children's program, Florida governor Jeb Bush congratulated Walsh on an exceptional career.[50]

One month later the venerated priest died, sparking an outpouring of Pedro Pan eulogies. Manuel Ramos called the priest "an adopted father."[51] Another referred to him as a "freedom bridge" for Cuban exiles.[52] The Latin music singer Willy Chirino dedicated his star on Calle Ocho to the nurturing man he knew in a frock and collar.[53] Catholic Charities changed the name of Boys' Town to Msgr. Bryan Walsh Children's Village, which lodged some of the children separated from their parents under the immigration policy established under Donald Trump.[54]

With its history complete, memory of the program took over. In 1978 the Operation Pedro Pan Foundation was established in Miami, and it presented the first of many glowing tributes to Bryan O. Walsh.[55] The Operation Pedro Pan Group, Inc. followed in 1990. There are now websites, social media venues, anniversary galas, and informal gatherings—from the Cuban eatery Versailles in Little Havana to banquet halls and living rooms around the nation—that commemorate this history. Throughout these virtual and material spaces, the politics of memory churns and reconfigures the contemporary meaning of Cuban exile identity.

More often than not, Pedro Pans fell into the upper echelon of the first wavers imbued with a sense of survival and success. "In that Florida City Camp," Pury Lopez reminisced, "every kid made an unconscious choice to either be a survivor or not." One's background was important. A lot of children were from the "crème de la crème" of society, she said. Parental expectations of opportunity and success preceded the children's coming to America.[1] The end of the Freedom Flights signaled a milestone in the production of Cuban America. A survey in 1972 showed that 79 percent of Cubans wanted to return to Cuba once Castro was overthrown, but two years later, after termination of the flights, less than 50 percent felt the impulse.[2]

Though representing a diverse body of people, Cuban Americans must contend with narratives retold over the years that are vital for community sustenance. Eventually refugees and exiles transformed into permanent residents and citizens, and they stood as an exceptional case in U.S. immigration history. The nomenclature is important. Scholar María Cristina García highlights that many Cubans prefer "exile" over "immigrant" because the second implies a choice.[3] "Exile," we might say, is a political identity, and preserving it delegitimizes the revolution in perpetuity. One is always fighting the regime that forced him or her out. Yet "refugee" is often a referent fraught with economic and racial associations. U.S. law has historically treated refugees as a special category when deciding alien admissions. The category in its current form is a twentieth-century invention, a term first employed when millions were displaced during World War I and after World War II to convey a legal and political status governed by national and international law.

But being labeled a refugee also has social implications. Joyce Carol Oates has distinguished the term from "expat" and "immigrant" thusly:

"Expat" suggests a cosmopolitan spirit and resources that allow mobility; to be an "immigrant" suggests some measure of need. . . .

A "refugee" is, by definition, desperate; he has been displaced from his home, has been rendered stateless, has few or no resources. The expat retains an identity as he retains his citizenship, his privileges; the refugee loses his identity amid the anonymity of many others like him.[4]

The refugee title often invites stigma, with one imagined to be a destitute outsider who takes from—rather than contributes to—the national welfare. Monsignor Bryan Walsh was uncomfortable with the term: "One of the barriers that has prevented us coming to grips with this problem has been the use of that word. For the Cuban it connotes the idea of political exile, and once identified thus, it leaves his family in Cuba subject to reprisal. So, many are reluctant to seek help because they fear this designation. . . . I regret that I have not found a suitable substitute, so I am going to refer to them simply as Cubans."[5]

Stuck between their exile and refugee appellations, Cubans found preferential treatment as well as stigma. The nomenclature is important whether one chooses it or is forced to accept it. Former U.S. senator and Pedro Pan Mel Martínez thought that his "compassionate conservativism" was rooted in the condition of exile.[6] Mario García both blames and credits his refugee status for making him the person he is today: "Although I don't consider myself a 'refugee' and always disliked that term even when I had just arrived in the U.S. and that was my immigration status, I am aware of the significance that my becoming a refugee continues to have on many of the decisions I make, what I tell my children, how I live my life, my approach to money, and the lessons I learned at the age of 14: don't attach yourself to anything physical, because it is here today and gone tomorrow."[7]

The exceptional status of Cuban Americans not only was codified in law and policy but also has produced a cohesive ideology of "Miami Cubans" with exile at the center. María de los Angeles Torres has described the importance of this location in the collective identity: "The Cuban community in the United States is held together by the powerful collective belief that we had no choice but to flee the island. There is no stronger proof of this than the fact that parents, fearful of the Communist government, sent their children abroad, alone. In effect, we, the children in exile, became living evidence of the terrible turn of events on the island. Leaving Cuba was a heroic deed. Living in exile was a patriotic sacrifice, and dying in exile was nearly elevated to an act of martyrdom."[8]

The decades of exile without return have built a Cuban American bloc that exerts disproportionate weight in federal politics. Well known is the conservative community based in Miami. One historian scoffs that the "residents of Miami joke that Florida is the only state in the union with its own foreign policy." Maurice Ferré said as much in the 1980s after the city commission had passed twenty-eight formal resolutions, ordinances, or motions that dealt with Cuban and Cuban American affairs. Local holidays were invented and landmarks renamed. March 25, 1983, turned into Orlando Bosch Day for the person who helped mastermind the 1976 explosion of a Cuban passenger jet that killed seventy-three people. Many exiles revered Bosch. Another example was the city's stinging condemnation of Universal Pictures' remake of *Scarface* (1932) starring Al Pacino for its portrayal of Cubans in the film.[9]

Separating Pedro Pan memory from this larger binding identity is impossible. Museum exhibits, blogs, group pages, and reunions are fixtures on the public and virtual slates of Pedro Pan history. The *muchachitas de Villa Maria* (Villa Maria girls) is a tight-knit group of Pedro Pan friends. The group's name derives from the residence where the girls lived under supervision of the Daughters of Mary Immaculate Order in San Antonio.[10] They numbered forty girls, housed first at the Florida City camp before alighting to San Antonio. They started having reunions in 1986 with a near-perfect thirty-eight in attendance. They continue to meet yearly.[11]

In 1997 muchachitas from around the country gathered at a gala celebrating their thirty-five years together. One attendee testified that the collective supplied her with unfailing "understanding" and "support." "They validate me," she said, "they complete me." Another expressed "deep love" for the group because the members were by her side when she felt loneliest. She had believed that either her parents were coming soon or that she would return to Cuba. Neither happened; her parents only showed up after she was married and had a son. One interviewee volunteered that "the unknown was more than I could handle," but the camaraderie of forty girls gave her hope. Still another compared their bond to soldiers in the trenches: "We fought a war," she said. Finally, another muchachita found the gatherings enabled her "to find out what I was. . . . Being with them reminds me of what I've forgotten."[12]

When observing the women today, instantly evident is the palpable sense of sisterhood in their rushing torrent of vivid memories. Remembering their days as Pedro Pans is a part of these reunions, but so are the ups and downs of life that have come with aging, the planned and unplanned events that began with their foundational experience in Texas. There is a nostalgia for these early days as well as murmurs of disquietude. One gleefully recounted her first ride in a limousine but also frowned at seeing racism for the first time in San Antonio. There were stern warnings not to associate with African Americans, and one regretted sitting in the "Negro" section of a lunch counter in Alabama and the embarrassing rebuke from white patrons that followed. Another said her first American political act was supporting Barry Goldwater for president in 1964. She was a renegade against the sixties counterculture of her generation. And still another was shocked to see so many people of Mexican descent in Texas. Unfamiliar with the state's Spanish and mestizo history, she at first thought Mexican Americans to be Indians and could not believe her ears when she heard Spanish spoken everywhere upon landing in Dallas. The women smiled when reliving the time they bought coats on layaway. They then jokingly posed in them on a blistering July day in San Antonio for photographs sent to their families. The tone of the gathering was also serious. Some women's parents were absent for more than five years. One was jolted by the uncomfortable time she endured first at an orphanage and then with a foster family in San Antonio before her transfer to Villa Maria.[13]

Reunions of this kind keep the past and present interlocked and are a crucial fixture in the Pedro Pans' adult lives. Out of the thirty who resided with Raul Alvaro at Brondel Hall, seven live in the New York City area. In 2014 the house parents, in their twenties in Helena but now retirees in Tacoma, came to visit Raul and the group in New York. Raul talks of them with extreme fondness. They were caring and nice people who came to exemplify the incidental and endless acts of kindness that helped Cubans habituate to living in the United States.[14]

The year before some other Pedro Pans of Helena popped champagne for the fiftieth-anniversary celebration of Operation Pedro Pan. The participants ran a notice in the local newspaper thanking the town's residents: "You did not know us, and we did not know you. You did not understand us, and we did not understand you. But in the end, you embraced us and made us part of your city."[15]

Curated spaces also serve the halls of memory. In 2015 the HistoryMiami Museum launched a Pedro Pan exhibit backed by a $300,000 grant from Florida's Division of Cultural Affairs.[16] Miami's Operation Pedro Pan Group was a key architect of the exhibition. To wander through it was to take a leap backward in time and across the ocean. Television footage streamed the famous executions Fidel Castro governed after he took control. The screens lit up with a frenzied and specious tribunal attended by seventeen thousand spectators in the Havana Sports Palace that enacted the illusion of justice and carried with it the sentence of capital punishment. As one wandered on, other video feeds displayed prominent Pedro Pans telling their stories, among them former Miami mayor Tomás Regalado, Florida senator Mel Martínez, and members of the Operation Pedro Pan board of trustees and board of directors. As is often the case in public depictions of the program, certain perspectives and truths prevailed while others fell silent. At the end of the retrospective rested several books on Operation Pedro Pan. All the major authorities on the program were available save one, Maria de los Angeles Torres's *The Lost Apple*. This oversight did not seem accidental. Over the course of writing this book, it became evident that her scholarship and views are anathema to what often constitutes official Pedro Pan history in Miami. The absence of her book is a further testament to the determinative ways remembering and forgetting function in the politics of memory.[17]

But as with all group identifications, the Pedro Pans' place in wider Cuban America is something more complex, something beyond monolithic notions of "Miami Cubans." Some have posed challenges to the "Cuban exile model," which trumpets success stories of the 1960s and 1970s in the making of Cuban American exceptionalism. "Golden exile" was a narrative shaped by the exiles themselves, and departing from it can risk retribution.[18] Refugees were to be representatives of what one historian termed "yesterday's Cuba" and the "Cuba that could be." Something between was not possible.[19] This constraint has always weighed on the 1.5 generation, which feels the pressure to live while recalling the Cuba that was, to renounce the Cuba that is, and to face scorn if wanting to rediscover the nation on one's own terms. Novelist Cristina García has lamented that the exile debate has long been "very black and white, very polarized, very unintegrated." Through her writing, she reaches "in the gap and shades of gray between the two extremes." She seeks variation and community through difference rather than homogeneity. "There are many ways to be Cuban and I resist the notion that to be Cuban is to hold particular political views or act in certain circumscribed ways." García has said that she does not consider herself an exile, but all writing in her mind is a kind of exile, to step "outside the stream of everyday life to try to make sense of it."[20]

Ruth Behar, who identifies as both Cuban and Jewish, similarly has been frustrated by the seeming irreconcilability of being both. She never thought of her "mixed identity" as strange, but it has befuddled others. She, too, has written about individuals in the diaspora who have distanced themselves from the Miami enclave "to find breathing space to articulate their sense of Cuban identity." She sees a conflicted zone between old and new, Cuban and Cuban American: "We didn't want to wage the same struggles as our parents, yet we were still caught in the frameworks, fears, and silences of their generation."[21]

Where one ends up in the United States affects this identity as well. Mario García views a sizable difference between Miami Cubans and those who resettled elsewhere. For him, a man whose education and professional life have been consumed by words and language, the telltale sign is one's accent. Those who left south Florida, he submits, inflect less of an accent than those who stayed. He thinks what also sets Miami Cubans apart is the bitterness of their parents. He says that some Miami Cubans—Pedro Pans included—sound like his dad. He points to Senator Marco Rubio (R-FL) as a product of this conservative thinking. García says Rubio should think differently about Cuba because of his age, but he's "a Miami product," which makes his ideas closer to those of García's parents than to those of his children.[22]

Raul Alvaro is of a similar mindset. He exhales with relief that he did not stay in Miami; leaving, he believes, permitted him to adapt more ably to U.S. culture. He did not see his father, sister, and step-mother again until 1969 when they arrived in Elizabeth, New Jersey, via Mexico. Raul was already an adult living in New York City, and time had passed and distance had grown. Seeing his father made him realize, he says, "I wasn't 100 percent Cuban anymore." Politically, it has been difficult to interact with other Cuban Americans who live in Miami. "The Cubans living there are living in the 1950s." Miami, he said, is "frozen." In the age of social media, fissures in the online world can turn to vitriol. As an ardent supporter of President Barack Obama and a longtime advocate of ending the U.S. embargo, he has endured name-calling and castigation for his political views. "They live in the past," he said, and that puts a void between him and some of his friends and even family.[23]

Cleaving the community are such tensions and divides; however, these rifts threaten but never fully achieve Cuban America's undoing. Adhering to a common account of the exile experience suggests that at some level the narrative is necessary to keep the community together and one's identity meaningful, even as detractors drift from the so-called Miami line. The group is still needed for ethnic survival; being a good, trustworthy, and well-connected Cuban American has meant keeping in step with truths about the Cuban past and present that have become the basis for cohesion. How to reject political claims when they make up the essence of an identity, of an ethnic nationalism? To let go of a particular worldview or to change it is to change one's being, one's family history, one's origin.

Raul says that one "betrays" Cuban America by going against the tide. He sees disunion between those who return to the island and the people who stay defiantly away. In the end, he confirms the children's program "was good for me" and that "it was great what my father did for me," though he swears he could not have done it with his own children.[24] For Mercedes Diaz Dash, the birth of her first child stopped her regular visits to Miami from Virginia. She did not return until 2010 when she was reconnecting with her sister. Mercedes is also against the embargo and urges a closer relationship between countries. She looks forward to a trip to Cuba one day, ideally with her sons. Like Raul, she has endured criticism of her politics. Striking a balance between her own Pedro Pan identity and those of Miami-based Cuban Americans, she confesses, "is very difficult."

The tension at times has escalated into contentious rounds of comments on social media, and she has even been kicked out of some groups. She has felt forced to censure her opinions. Her reverence for her parents, however, is unyielding. "We all hail our parents as heroes, all of us." Castro was to blame, not the family. Her father resolved to break definitively with the homeland. Mercedes says it was his motive for leaving Miami—to get out of the routine of "constantly talking about the same thing." To break out of the shell, her father moved the family out of Miami, only returning to visit two weeks a year. Then he was adamant that the family stay at the beach, not with relatives.[25]

José Arenas reasons that he is both Cuban and Cuban American. Proud of his Pedro Pan heritage, he excoriates the glossed-over histories of the program, such as the record of abuse.[26] Pury Lopez holds no grudge and rationalizes Operation Pedro Pan as a product of the circumstances and "a logical alternative" to the writing on the wall. While she knows some suffered abuses, she points out that abuses of all kinds have occurred in foster homes and orphanages, and Operation Pedro Pan was no exception. She has a friend whose brother was a Pedro Pan and ended up in a halfway house. But she is convinced that the United States and the Catholic Church did the best they could to care for thousands of children. In other countries, she surmises, those kids would have become petty thieves or prostitutes. "We did not."[27]

Pury has long conceived of herself as the product of "two cultures." Her paternal grandparents emigrated from Spain to Cuba just before the Spanish Civil War. Her mother's grandparents were also Spanish but landed in Cuba earlier to fight for the crown in Cuba's War of Independence. This made her family's life akin to one of expats. She credits this diverse growing up with a resilience that helped her to succeed as a Pedro Pan. Her parents were able to rejoin her when her father miraculously obtained a forged permit for a vacation. In one of the last Cubana de Aviación flights to Miami before the missile crisis, they arrived along with masses of Cubans seeking asylum, including the flight crew; thus, the plane was effectively stranded until the airline could find replacements. As a well-connected sugar expert who could speak English, Pury's father was able to find work as an accountant in an American mill.[28]

Pury unequivocally views her parents' act of sending her to the States as one of love. Her father was at peace with the decision, but it took a long time for her mother to release the guilt. Pury considers herself Cuban American but "more American than anything else." She "respects Cuba and the heritage that it brought," even though she thinks of hers as "split." In terms of when she first *felt* American, Pury chuckles that it was in the fifth grade when her class sang "The House I Live In," the title song from the film starring Frank Sinatra.[29] It contains the recurring line, "What is America to me?" It is an ironic composition to mark the occasion. The music was written by Earl Robinson, a legendary left-wing American composer who composed labor jingles such as "Joe Hill" and the nationalist tune "Ballad for Americans." He also was blacklisted in the Cold War for his communist ties.[30]

Pury has never felt racial discrimination but has stared down prejudice as a woman. The segregation Cubans faced, she thinks, was more self-imposed than anything: "We created our own ghettos in Miami." She seconds the opinions of other early exiles in thinking that the newer ones are poor representatives of the old country, interpreting their behavior as conditioned by a "particular sociological structure" that forced them to subvert domestic authority to survive in Cuba. It is not unlike the white-collar crime she sees in Florida in the fraud cases strewn across her desk.

Pury concludes that she and her father made peace with the decision to send her to Miami, but her mother, tortured by guilt, would not talk about it. The family moved on. A sister was born in the United States, and Pury attended a Belgian Catholic school on Brickell Avenue, graduating in 1969. She is proud to be a Pedro Pan because she believes the event is of larger significance. It is something that "happens to us while we're sleeping, eating, and then we flip around, and say, 'Oh wow, hey, we're part of history.'" Such are the accidents in an unchosen game of chance: "It was happenstance that put you on the right path or the wrong path. . . . Some of us were extremely lucky."[31]

16 | THE RETURN

As U.S.-Cuban relations change and exiles age, more Pedro Pans are making the return trip to Cuba. The topic can be a delicate one, as the choice is not always easy and the implications enormous. Before Mercedes Diaz Dash books a flight for Cuba, she would like to see diplomatic ties fully normalized. Her biggest fear is that she would be unable to come back to Virginia. But the larger badge of betrayal looms in her mind. Cuban Americans can suffer immense criticism and shame from the community. Eloy Cepero thinks the same and will stay away from his country of birth because he does not want the negative attention. A prominent member of the Miami Pedro Pan community, he places his allegiance to this collective first. Traveling to Cuba is tantamount to treason. Though she is determined to go at some point, Mercedes knows that it will alter her standing in Cuban America when she does it.[1]

Meanwhile, Roberto Rodriguez has only positive impressions of his decision to return. He thinks the obligation to stay away delayed many satisfying moments as well as the ability to heal from the trauma of his childhood. "It's just that what I was thinking was, what a waste. . . . I've wasted fifty years of my life," he says, regretting his delay to return. Rodriguez has enjoyed hospitality on his trips and in due course has changed himself. He steers clear of Miami and prefers to make his home in Puerto Rico. "There are a lot of lies in Miami," he said. Many in that circle warned him of the bad encounters he could have in Cuba, yet they did not happen. During his first trip, the woman who owned the house he grew up in welcomed him and comforted him when he became emotional at the first sight of a place he had not seen in fifty years. "It's like being a kid again." When he returns from Cuba, people tell him that he "looks ten years younger." He says, "I become alive again."[2]

The sojourn back exposes change, updating how people look and act, or the ways environments have altered. Staying put, by contrast, permits exiles to hold onto the impressions they have in their memories. It can be agonizing to update these impressions. As a defense mechanism, it may be preferable to keep the thoughts of one's childhood home or neighborhood locked away and not revisit them. Altering these associations can be excruciating. It may be easier to latch onto the nostalgia of childhood or the painful recollections of the revolution that validated the parents' choice to leave. That one may return can actually make the condition of one's exile more daunting. When one's self-worth hinges on political circumstances that made flight necessary, returning to the island affects one's Cuban American identity. Indeed, lamenting the inability to return can be emotionally easier than actually returning, for there are decades of antipathy to overcome. Even though the chief object of the exiles' ire—Fidel Castro—has died, the revulsion for him and the system he championed remain. Carlos Eire called Castro's Cuba the "deepest circle of hell" and his nation of origin "wrecked in the name of fairness."[3] The ongoing vitriol has sustained generations of family separation and emotional crisis, even as Cuba itself has changed.

Iraida López has written at length on what she calls a "typology of return." The members of the 1.5 generation living in the diaspora have a distinct collective consciousness. For their parents, a return is perceived as an act of disloyalty, an affront to the principles and the agonizing sacrifices that leaving required in exchange for a sea of opportunity in the United States. One of the outcomes of this static line is that the younger generation shares a weight, a feeling of "dislocation and dispossession." Because they were children, young exiles were still in the age of innocence, at a time when their outlooks on life and political sensibilities had yet to congeal. Their focus is on what is lacking or what is absent. There is a difference, then, between a community rooted in diaspora and one that is transnational, or between those who remain distant from the homeland and those who make the return.

Over the entirety of its lifetime, the revolution has vilified those who fled the island as gusanos who took everything but their patriotism. For those in the first wave, the cut was clean and clear, their exile emotions always vengeful. But for a portion of their children, aging in exile planted the desire to enhance their Cuban heritage by re-rooting themselves in Cuban soil. They have a persistent feeling that some part of them lies dormant or left unfinished. Returning brings one into a different psychic and emotional space; it can "confirm the elusiveness of home in concrete ways," López points out. It can bridge the distance between imagining or remembering one's original home and seeing it again. It can also shore up the "Cuban" side of one's Cuban American identification. "Healing" is a word so many use to describe the process of returning. Doing so does not necessarily make the pain of exile go away, but it does reconfigure it. The past can become more manageable in the present.[4]

Coming of age in the 1960s and 1970s helped diversify Cuban America, with the era's radical, countercultural zeitgeist piercing high school classrooms and college dorm rooms. The air of freethinking experimentation and political engagement sparked interest in a Cuban journey for a contingent of the 1.5 generation, even if it meant facing criticism from their forebears. The first en masse return for this cohort, including some Pedro Pans, took place in 1977 in the Antonio Maceo Brigade. What united the members was their opposition to the U.S. embargo, their support for normalizing ties between the countries, and, of course, their obligatory requirement of being Cuban American. When Joan Didion interviewed some of them, she discovered that "they were Americans, yet they were not. *Somos Cubanos* [We are Cuban]. They remained Cubans, and they remained outside Cuba, and as Cubans outside Cuba but estranged from *el exilio* [exile] they came to occupy a particularly hermetic vacuum, one in which, as in *el exilio* itself, positions were defined and redefined and schisms were divined and dissected and a great deal of what went on floated somewhere in a diaspora of its own."[5]

Among the Pedro Pan *brigadistas* (members of the brigade) was Nelson Valdés, whose initial visit to Cuba was enabled by President Jimmy Carter's opening of dialogue and exchange between countries. His trip, he remembered, "had personal, political and existential consequences for me." Juan Monje joined the brigade by working for a company that brought exiles to Cuba. Coming to the United States from a Cuban village in 1962, he spent four long years in CWB camps. His memory of the terrible punishments by Marist priests lingered. Returning to Cuba presented him with a new spin on his childhood and his transition to America, something difficult that enabled him to put the puzzle pieces of the past and present together.[6]

To be sure, the exhilarating trip to Cuba could saddle a traveler with resentment once back in the United States. During the heyday of the New Left, María de los Angeles Torres sometimes felt out of step with groups that fought for civil rights, women's liberation, and the war on poverty. After becoming an activist, she applied to the Venceremos Brigades, a multiracial leftist organization that brought hundreds of radicals to Cuba to cut sugarcane and imbibe revolutionary socialism. Her application was denied; Cuban exiles were not allowed to become members. Torres called into question the widespread glorification of the revolution and the idolatry of Che Guevara on college campuses. "I began wondering, why is he a hero? I began to confront everything my parents had taught me about the revolution."[7] When three thousand orphans were transported from war-ravaged Vietnam to the United States in 1975 in Operation Babylift, Torres was flooded with memories of her own childhood crossing.[8] She joined the Antonio Maceo Brigade, angering members of her family. They saw it as an act of betrayal, and she received constant admonition from the Miami exile community. But in her journey, she realized an instant metamorphosis: "As soon as I deplaned, I knew I was home. . . . Somewhere deep in my memory, I had kept these images intact." Some semblance of wholeness appears in the return. Torres reflects that Pedro Pans who go back are "no longer dealing with only memories or ghosts." Another returnee reiterated the sensation of "feeling whole" when he visited Cuba. For him, "it was a sense of completeness, that the branch was connected to the trunk of the tree."[9]

As a Cuban, however, fitting in with protest movements of the period that took group identity seriously proved difficult. There were Latino nationalist groups—Chicanos or Puerto Rican anticolonialists—but Cubans were different. Torres longed to see the nation of her birth, but it came with a cost: to friends and family, "traveling to Cuba would be the definitive break." The reality was, however, that "the further I got from Cuba, the more I wanted to return." The brigades took her in December 1978.[10] It changed the way she thought about memory: "Memory becomes a central force in creating a diasporic identity. The inability to reproduce the past or to return to a prior status compels the re-creation of memory of what was left behind. . . . Memory, remembering, and re-creating become individual and collective rituals, as does forgetting. In this sense the formation of an exile community is a process similar to that of nation building, one in which collective symbols form a constellation of reference points that endow upon disparate fragments a sense of congruity."[11]

Becoming whole again, filling a void—the return reorients one's memories of childhood and one's adult self-conception. Pedro Pans experience this evolution uniquely because it is wrapped up with issues of parental abandonment.

When he visited in 1994, Ed Canler said doing so "helps one heal." Elly Chovel sensed something similar when she returned to Cuba to see the pope in 1998 and visited her old home in Guanabacoa. She called the experience "absolutely marvelous" and the people occupying her former house very welcoming.[12] Both Chovel and Canler were among a group of Pedro Pans who became subjects of Estela Bravo's documentary *Operación Peter Pan: Cerrando el Círculo en Cuba* (Operation Pedro Pan: Completing the Circle in Cuba).[13] Candi Sosa, another participant, also yearned to see her home. Upon doing so, she cried.[14] Flora González was there, too, but it was not her inaugural trip back. She first returned in 1980 and went to her old house in Camaguey. After a knock on the door, she found out that she still had family in the area. She has returned several times. Each expedition peels back a new layer and reveals her contemporary identity: "I think that it took me like 10 times . . . until I began to live in the present. The first 5 or 6 visits I was still a little girl that had gone and carried with me all the emotions that I had when I left, so I wasn't looking at Cuba like it was 1980 or 1990."

As a child, González attended a public school in Cuba. At age thirteen, she arrived in the States in January 1962 with her eleven-year-old sister. Their parents arrived a year and a half later.[15] Today she views herself as Cuban American, but for a long time she was only Cuban. Cuba and its history are substantial in her self-perception, which became more vivid on a life-changing trip with her sister in 1994. She recalls, "It was very confusing for me, because I had been there so many times and could show her things, and in some way I allowed myself to become a little girl, though she was younger. On that trip I changed. She had to take care of me emotionally, but I allowed myself to be a little girl again." The return is a bid to heal, a way to authenticate the importance of origin in her identity because, as González notes, Cubans consider her Cuban.[16]

For author Cristina García, the return modified her self-image and literary voice. Retracing her steps to Cuba in 1984 exposed her to refreshing gradations in what had been a reductive bivalent fraction: "Cuba had been a black and white situation up to that point." But then seeing her Cuban family and resuming her life in Miami made for a richer palette of Cubanness. Still, she took heat from the Miami community. "Alienated" is how she felt when she was called a communist for registering as a Democrat.[17]

Gerardo Simms does not rule out returning to Cuba one day. When "individual liberties are restored," he would like to revisit his old neighborhood, even though regrettably he would "probably feel like a tourist."[18] Pury Lopez has no interest in returning to Cuba. Leaving was a frightening experience, moments she does not want to relive, nor does she feel the need to reassess anything from her childhood. However, if she were to return, it would be with a grandchild or charity group.[19] For his part, José Arenas was warm to the idea of going back but only after the government changes. Class consciousness plays a part in his hesitation. He is uncomfortable with the prospect of visiting as a well-off Cuban American. Some returnees are ostentatious about their success. The material possessions they bring back for family and friends are extravagant proof that their decision to leave was the correct one. Like Mercedes, José would want to return with his son or daughter. He would first scout out his onetime home on Obrapía Street, where he remembers family gatherings to watch baseball games on the black-and-white television.[20]

Mario García has kept away from Cuba to honor the memory of his father, a man who detested Castro and the revolution. But he is open to the possibility of going with a college program to promote a free press, his field of expertise. This option would have been acceptable to his father. García is keen to "complete the circle" but dreads seeing a Havana that he does not remember. His children's curiosity spurs his own, and he fantasizes about shouting to Cubans, "I am the American dream!" García is eager for "normalcy" on the island and would welcome the change: "I want to see before I die that Cuba gets itself on the map again as an example of what a society can do."[21]

José Azel also stays away out of respect for his father's memory. Exile, he imparts, means working hard and keeping one's home country inside. "The family name was important to us." Without much family there, he feels no urgency to go. Nostalgia constantly lingers, but he stops short from buying a ticket because it would dilute his identification as a "political exile." In his mind, returning to Cuba would reclassify him as an immigrant. "By definition, a political exile does not return until the conditions that brought about his exile change," he explains. A churning tension exists between exile and immigrant, personal and political considerations, and one's childhood gets tossed around in the maelstrom.[22]

And for others, the decision to stay put is an easy one. "Go back to what?" Mayda Riopedre snorts. "God knows who lives in my house." Better for her is to have the ideal past unchanged in her memory: "I want to remember Cuba the day I left back in 1961." She has absolutely no desire to see her old neighborhood using Google Maps, although she is slightly open to her granddaughter seeing the island one day.[23]

CONCLUSION

Echoes of Operation Pedro Pan drifted ashore in 1999 when two fishermen found six-year-old Elián González alone on a raft on Thanksgiving Day. Elián's mother and ten fellow Cubans had drowned, leaving him the lone survivor. The U.S. Immigration and Naturalization Service first placed the boy in the custody of his great uncle but then ordered him returned to his father in Cuba. The decision was upheld by a U.S. court of appeals and enforced by the U.S. Department of Justice under the direction of Attorney General Janet Reno, a former prosecutor in Dade County. The event garnered international attention and reinvigorated Cold War passions as another standoff occurred between Cuban Americans and Fidel Castro. Miami mobilized to keep Elián in the United States, with the boy's astonishing survival elevated to biblical proportions, and requests not to remove him during Holy Week were granted.[1]

Elián's father in Cuba, Juan Miguel González, refused financial offers teetering on $2 million to allow the "Miracle Boy" to stay in the United States. One church reportedly promised $4 million. Undulations of protests in the Magic City fell on deaf ears in Washington as the federal government decided to return the boy to Cuba. Demonstrators in Havana demanded the father's right to his child. Whereas all fought for the "interests of the boy," the row stood inextricably linked to Cold War passions and the issue of the sanctity of the family. For Cuban Americans, it hit at the heart of their own exile existence; Elián's return in a sense would minimize refugee displacement. Letting him go threatened the exiles' raison d'être—the painful memory of forced separation from the home country—and would undercut the strong political value of transplanted cubanidad.[2]

But the Elián case also illustrated that a Cold War policy had changed in the United States, at least in the executive branch. Kennedy's mandate of accepting the world's refugees had lost some of its bravado when President Bill Clinton responded to the ordeal with the wish that

Elián's fate be decided in accordance with U.S. immigration law and with a calculation that inflicted the least trauma for the child. While members of the Republican-led Congress were debating a bill to grant Elián citizenship and the boy's two grandmothers pleaded before legislators for his return, Clinton was not sure that the United States should automatically open its doors to Cubans as it once had. He remarked:

> Let me just say for the moment, if you take [the case] out of the combustible, emotional nature of our relationship with Cuba and particularly the Cuban American community in South Florida's relationship with Cuba, and you think about the issue, one of the things that I think we all need to think about is this could happen again. I mean, this sort of thing could happen again because you have so many people coming to our shores from all these different countries, and then shifting governments, shifting policies within countries. . . . I'm just trying to minimize the politics of it, because I think if you take this one decision out of context, it's not just Cuba and it's not just this little boy, there are likely to be a lot of these things in the future as immigration flows increases, upheavals increase elsewhere, and as we know more and more about what goes on in other countries.[3]

Clinton had refused entry to Cubans before. A few years prior, tens of thousands of Cuban *balseros* (rafters) made desperate attempts, some fatal, to reach the United States. The event brought about an emendation of the 1966 Cuban Adjustment Act in a policy known as "wet foot, dry foot": Cuban refugees reaching U.S. land would be admitted, but those intercepted in international waters would be returned to Cuba or sent to a third country. On the Elián matter, Clinton decided to side with his attorney general in a legal decision that seemed to choose family over politics, a position that put Clinton at odds with Cuban Americans in Miami, congressional members, and even Vice President Al Gore. Some would conclude this decision led to Gore's controversial loss of Florida in the 2000 election.[4]

Castro made the symbolic significance no less important. Elián's return made the boy a cause célèbre, and he received a hero's welcome.

In a follow-up story in 2005, the BBC reported that Elián was happy living in Cuba but still felt resentment toward the way his family in Miami had tried to turn him against his father. Then eleven years old, Elián not only called Castro his "friend" but also viewed him "as a father." Cuban American detractors promptly dismissed the fanfare and his claims to contentment as mere "brainwashing" by the Cuban government.[5]

One suspects that Pedro Pans must have looked at the ordeal with dismay. Here was a later version of their own story, but the boy was turned away from a post–Cold War America. Clinton in effect chose patria potestad, the right of Elián's biological father to his son, over those of other relatives. That right, which was so passionately fought for and the underlying polemic that caused so many Pedro Pan parents to send their children, was no longer the rallying call of Cuban Americans. Now greater than the parent-child relationship was political freedom. The community would not budge from the claim that Elián would be better off in the United States than in Cuba, even if it meant losing his father.

The Cuban American exile line has held up, but in recent years, the sands of time also have shifted perspectives. Today, two-thirds of the 2.3 million people who identify as Cuban in the United States live in Florida. Nearly 60 percent of this group was born in Cuba, and of those who were foreign born, approximately two-thirds are U.S. citizens.[6] As of 2013, across the country 75 percent of Cuban Americans had U.S. citizenship, but only 18 percent of those who have arrived since 1990 are citizens. The latter group, in Lillian Guerra's words, is "the least prosperous segment of the community and the most connected to the island."[7] Also unique is that young Cuban Americans are a minority of this demographic. With an average age of forty, Cuban Americans are older compared with other Latinos in the United States, who across the board are on average twenty-nine years old.[8]

In 2012, in a departure from prior elections, 48 percent of this bloc in Florida backed Democratic candidate Barack Obama.[9] More people in the diaspora were cheering normalization, and there were growing numbers of returnees, particularly among older Cubans after President Raúl Castro allowed emigrants to apply for repatriation.[10] When Presidents Obama and Castro shook hands in Havana in 2016, it seemed as if a full restoration of ties between the countries could be around the corner.[11] Embassies reopened, and Obama ended the wet foot, dry foot policy.

In 2016, however, Trump's team restoked the conservative wing of this conglomerate and did so with even greater success in the election of 2020. Yet in the time since, fissures have appeared. The administration's crackdown on immigration has included the removal of Cuban nationals from the United States, going against the decades-old practice of granting asylum to refugees and fast-tracking them to permanent residency. Half of Cuban Americans between the ages of eighteen and forty-four disapproved of President Trump, and those in Florida from this group tend to lean Democrat or independent.[12] Yet in the 2018 midterm elections, even as they squeaked by in their victories, Governor Ron DeSantis and Senator Rick Scott (R-FL) enjoyed sizable support from Cuban Americans, and Trump's electoral success in Florida in 2020 suggests that the conservative line is durable.

President Joe Biden has done little to advance U.S.-Cuban relations. He has ignored a growing choir of voices in his party, such as the letter signed by 114 representatives in December 2021 that called upon the White House to ease restrictions and restore Obama-era standards. But anti-government protests in Cuba and the chilling diplomatic effects of the illness the press calls "Havana Syndrome" have slowed Biden's promises to restore ties.[13]

The willingness of Americans to host refugees has also declined in recent years. The office of the United Nations High Commissioner for Refugees estimates that 25.4 million of today's 68.5 million forcibly dislocated people are refugees, half of whom are children and nearly 175,000 of them unaccompanied.[14] In 2017 Turkey hosted 3.5 million refugees; the United States took in 33,000.[15] America's yearly allotments fell further to just 18,000 in 2019.[16] The weight of this global calamity was felt more acutely when tens of thousands of Central American nationals—unaccompanied children included—sought haven at the U.S. border during the Obama administration. Those coming out of desperation, fleeing various forms of violence and unimaginable poverty, are not seen as heroes or tokens of America's capacity for sanctuary. Rather, the swelling masses at the border have been derided as a burden at best, a threat at worst. Stuck in rolling detention and legal limbo, they are bereft of adequate humanitarian aid. What a different country they have encountered in contrast to the Cubans of the 1960s. Demands to extend the wall at the southern border and policies that have separated families in detention camps have painted a disfigured likeness of Uncle Sam when compared to the earlier version.

In the Cold War, succoring refugees was part of the anti-Castro strategy by Washington. Draining Cuba of its valuable citizen assets brought material consequences in labor and economics, but it was also part of the psychological war. Americans feared communist subversion from the Cubans crossing the border but ultimately accepted them. Today, tens of thousands of children have passed through detention camps. While the extent of suffering incurred by Pedro Pans in care is unknown (record keeping was poorer than it is today), current research makes clear that child detention breeds psychological, emotional, and sexual violence. Central American child detainees today writhe in conditions far worse than their Cuban counterparts experienced decades ago. The New York Times reported that between October 2014 and July 2018, the Office of Refugee Resettlement fielded "4,556 allegations of sexual abuse or sexual harassment" of minors.[17] Lawyers for the Trump administration even argued in federal court that overcrowding migrants without access to soap, towels, or toothbrushes should be entirely legal.[18] In 2019 three thousand migrant children were kept at a center in Homestead, Florida, not far from where several thousand Pedro Pans spent their first weeks in the United States.[19] What to make of these two vastly imbalanced scenarios, the 1960s and our own era?

The Pedro Pans and the larger refugee waves threw themselves into the building of modern Miami. One of the ironies of this story is that the exiles' enemy, the Cuban Revolution, was necessary for the production of Cuban America and the city it transformed. The metropolis now continues to morph under the weight of hemispheric forces. Seventy percent of the city is Latino/a today, with Cuban Americans composing half the city's population. Venezuelans, Nicaraguans, Colombians, and people of several other nationalities have added to their ranks.[20]

Marvin Dunn says Miami did not "grow up" until the 1970s under the mayoral tenure of Maurice Ferré, the first Puerto Rican–born mayor on the mainland and the first Hispanic one in Miami. He catered to the "Black political machine" after a tumultuous period of racial violence in the late 1960s, but not much changed for African Americans, Dunn laments, because the municipality forever felt like a "Latin city." Too often presidential candidates landed to court Cubans, not African Americans. This changed in the 1980s, when Miami Blacks achieved new political capital as the local swing vote and sat in greater numbers on the city commission alongside whites and Hispanics. Liberal whites found their olive branches. Janet Reno, for example, invited Dunn to sit on the judicial nominating commission for the Eleventh Circuit. When Bill Clinton campaigned as a candidate in 1992, he not only surveyed the devastation left by Hurricane Andrew but also canvassed African American interest in his presidential run.[21]

Even Little Havana has shape-shifted and barely resembles what it once did. Mario García's father bought a jewelry store in the area from a Jewish businessman who vacated downtown along with other white ethnics of the day. When his father sold the store decades later, Nicaraguans and Salvadorans were the new immigrants, and his father was of the generation leaving an urban landscape he no longer recognized. Little Havana had become Central American. García, who is still a practicing Catholic, says Pope John Paul II's visit to Cuba was seen as a major moment for Cubans and Cuban Americans. On the island, the visit was momentous because it showed the standoff between the revolution's leaders and the Catholic Church had tempered.[22] Today, 25 percent of U.S. residents are Catholic.[23] The church is facing its own reckoning, with the revelation of ever-climbing numbers of sexual crimes perpetrated against minors long veiled by the Vatican. But Rome is now a key conduit of U.S.-Cuban normalization. Pope Francis was instrumental in the back-channel dialogue between Havana and Washington, and without his insistence, Raúl Castro and President Obama most likely never would have shaken hands.

In the end, Cuba, too, has faced undue challenges with the exile of so many of its sons and daughters. Cuban American writer Gustavo Pérez Firmat thinks both sides have lost too much: "Exile mutilates the country that is left no less than the people who leave it. Even those exiles who arrived with only the clothes on their backs brought with them all kinds of precious baggage, a cache of expertise and talent whose loss changed the island, for the worse. . . . Years later residential Cuba is still paying the price of exile, and so are we."[24]

Pedro Pans continue to sift through the sands of time to find their own balance sheets in the price of exile. Though a mere fraction of the more than fourteen thousand voices are represented in this book, through them we learn that the relationship between memory and "official" history is not predetermined or evenhanded. We would do well to heed philosopher Paul Ricoeur's thinking on this relationship. Whereas the historian "does history" professionally, everyday individuals remember, setting up what he called a "confrontation between memory and history." Yet these enterprises also overlap, and this account has attempted to make the two compatible. Memory is intensely personal but is also part of a collective. It operates within an individual but is also mobilized in the context of a group identity such as an ethnicity or nation. For Ricoeur, history is vaster than memory; "its time is layered differently."[25] For Pedro Pans, it is undeniable that there is no history without memory.

Mercedes Diaz Dash has worried where Operation Pedro Pan will end up in history: "I'm afraid we'll be forgotten."[26] This is where memory takes over. Pedro Pan memory is an axis within Cuban America that has sprung to life as a distinctive narrative of the nation. The work of memory can depend on truths frozen in time that at some level cannot be extricated from the push-pull demands of national allegiances. The children who were saved from communism were afforded an exceptional space in the United States not granted to other immigrants, and to this day it generates affiliations and political meaning in the crafting of their adult selves. It is a testament that the work of remembering is never finished in producing the nation.

NOTES

Introduction

Epigraph: Marcel Proust, *Swann's Way*, trans. Lydia Davis (New York: Penguin, 2004), 46–47.

1. Interview with Mercedes Diaz Dash, July 6, 2015, Fairfax VA; and email correspondence with Mercedes Diaz Dash, February 10, 2017.
2. Interview with José Azel, November 25, 2014, University of Miami.
3. Phone interview with Roberto Rodriguez Diaz, September 4, 2014.
4. Letter to Jean Lang from Frances Davis, June 29, 1967, Folder: Cuban Refugee Children, Florida State Agency, Correspondence—General, January 1, 1966–December 31, 1967, RG 363, Records of the Social and Rehabilitation Service, Unaccompanied Cuban Children's Refugee Program, 1961–1967, Box 3, National Archives and Records Administration, College Park MD (hereafter NARA).
5. Catholic Welfare Bureau (CWB), "Memorandum to All Contracting Agencies," October 31, 1968, Operation Pedro Pan/Cuban Children's Program Records (hereafter OPP/CCP), Series D, Folder: Contracts, 1965–1971, Barry University, Miami.
6. Alicia A. Caldwell, "Immigrant Arrests Smash Records, and U.S. Border Struggles to Handle the Crush," *Wall Street Journal*, May 8, 2019, https://www.wsj.com/articles/not-built-for-this-u-s-border-struggles-to-handle-crush-of-migrant-families-11557334318; and Anna Giaritelli, "Top US Border Official: 'The Breaking Point Has Arrived,' with 100,000 Encounters in March," *Washington Examiner*, March 27, 2019, https://www.washingtonexaminer.com/news/top-us-border-official-the-breaking-point-has-arrived-with-100-000-encounters-in-march.
7. Franco Ordoñez, "Almost 19,000 Migrant Children Stopped at U.S. Border in March, Most Ever in a Month," *Morning Edition*, NPR, April 8, 2021, https://www.npr.org/2021/04/08/985296354/almost-19-000-migrant-children-stopped-at-u-s-border-in-march-most-ever-in-a-mon; and Camilo Montoya-Galvez, "U.S. Shelters Received a Record 122,000 Unaccompanied Migrant Children in 2021," CBS News, December 23, 2021, https://www.cbsnews.com/news/immigration-122000-unaccompanied-migrant-children-us-shelters-2021/.

8. Catholic Welfare Bureau/Cuban Children's Program, "Fact Sheet," n.d. (1963), Bryan O. Walsh (hereafter BOW) Papers, Personal Files, Appointments, Box 5, Folder I, BOW Appointments, Catholic Welfare Bureau/Cuban Children's Program, 1963, 1969, Operation Pedro Pan Collection, Barry University (hereafter OPPC).

9. Deborah Shnookal, *Operation Pedro Pan and the Exodus of Cuba's Children* (Gainesville: University of Florida Press, 2020), 8.

10. Brian [*sic*] O. Walsh, "Un Católico Americano mira a la Iglesia Católica en Cuba," in *Razón y pasión: Veinticinco años de estudios Cubanos*, ed. Leonel Antonio de la Cuesta and María Cristina Herrera (Miami: Ediciones Universal, 1996), 26.

11. Catholic Charities of the Archdiocese of Miami, Inc., "Our History," accessed July 28, 2014, https://www.ccadm.org/about-us/our-history/.

12. Gustavo Pérez Firmat, *Life on the Hyphen: The Cuban-American Way* (Austin: University of Texas Press, 1995).

13. Carlos Cortés, ed., *Cuban Refugee Programs* (New York: Arno Press, 1980), 288.

14. María Cristina García, *Havana USA: Cuban Exiles and Cuban Americans in South Florida, 1959–1994* (Berkeley: University of California Press, 1996), 13.

15. García, *Havana USA*, 1; Everett M. Ressler, Neil Boothby, and Daniel J. Steinbock, *Unaccompanied Children: Care and Protection in Wars, Natural Disasters, and Refugee Movements* (New York: Oxford University Press, 1988), 51; Félix Roberto Masud-Piloto, *With Open Arms: Cuban Migration to the United States* (Totowa: Rowman & Littlefield, 1988), 1; and Gustavo López, "Hispanics of Cuban Origin in the United States, 2013," PewHispanic.org, September 15, 2015, http://www.pewhispanic.org/2015/09/15/hispanics-of-cuban-origin-in-the-united-states-2013/.

16. Karen Dubinsky, *Babies without Borders: Adoption and Migration across the Americas* (New York: New York University Press, 2010), 7.

17. Paula S. Fass, *Children of a New World: Society, Culture, and Globalization* (New York: New York University Press, 2007), 2–7, 103.

18. BOW, "Cuban Refugee Children: The Origins of Operation 'Pedro Pan,'" unpublished manuscript, n.d. (probably 1971), 2, BOW Papers, BOW Works, Folder: Cuban Refugee Children: The Origins of Operation Pedro Pan 1971, OPPC.

19. Catholic Welfare Bureau/Cuban Children's Program, "Fact Sheet," OPPC.

20. Florida State Department of Public Welfare, "1963 Program Report of the U.S. Cuban Refugee Assistance Program Administered by the Florida

State Department of Public Welfare," 31, Series 325, Box 3, Folder: 1963
Program Report of the U.S. Cuban Refugee Assistance Program Admin-
istered by the Florida State Department of Public Welfare, ff1, State
Archives of Florida, Tallahassee (hereafter SAF).

21. "Report on Services Rendered by the Health and Welfare Agencies of the
Diocese of Miami to the Cuban Refugees for Period Ending December
31, 1962," 14, 19–20, OPP/CCP, Subject Files, Series E, Folder: HEW (Department of Health, Education, and Welfare), OPPC; and R. Hart Phillips,
"14,072 Children Sent out of Cuba," New York Times, March 9, 1963, 2.

22. Letter to Edward S. Skillin from BOW, December 20, 1965, BOW Papers,
Personal Files, Correspondence 1963–1965, Box 20, Folder I, OPPC.

23. Estela Bravo, Operación Peter Pan: Volando de Vuelta a Cuba, segment 1,
accessed August 20, 2014, https://www.youtube.com/watch?v=e2PPfPWygBQ;
and Olga Rosa Gómez Cortés, Operación Peter Pan: Cerrando el círculo en
Cuba (Havana: Fondo Editorial Casa de las Américas, 2013), 203, 205.

24. Eric Pace, "Msgr. Bryan Oliver Walsh, 71; Led Effort to Aid Cuban Children," New York Times, December 29, 2001, http://www.nytimes.com
/2001/12/29/us/msgr-bryan-oliver-walsh-71-led-effort-to-aid-cuban
-children.html.

25. See, for example, an obituary for a woman who worked at the CWB
between 1963 and 1965 and was praised for her work on "Operation
Pedro Pan." Lisette Garcia, "Eloisa M. Fajardo, Patron of Cuban Children," Miami Herald, June 2, 1998, 4B.

1. Takeoff

1. Bravo, Operación Peter Pan, segment 1.
2. Estela Bravo, Operación Peter Pan: Volando de Vuelta a Cuba, segment 2, accessed August 20, 2014, https://www.youtube.com/watch?v=
rTXc2vrj2vI.
3. Maya Bell, "Operation Pedro Pan," Florida Magazine (Orlando Sentinel
insert), December 10, 1995, 12, OPP/CCP, Newspaper Clippings, OPPC.
4. Gómez Cortés, Operación Peter Pan, 206.
5. "Catholic Welfare Bureau, Cuban Children's Program," December 31,
1963, BOW Papers, Personal Files, BOW Appointments, Catholic Welfare
Bureau, Cuban Children's Program, 1963, 1969, Box 5, OPPC; and Yvonne
M. Conde, Operation Pedro Pan: The Untold Exodus of 14,048 Cuban
Children (New York: Routledge, 1999), 50.
6. María de los Angeles Torres, The Lost Apple: Operation Pedro Pan, Cuban
Children in the U.S., and the Promise of a Better Future (Boston: Beacon

Press, 2003), 239–40. New Orleans was also a site steeped in Catholic history, with other Pedro Pans landing there. Interview with Dr. Mario R. García, July 12, 2015, New York City.

7. Gómez Cortés, *Operación Peter Pan*, 219, 221; and Torres, *Lost Apple*, 47.

8. Quoted in Ramón Torreira Crespo and José Buajasán Marrawi, *Operación Peter Pan: Un caso de guerra psicológica contra Cuba*, 3rd ed. (Havana: Editora Política, 2000), 172.

9. Torreira and Buajasán, *Operación Peter Pan*, 125.

10. Letter from BOW to Honorable Daniel Braddock, December 12, 1960, OPP/CCP, Subject Files, Series E, Folder: Cuban Children's (CC) Program History 1960–1967, 1980, OPPC.

11. Agustín Blázquez and Jaums Sutton, "Operation Peter Pan: The Largest Exodus of Children in the Western Hemisphere," February 24, 2022, https://pedropanca.tripod.com/cubankidsfromthe60sexodus2/id1.html; Victor Andres Triay, *Fleeing Castro: Operation Pedro Pan and the Cuban Children's Program* (Gainesville: University Press of Florida, 1998), 35–36; García, *Havana USA*, 24; BOW, "Cuban Refugee Children," 19–23, OPPC; and Operation Pedro Pan Group, "The History of Operation Pedro Pan," accessed January 18, 2017, https://www.pedropan.org/history. For confirmation that the author was Monsignor Walsh and its date of origin, see Monsignor Bryan O. Walsh, "The History of Operation Pedro Pan," March 1, 2001, http://www.bishop-accountability.org/news5/2001_03_01_Walsh_TheHistory.htm; Gómez Cortés, *Operación Peter Pan*, 207; James Baker interview by Miguel Gonzalez-Pando, part 1, Florida International University Cuban Living History Project (hereafter FIU CLHP), online, 1997, http://libtube.fiu.edu/Play/50; Conde, *Operation Pedro Pan*, 50–51; and Torres, *Lost Apple*, 67–68.

12. BOW, "Cuban Refugee Children," 1, OPPC; and Susan Maret and Lea Aschkenas, "Operation Pedro Pan: The Hidden History of 14,000 Cuban Children," in *Government Secrecy*, ed. Susan Maret, vol. 19, *Research in Social Problems and Public Policy* (Bingley: Emerald Group, 2011), 176.

13. Blázquez and Sutton, "Operation Peter Pan."

14. BOW, "Cuban Refugee Children," 27, 32, OPPC.

15. Triay, *Fleeing Castro*, 20–21.

16. Gómez Cortés, *Operación Peter Pan*, 207.

17. Letter from BOW to Frank L. Auerbach, December 30, 1960, OPP/CCP, Subject Files, Series E, Folder: CC Program History 1960–1967, 1980, OPPC.

18. BOW, "Cuban Refugee Children," 33–34, OPPC.

19. Donald P. Baker, "A Journey out of the Past for 'Pedro Pan' Project," *Washington Post*, January 26, 1998, OPP/CCP, Newspaper Clippings, Barry University.

20. Letter from James Baker to BOW, December 14, 1960, OPP/CCP, Subject Files, Series E, Folder: CC Program History 1960–1967, 1980, OPPC; and "39 Cuban Youths Find Refuge in Diocese," *Nevada Register*, December 8, 1961, front page, OPP/CCP, Newspaper Clippings, Folder: 1961, OPPC.

21. BOW, "Cuban Refugee Children," 35, OPPC. Baker's love for Cuba ran deep. In an interview a few years before his death, Baker teared up when remembering his life in Cuba. See James Baker interview by Miguel Gonzalez-Pando, part 2, FIU CLHP, online, 1997, http://libtube.fiu.edu /Play/51, August 14, 2014.

22. Blázquez and Sutton, "Operation Peter Pan"; letter from BOW to Abraham Ribicoff, February 1, 1961, OPP/CCP, Subject Files, Series E, Folder: CC Program History 1960–1967, 1980, OPPC; and BOW, "Cuban Refugee Children," 37–42, OPPC.

23. Marjorie L. Donahue, "100s Thank Priest 'Who Cared,'" *The Voice*, March 3, 1978, 5, OPP/CCP, Newspaper Clippings, OPPC.

24. Memorandum from BOW to Bishop Coleman F. Carroll, March 1, 1968, and memorandum from BOW to Bishop Coleman F. Carroll, January 26, 1968, OPP/CCP, Subject Files, Series E, Folder: Cuban Children Arriving from Spain, Barry University; memorandum from BOW to Bishop Coleman F. Carroll, March 7, 1966, OPP/CCP, Subject Files, Series E, Folder: CC Program History 1960–1967, 1980, OPPC; and Mirta Ojito, "The Second Father," *Miami Herald*, June 18, 1994, 1G, 2G. The numbers are difficult to reconcile. Walsh made such problems known in regular progress reports to Bishop Carroll. In 1966 Walsh estimated ten thousand Cuban refugees, including parents of unaccompanied children in the United States, were stranded in Mexico and Spain. Torreira and Buajasán say two thousand to three thousand children left for Spain on a parallel program. See Torreira and Buajasán, *Operación Peter Pan*, 369.

25. BOW, "Cuban Refugee Children," 42, OPPC.

26. Torres, *Lost Apple*, 76–77.

27. Interview with Raul Alvaro, June 23, 2015, New York City.

28. Letter from BOW to Frank Auerbach, February 14, 1961, OPP/CCP, Subject Files, Series E, Folder: U.S. State Department, Visa Section, 1961–1962, OPPC.

29. Letter from BOW to George W. Philips, March 10, 1961, OPP/CCP, Subject Files, Series E, Folder: U.S. State Department, Visa Section, 1961–1962,

OPPC; and letter from Charles G. Sommer to BOW, July 17, 1961, OPP/CCP, Subject Files, Series E, Folder: U.S. State Department, Visa Section, 1961–1962, OPPC.

30. Bell, "Operation Pedro Pan," 10.

31. Note from John J. Nevins to BOW, June 29, 1962, OPP/CCP, Subject Files, Series E, Folder: U.S. State Department, Visa Section, 1961–1962, OPPC.

32. Gómez Cortés, *Operación Peter Pan*, 13.

33. Bell, "Operation Pedro Pan," 12.

34. Donahue, "100s Thank Priest," 15.

35. Lillian Nitcher, "They Come Alone from Cuba," *Wisconsin State Journal*, February 11, 1963, 8, OPP/CCP, Newspaper Clippings, OPPC.

36. Letter to Martha Hynning from Frank Craft, August 27, 1962, Folder: Florida State Agency, Child Welfare Unit, RG 363, Records of the Social and Rehabilitation Service, Unaccompanied Cuban Children's Refugee Program, 1961–1967, Box 3, NARA.

37. Letter from BOW to George Phelan, July 20, 1962, OPP/CCP, Subject Files, Series E, Folder: U.S. State Department, Visa Section, 1961–1962, OPPC.

38. Torres, *Lost Apple*, 78.

39. Marilyn Holt, *Cold War Kids: Politics and Childhood in Postwar America, 1945–1960* (Lawrence: University Press of Kansas, 2014), 106, 108–9.

40. García, *Havana USA*, 21; and Ressler, Boothby, and Steinbock, *Unaccompanied Children*, 15–16, 49.

41. García, *Havana USA*, 21.

42. Tracy S. Voorhees, "Report to the President of the United States on the Cuban Refugee Problem," in Cortés, *Cuban Refugee Programs*, 6–7.

43. Tracy S. Voorhees, "Interim Report to the President of the United States on the Cuban Refugee Problem" (Washington DC: GPO, December 19, 1960), 9.

44. John F. Kennedy, "Letter to the President of the Senate and to the Speaker of the House Proposing Reorganization and Reenactment of Refugee Aid Legislation," July 21, 1961, https://www.presidency.ucsb.edu/documents /letter-the-president-the-senate-and-the-speaker-the-house-proposing -reorganization-and.

45. Text of President John F. Kennedy's Letter to Secretary Ribicoff, n.d., OPP/CCP, Subject Files, Series E, Folder: CC Program History 1960–1967, 1980, OPPC.

46. García, *Havana USA*, 22–23; and Triay, *Fleeing Castro*, 45.

47. Irving Spiegel, "Director Chosen for Cuban Relief," *New York Times*, February 2, 1961, 5.

48. García, *Havana USA*, 23.

49. John W. Finney, "President Orders Cuba Refugee Aid," *New York Times*, February 4, 1961, 1.

50. Gómez Cortés, *Operación Peter Pan*, 25; Conde, *Operation Pedro Pan*, 23, 28; García, *Havana USA*, 16–17, 20–21; and Torres, *Lost Apple*, 58, 125.

51. María de los Angeles Torres, *In the Land of Mirrors: Cuban Exile Politics in the United States* (Ann Arbor: University of Michigan Press, 1999), 62–63.

52. John F. Thomas, "The Cuban Refugee Program," in Cortés, *Cuban Refugee Programs*, 4–6; and García, *Havana USA*, 16.

53. Department of Health, Education, and Welfare, Social Security Administration, Bureau of Family Services, "Financial Assistance for Resettled Cuban Refugees," August 1962, 2, 3, 5, 9, OPP/CCP, Subject Files, Series E, Folder: HEW, OPPC.

54. Anita Casavantes Bradford, *The Revolution Is for the Children: The Politics of Childhood in Havana and Miami, 1959-1962* (Chapel Hill: University of North Carolina Press, 2014), 126–27.

55. Torres, *Lost Apple*, 73–74.

56. Victor Andres Triay, *The Mariel Boatlift: A Cuban-American Journey* (Gainesville: University of Florida Press, 2019), 5.

2. Landing

1. Interview with Mayda Riopedre, August 19, 2014, Florida International University, Miami.

2. "Los Campamentos de Miami," Miami Child Care Shelters, 1960–1966, Memorandum to Elly Chovel from Walsh, September 24, 2001, Subject Files, Ce-D, Box 26, Folder II, BOW Subject Files, Cuban Children's Program, 1964–2001, OPPC; and Conde, *Operation Pedro Pan*, 89–90.

3. Interview with Riopedre.

4. Triay, *Fleeing Castro*, 72–74.

5. Conde, *Operation Pedro Pan*, 108; and Shnookal, *Operation Pedro Pan*, 52.

6. Conde, *Operation Pedro Pan*, 73.

7. Bell, "Operation Pedro Pan," 12.

8. Memorandum from BOW to Father Dominick Adessa, May 5, 1964, 3, OPP/CCP, Subject Files, Series E, Folder: Adessa, Dominick, Jr., Fr., 1963–1965, OPPC.

9. Florida State Department of Public Welfare, "1963 Program Report," 29, SAF; and memorandum to State Public Welfare Administrators and Child Welfare Directors from Mildred Arnold, Director, Division of Social

Services of Children's Bureau, May 24, 1962, 1, Series 325, Box 1, Folder: Cuban Refugee—Tampa, ff25, SAF.

10. Memorandum from Fern M. Pence (Dir., Cuban Refugee Assistance Program) to Grace H. Stewart (Dir., Public Assistance Division), July 31, 1961, Series 325, Box 1, Folder: Cuban Situation—Historical, ff10, SAF; García, *Havana USA*, 19; and "Report on Services Rendered by the Health and Welfare Agencies," OPPC.

11. Triay, *Fleeing Castro*, 58; and Gómez Cortés, *Operación Peter Pan*, 216.

12. Garcia, "Eloisa M. Fajardo," 4B.

13. Helen Ferguson, "Unwanted Children Find Love," *Miami Herald*, January 17, 1963, OPP/CCP, Newspaper Clippings, Folder: January 1963, OPPC.

14. Ana Rodriguez-Soto, "Pedro Pan Children May Number More than 14,000, Experts Say," *Florida Catholic*, November 29, 2001, A5, OPP/CCP, Newspaper Clippings, OPPC.

15. Daniel Shoer Roth, "The Jewish Children of Pedro Pan: Secret Exodus, New Left," *Miami Herald*, August 24, 2008, 1A, 4A, OPP/CCP, Newspaper Clippings, OPPC.

16. Triay, *Fleeing Castro*, 54.

17. Carlos Eire, *Waiting for Snow in Havana: Confessions of a Cuban Boy* (New York: Free Press, 2004), 348.

18. HEW, "State Plan for Assistance to Cuban Refugees, Florida," February 1961, Series 325, Box 1, Folder: State Plan for Assistance to Cuban Refugees in Florida, ff1, SAF; Operations Letter Number 975 from Grace H. Stewart to District Directors, January 26, 1962, Series 325, Box 1, Folder: Informational Pamphlet Cuban Refugee Assistance (CRA) Program, ff2, SAF; and Florida State Department of Public Welfare, "Policy Manual: United States Cuban Refugee Assistance Program, Distribution of Federally Donated Commodities, Child Welfare Services," May 1963, Series 325, Box 1, Folder: Informational Pamphlet CRA Program, ff2, SAF.

19. HEW, "History of the Federal Unaccompanied Cuban Refugee Children's Program," report, n.d., 2, 25, Folder: History of the Federal UCRC Program, RG 363, Records of the Social and Rehabilitation Service, Unaccompanied Cuban Children's Refugee Program, 1961–1967, Box 1, NN3-363-095-001, NARA; and Martin Gula, memorandum to Mildred Arnold, "Cuban Refugee Children—HEW Conference with Florida State Department of Public Welfare, December 15, 1960," December 19, 1960, Folder: Refugee Problems, 1958–1962, RG 102, Records of the Children's Bureau, Central File, 1958–1962, Box 761, NN3-102-83-1, NARA.

20. Letter to Frank M. Craft from Wave L. Perry, March 27, 1963, Series 325, Box 1, Folder: Informational Pamphlet CRA Program, ff2, SAF.

21. "Agreement between the United States of America and the Florida State Department of Public Welfare for the Administration of the Cuban Refugee Program in Dade County Florida," n.d., 1961, Folder: Refugee Problems, 1958–1962, RG 102, Records of the Children's Bureau, Central File, 1958–1962, Box 761, NN3-102-83-1, NARA.

22. Letter from Katherine B. Oettinger to BOW, June 25, 1964, BOW Papers, Personal Files, Correspondence, Box 20, Folder I, BOW Correspondence, 1963–1965, OPPC; Dorothy Bradbury and Katherine B. Oettinger, *Five Decades of Action for Children: A History of the Children's Bureau* (Washington DC: Dept. of HEW, 1962), 120; and letter to BOW from Lucille Batson, Consultant on Services for Cuban Refugee Children, from Children's Bureau in Dept. of HEW, November 26, 1965, BOW Papers, Personal Files, Correspondence, Box 20, Folder I, BOW Correspondence, 1963–1965, OPPC.

23. Memorandum from (Mrs.) Fern M. Pence, Director of US Cuban Refugee Assistance Program, to Mrs. Grace H. Stewart, Director of Public Assistance Division, April 30, 1962, Series 325, Box 1, Folder: Cuban, ff3, SAF.

24. HEW, "History of the Federal Unaccompanied Cuban Refugee Children's Program," 39.

25. HEW, "History of the Federal Unaccompanied Cuban Refugee Children's Program," 37–39.

26. In September 2001 Walsh sent Pedro Pan and founding member of the Operation Pedro Pan Group Elly Chovel a memo that provided details of the various OPP camps. See "Los Campamentos de Miami," OPPC.

27. Conde, *Operation Pedro Pan*, 75; Clemente C. Amézaga and Eloísa Echazábal, "Unaccompanied Cuban Children's Program Florida Camps and Group Homes, 1960–1978," December 26, 2013, OPPC; "Los Campamentos de Miami," OPPC; and Blázquez and Sutton, "Operation Peter Pan."

28. Conde, *Operation Pedro Pan*, 91.

29. Conde, *Operation Pedro Pan*, 76–78; Triay, *Fleeing Castro*, 59–60; BOW, "Brief History of Camp Matecumbe/Boystown of South Florida," April 21, 1999, Digital Library of the Caribbean, https://original-ufdc.uflib.ufl.edu/AA00053009/00001?search=brief+=history+=camp+=matecumbe; "Los Campamentos de Miami," OPPC; and "Memo to Brother Maxi-

miliano from BOW," September 24, 1962, OPP/CCP, Series D, Folder: Camp Matecumbe, 1962, OPPC.

30. HistoryMiami Museum, "Operation Pedro Pan: The Cuban Children's Exodus," July 26, 2015–January 17, 2016, Miami, http://www.historymiami .org/exhibition/operation-pedro-pan-the-cuban-childrens-exodus/.

31. Conde, *Operation Pedro Pan*, 83–85; and memo to James Haverty from Carlos Florido, April 25, 1963, OPP/CCP, Administrative Files, Series D, Folder: Camp Matecumbe: School, 1962–1964, OPPC.

32. Gómez Cortés, *Operación Peter Pan*, 41, 43–44, 46.

33. Memo to Father Joseph H. O'Shea from BOW, April 5, 1963, OPP/CCP, Administrative Files, Series D, Folder: Camp Matecumbe: School, 1962– 1964, OPPC.

34. Torres, *Lost Apple*, 156.

35. Conde, *Operation Pedro Pan*, 86; Amézaga and Echazábal, "Unaccompanied Cuban Children's Program," OPPC; and "Los Campamentos de Miami," OPPC.

36. "Los Campamentos de Miami," OPPC; Operation Pedro Pan Group, "Florida City," accessed January 5, 2017, https://www.pedropan.org /locations/florida-city-camp; and Conde, *Operation Pedro Pan*, 95.

37. Memo to R. P. Salvador De Cistiema from Dr. Alfonso Matas, May 14, 1962, OPP/CCP, Administrative Files, Series D, Folder: Florida City Shelter, 1962–1964, OPPC.

38. Conde, *Operation Pedro Pan*, 92.

39. Gómez Cortés, *Operación Peter Pan*, 15–17.

40. Interview with Pury Lopez Santiago, July 30, 2015, Miami FL; and email correspondence with Pury Lopez Santiago, February 10, 2017.

41. Lars Schoultz, *That Infernal Little Cuban Republic: The United States and the Cuban Revolution* (Chapel Hill: University of North Carolina Press, 2009), 159; Triay, *Fleeing Castro*, 64; Conde, *Operation Pedro Pan*, 98– 99; "Memo from Bro. Maximiliano to BOW," April 30, 1963, OPP/CCP, Administrative Files, Series D, Folder: Opa-Locka Shelter 1963, OPPC; "Los Campamentos de Miami," OPPC; "Memo to Brother Maximiliano from BOW"; and Amézaga and Echazábal, "Unaccompanied Cuban Children's Program," OPPC.

42. "Memo from Daniel R. Morgan to BOW," April 10, 1963, OPP/CCP, Series D, Folder: Miami Memorandum, 1962–1971, OPPC.

43. Gómez Cortés, *Operación Peter Pan*, 205.

44. Conde, *Operation Pedro Pan*, 86–87.

45. Torres, *Lost Apple*, 157.

46. Conde, *Operation Pedro Pan*, 93.
47. Until 1966, Dorothea Sullivan worked as the CCP's director of social services. At one point, Brother Maximiliano Mediavilla ran Opa-locka, while Tomás de la Aguilera and his wife, Pilar Fortún, took charge of St. Raphael's Hall, aided by Carmen García and Walter Wilson Jr. Florida City's leadership was guided by Father Salvador de Cistierna and Joan Gross, the head social worker, while Matecumbe's chief administration landed on the Piarist Father Francisco Palá, who was later succeeded by Father Joaquín Guerrero and the social worker Raymond McGraw. See OPP/CCP, Administrative Files, Series A, Folder: Memorandum, Apr-Aug 1963, OPPC; "Telegram to Dorothea F. Sullivan from Walter B. Wilson, Jr.," February 1, 1963, OPP/CCP, Series D, Folder: Miami Memorandum, 1962–1971, OPPC; memo to Dorothy McCrary [director, Child Welfare in CCP] from D. F. Sullivan, August 31, 1966, OPP/CCP, Administrative Files, Series A, Folder: Memorandum, Dorothea F. Sullivan, Director of Social Services, 1963–1964, OPPC; and Amézaga and Echazábal, "Unaccompanied Cuban Children's Program," OPPC.
48. CWB, "Camp Matecumbe Daily Schedule," OPP/CCP, Series D, Folder: Camp Regulations, 1963, OPPC.
49. BOW and CWB, "Cuban Boys' Home Boys' Handbook," 1966, OPP/CCP, Administrative Files, Series D, Folder: Cuban Boys' Home handbook, OPPC.
50. "Telegram to Dorothea F. Sullivan from Walter B. Wilson, Jr."
51. Interoffice memorandum from Walter B. Wilson Jr. to BOW, February 15, 1963, OPP/CCP, Subject Files, Series E, Folder: Medical & Health Issues 1962–1963, 1965, OPPC; and memorandum from BOW to Dr. Crissey et al., February 20, 1963, OPP/CCP, Subject Files, Series E, Folder: Medical & Health Issues 1962–1963, 1965, OPPC.
52. Letter from Daniel R. Morgan to Father Joaquin Guerrero, January 25, 1963, OPP/CCP, Series D, Folder: Camp Matecumbe, 1963, OPPC.
53. Letter from BOW to Reverend Joaquin Guerrero, March 6, 1963, OPP/CCP, Series D, Folder: Camp Matecumbe, 1963, OPPC.
54. "Memo from Dorothea F. Sullivan to BOW," February 21, 1963, OPP/CCP, Series D, Folder: Miami Memorandum, 1962–1971, OPPC.
55. Dorothea F. Sullivan, "Case of Juan," March 22, 1966, OPP/CCP, Subject Files, Series E, Folder: Juan, case of, 1966, OPPC.
56. Letter to Zelma J. Felten from Frances Davis, December 15, 1964, Folder: Cuban Refugee Children, Florida State Agency, Correspondence—General, January 1, 1965–December 31, 1965, RG 363, Records of the Social

and Rehabilitation Service, Unaccompanied Cuban Children's Refugee Program, 1961–1967, Box 3, NN3-363-095-001, NARA.

57. CWB, "Instructions—St. Raphael's Hall," OPP/CCP, Series D, Folder: Camp Regulations, 1963, OPPC.

58. Memo to BOW from Dorothea F. Sullivan, February 18, 1963, OPP/CCP, Administrative Files, Series A, Folder: Memorandum, Jan–March 1963, OPPC.

59. "Reglamento," Pedro Pan Collection, CHC0350, Box 1, Folder 1, Amézaga, Clemente, 1961, Operation Pedro Pan Files, Cuban Heritage Collection, University of Miami (hereafter CHC).

60. "Jesuit Preparatory School, School Regulations," Pedro Pan Collection, CHC0350, Box 1, Folder 1, Amézaga, Clemente, 1961, Operation Pedro Pan Files, CHC.

61. Memorandum to All Shelter Administrators from BOW, October 29, 1963, OPP/CCP, Administrative Files, Series A, Folder: Memorandum, Sept–Dec 1963, OPPC.

62. Memorandum from Dorothea Sullivan to BOW, February 10, 1964, OPP/CCP, Administrative Files, Series A, Folder: Memorandum, Jan–April 1964, OPPC.

63. Memorandum to All Shelter Administrators from Ann Unterman, Social Group Worker, March 2, 1964, OPP/CCP, Administrative Files, Series A, Folder: Memorandum, Jan–April 1964, OPPC.

64. "Survey: Overweight Girls in Florida City," n.d., 1, 3–4, OPP/CCP, Administrative Files, Series D, Folder: Florida City Shelter: Medical Services, 1963–1965, OPPC.

65. CWB, "Rules for Cuban Girls Home," January 8, 1973, OPP/CCP, Subject Files, Series E, Folder: Rules for Cuban Girls Home, 1973, OPPC.

66. Memo to Aileen Shea Zahn from Valdes Romero, July 26, 1963, OPP/CCP, Series D, Folder: Camp Matecumbe, 1963, OPPC.

67. "Memo to BOW from Brother Maximiliano," March 11, 1963, OPP/CCP, Administrative Files, Series D, Folder: Opa-locka Shelter 1963, OPPC.

68. "Memo from BOW to Brother Maximiliano," March 11, 1963, OPP/CCP, Administrative Files, Series D, Folder: Opa-locka Shelter 1963, OPPC.

69. Letter to Miguel Estades Navarro from John J. Fitzpatrick, October 28, 1964, Pedro Pan Collection, CHC0350, Box 1, Folder 4, Estades Navarro, Miguel, 1962–64, Operation Pedro Pan Files, CHC.

70. Letter from Brother Santiago Fernández to BOW, November 24, 1961, OPP/CCP, Subject Files, Series E, Folder: Marist Brothers, 1961–1964, OPPC.

71. Letter from Brother H. Maximiliano to BOW, August 2, 1964, OPP/ CCP, Subject Files, Series E, Folder: Marist Brothers, 1961–1964, OPPC; letter from Monsignor John J. Fitzpatrick to Brother Maximiliano Mediavilla, September 16, 1964, OPP/CCP, Subject Files, Series E, Folder: Marist Brothers, 1961–1964, OPPC; letter from BOW to Brother Maximiliano Mediavilla, September 17, 1964, OPP/CCP, Subject Files, Series E, Folder: Marist Brothers, 1961–1964, OPPC; and letter from BOW to Bishop Coleman F. Carroll, September 21, 1964, OPP/CCP, Subject Files, Series E, Folder: Marist Brothers, 1961–1964, OPPC.

72. Letter from BOW to Miguel A. González, February 19, 1965, OPP/CCP, Subject Files, Series E, Folder: Marist Brothers, 1961–1964, OPPC; and letter from Miguel A. González to BOW, January 25, 1965, OPP/CCP, Subject Files, Series E, Folder: Marist Brothers, 1961–1964, OPPC.

73. CWB, "Cuban Children's Program Minutes, Meeting of Social Service Supervisors," September 5, 1963, OPP/CCP, Subject Files, Series E, Folder: Social Service, 1958–1963, OPPC.

74. E. L. Matta, memorandum to T. E. Cato, "Handicapped Cuban Refugee Children," April 20, 1962, Folder: Refugee Problems, 1958–1962, RG 102, Records of the Children's Bureau, Central File, 1958–1962, Box 761, NN3-102-83-1, NARA.

75. Sara Fieldston, *Raising the World: Child Welfare in the American Century* (Cambridge MA: Harvard University Press, 2015), 25, 47.

76. Carolina Garzón Papers, CHC5233, Box 1, Untitled Folder (blue), Operation Pedro Pan Files, CHC.

77. Carolina Garzón Papers, CHC5233, Box 1, Untitled Folder (manila), Operation Pedro Pan Files, CHC.

78. "Confidential Information," n.d., Carolina Garzón Papers, CHC5233, Box 1, Untitled Folder (blue), Operation Pedro Pan Files, CHC.

79. "CRS #779-C, May 22, 1963, Opa-locka, Shelter, Social History," Carolina Garzón Papers, CHC5233, Box 1, Untitled Folder (manila), Operation Pedro Pan Files, CHC.

80. "CRS #4294, Cuban Boys School (Opa-locka), June 26, 1963, Summary Social History," Carolina Garzón Papers, CHC5233, Box 1, Untitled Folder (manila), Operation Pedro Pan Files, CHC.

81. "CRS #3473B, 2/6/1963," Carolina Garzón Papers, CHC5233, Box 1, Untitled Folder (manila), Operation Pedro Pan Files, CHC.

82. Letter from José I. Lasaga, PhD, to BOW, July 8, 1964, OPP/CCP, Subject Files, Series E, Folder: Psychological Services, 1964–1968, OPPC.

83. Memorandum from Katherine Sheridan to Dorothea F. Sullivan, "Use of Psychological Services at Matecumbe and Opa-Locka Shelters," March 17, 1964, OPP/CCP, Subject Files, Series E, Folder: Psychological Services, 1964–1968, OPPC.

84. "Memo from Rev. Francisco Palá to BOW," March 5, 1962, OPP/CCP, Series D, Folder: Camp Matecumbe, 1962, OPPC.

85. Letter to Father Joaquin Guerrero from BOW, September 23, 1963, OPP/CCP, Series D, Folder: Camp Matecumbe, 1963, OPPC.

86. Memo from Dorothea F. Sullivan to BOW, February 7, 1964, OPP/CCP, Administrative Files, Series A, Folder: Memorandum, Jan–April 1964, OPPC.

87. Email correspondence with Jay Castano, June 25, 2015.

3. From Camps to Resettlement

1. Interview with Lopez Santiago; and email correspondence with Lopez Santiago.

2. Shnookal, *Operation Pedro Pan*, 15.

3. "Aid for Cuban Children Asked," *New York Times*, March 8, 1962, 35; Erwin Potts, "8,000 Cuban Children Saved from Castro Brainwashing," *Miami Herald*, March 8, 1962, 1, 2A; "Cuban Children Find Haven Here," *The Oregonian*, March 8, 1962, 1, 18; George Southworth, "80 Cuban Boys in Miami—a Day in Their New Life," *Miami Herald*, March 8, 1962, 10A; Gene Miller, "'Peter Pan' Means Real Life to Some Kids," *Miami Herald*, March 9, 1962, 11A—all from OPP/CCP, Newspaper Clippings, Folder: March 1962, OPPC; Casavantes, "Remembering Pedro Pan," 290; and Torres, *Lost Apple*, 150.

4. "Cuban Children Helped in Florida," *New York Times*, May 27, 1962, 41.

5. Letter from BOW to Directors of Catholic Charities, March 6, 1962, OPP/CCP, Administrative Files, Series A, Folder: Memorandum, Feb–Aug 1962, OPPC.

6. Bruce Broussard, "Young Refugees from Cuba Arrive Here, Get New 'Home,'" *Alexandria Daily Town Talk*, February 1, 1962, 18, OPP/CCP, Newspaper Clippings, Folder: February 1962, OPPC.

7. For example, see "Refugee Children Placed throughout Diocese," *The Observer*, April 1962, 9, OPP/CCP, Newspaper Clippings, Folder: April 1962, OPPC.

8. Phillips, "14,072 Children," 2; Torres, *Lost Apple*, 186; and Blázquez and Sutton, "Operation Peter Pan."

9. New York took 58,478 people; New Jersey, 35,519; and California, 24,843. Alaska received only 1 during these years. See BOW Papers, II. Subject

Files, Ha–He Box 29, Folder: HEW Cuban Refugee Program, 1964–1970, OPPC.

10. Torres, *Lost Apple*, 151–52.

11. HistoryMiami Museum, "Operation Pedro Pan."

12. "Agencies under Contract," OPP/CCP, Administrative Files, Series D, Folder: Agency Lists, 1962–1963, OPPC.

13. Letter to Joseph M. Fitzgerald, Attorney in Miami, from Bryan Walsh, October 13, 1965, BOW Papers, Personal Files, Correspondence, Box 20, Folder I, BOW Correspondence, 1963–1965, OPPC.

14. CWB, "Contract for Provision of Foster Care for Unaccompanied Cuban Refugee Children," June 10, 1962, and October 6, 1972, OPP/CCP, Subject Files, Series E, Folder: Cuban Children's Program: Contracts, 1962–1972, OPPC.

15. "Memorandum to All Agencies of the Catholic Welfare Bureau—Cuban Children's Program from BOW," July 17, 1962, OPP/CCP, Administrative Files, Series A, Folder: Memorandum, Feb–Aug 1962, OPPC.

16. Memorandum to All Agencies Participating in Cuban Children's Program from BOW, July 2, 1962, OPP/CCP, Administrative Files, Series A, Folder: Memorandum, Feb–Aug 1962, OPPC.

17. Letter to G. E. Martini from Frances Davis, April 13, 1964, Series 897, Box 2, Folder: Alabama-Connecticut Foster Parent Inquiries, SAF.

18. Torres, *Lost Apple*, 162.

19. *Resettlement Re-cap*, November 1963, 1, BOW Papers, BOW Works by Others, Folder: Resettlement Re-cap, 1963–1966, OPPC.

20. *Resettlement Re-cap*, 3.

21. *Resettlement Re-cap*, January 1964, 1, BOW Papers, BOW Works by Others, Folder: Resettlement Re-cap, 1963–1966, OPPC.

22. "39 Cuban Youths Find Refuge in Diocese."

23. Sample Letter by Milton E. Sellars, OPP/CCP, Subject Files, Series E, Folder: Foster Home Care, 1961–1974, OPPC.

24. Letter to BOW from Dorothea F. Sullivan in Washington DC, the Catholic University of America, October 26, 1962, BOW Papers, Personal Files, Correspondence, Box 20, Folder: BOW Correspondence, 1947–1962, OPPC.

25. Memorandum from BOW to All Agencies Participating in Cuban Children's Program, July 2, 1962, OPP/CCP, Subject Files, Series E, Folder: Change of Care, 1962–1964, OPPC.

26. "Memorandum from Dorothea F. Sullivan to BOW," November 19, 1963, OPP/CCP, Administrative Files, Series A, Folder: Memorandum, Sept–Dec

1963, OPPC; and memorandum from BOW to All Participating Agencies, Cuban Children's Program, October 29, 1962, OPP/CCP, Subject Files, Series E, Folder: Complaint Procedures, 1962–1963, OPPC.

27. "Memo from Bro. Maximiliano to BOW," April 30, 1963, OPPC.
28. Letter to Bishop Coleman F. Carroll from BOW, April 26, 1963, OPP/CCP, Series D, Folder: Camp Matecumbe, 1963, OPPC.
29. Letter to Father Joaquin Guerrero from BOW, March 12, 1963, OPP/CCP, Series D, Folder: Camp Matecumbe, 1963, OPPC.
30. Torres, *Lost Apple*, 168–70.
31. Clint Attebery, "From Havana to Montana: Cuban Refugee Children, Operation Pedro Pan, and the Cold War Catholic Church," *Montana: The Magazine of Western History* 64, no. 1 (Spring 2014): 62–66, 69, 71.
32. "Russell D. Giesy, 90," *Daily Inter Lake*, October 31, 2012, https://dailyinterlake.com/news/2012/oct/31/russell-d-giesy-90-6/; and Attebery, "From Havana to Montana," 71–72.
33. Conde, *Operation Pedro Pan*, 106, 128–29.
34. "Psychiatric Resources," November 5, 1963, OPP/CCP, Subject Files, Series E, Folder: Emotionally Disturbed Children, 1963, OPPC.
35. Operation Pedro Pan Group, "History of Operation Pedro Pan."
36. Conde, *Operation Pedro Pan*, 118–21; Gómez Cortés, *Operación Peter Pan*, 143–47; Torres, *Lost Apple*, 167–68; and Bravo, *Operación Peter Pan*, segment 2.
37. Conde, *Operation Pedro Pan*, 121–22.
38. Gómez Cortés, *Operación Peter Pan*, 165–69, 172–73.
39. Betty Cortina and Elaine de Valle, "Exodus Unleashes a Flood of Memories," *Miami Herald*, August 29, 1994, 1A, 8A.
40. Mario R. García, "40 Years/40 Lessons (2)—Refugee," *Garcia Media* (blog), February 8, 2010, http://www.garciamedia.com/blog/40_years_40 _lessons_2-refugee.
41. Conde, *Operation Pedro Pan*, 125–26, 134–36.
42. Shnookal, *Operation Pedro Pan*, 9.
43. Rough draft of "Need for Group Facilities for Teenage Boys," October 1, 1963, BOW Papers, Works by BOW, Box 43, Folder: Need for Group Facilities, OPPC.
44. HEW, Bureau of Family Services and Children's Bureau, "Cuban Refugee Program—Recent Policy Changes Affecting Children," May 3, 1963, 1, Series 325, Box 1, Folder: Wayne Perry Correspondence 1964 Clarification of Policy, ff9, SAF.
45. Catholic Welfare Bureau/Cuban Children's Program, "Fact Sheet," OPPC.

46. BOW, "Commentary on Draft Copy of the Report to the Congress of the United States—Inadequate Administration of the Contract to Provide Foster Care for Unaccompanied Cuban Refugee Children, Welfare Administration Department of Health, Education, and Welfare, by the Comptroller General of the United States," December 21, 1964, 1, 2, 12, BOW Papers, BOW Works, Folder: Cuban Children's Program, Miami FL, 1964, OPPC.

4. Americanize a la Cubana

1. Interview with Azel.
2. "Cuban Children Helped in Florida," 2, 41; and Torres, *Lost Apple*, 156–57.
3. Interview with Lopez Santiago; email correspondence with Lopez Santiago; and Eire, *Waiting for Snow*, 14.
4. Carlos Eire, *Learning to Die in Miami: Confessions of a Refugee Boy* (New York: Free Press, 2010), 56–57, 162–63.
5. Email correspondence with Gerardo Simms, December 31, 2015.
6. Interview with José Antonio Arenas, July 30, 2015, Pérez Trading Company, Miami; Bob Drogin, "Chief Justice Leads Massive Swearing in of New Citizens," *LA Times*, July 4, 1986, https://www.latimes.com/archives/la-xpm-1986-07-04-mn-746-story.html; and Robert A. Liff, "14,000 Become Citizens in Orange Bowl Ceremony," *Orlando Sentinel*, July 4, 1986, https://www.orlandosentinel.com/news/os-xpm-1986-07-04-0230340026-story.html.
7. Ressler, Boothby, and Steinbock, *Unaccompanied Children*, 153, 174–75, 177.
8. Conde, *Operation Pedro Pan*, 146–47; and Ellis Island Honors Society, Ellis Island Medal of Honor Database, accessed February 25, 2022, http://medalists.eihonors.org/index.html.
9. Interview with Eloy Cepero, March 2, 2017, Miami.
10. Interview with García.
11. Conde, *Operation Pedro Pan*, 79, 125–26, 153.
12. HistoryMiami Museum, "Operation Pedro Pan."
13. Torres, *Lost Apple*, 165.
14. Letter from Dorothea F. Sullivan to Ellen O'Donoghue, July 10, 1963, OPP/CCP, Subject Files, Series E, Folder: Group Homes/Care, 1962–1977, OPPC.
15. Eire, *Waiting for Snow*, 160.
16. Eire, *Learning to Die*, 17, 174.
17. Conde, *Operation Pedro Pan*, 127; and Nitcher, "They Come Alone," 8.
18. Phone interview with Rodriguez.
19. Interview with García.

20. Torres, *Land of Mirrors*, 5–6.

21. Nancy Traver, "Memories of Cuba Inspire Book by DePaul Professor," *Chicago Tribune*, June 4, 2003.

22. Interview with Cepero.

23. Interview with Riopedre.

24. Carlos Eire, "Carlos Eire: A Cuban American Searches for Roots," interview by Terry Gross, *Fresh Air*, NPR, November 22, 2010, http://www.npr.org/templates/transcript/transcript.php?storyId=131449904.

25. Eire, *Learning to Die*, 99–100, 239.

26. "Memorandum to All Social Work Supervisors from Dorothea F. Sullivan," June 2, 1965, OPP/CCP, Administrative Files, Series A, Folder: Memorandum, 1965, OPPC.

27. Memorandum to Directors of Participating Agencies, Cuban Children's Program, from BOW, August 1, 1963, OPP/CCP, Subject Files, Series E, Folder: Segregation, 1963, OPPC.

28. Memorandum to Directors of Participating Agencies, Cuban Children's Program, from BOW, August 1, 1963, OPP/CCP, Administrative Files, Series A, Folder: Memorandum, Apr–Aug 1963, OPPC.

29. Letter from Katharine Black to BOW, August 20, 1963, OPP/CCP, Subject Files, Series E, Folder: Segregation, 1963, OPPC.

30. Catholic Charities of the Diocese of Harrisburg, "Confidential Questionnaire on Segregation," September 6, 1963, OPP/CCP, Subject Files, Series E, Folder: Segregation, 1963, OPPC.

31. Letter to Mildred Arnold from Frank Craft, April 30, 1962, Folder: Cuban Refugee Children, Florida State Agency, Children's Service Bureau, RG 363, Records of the Social and Rehabilitation Service, Unaccompanied Cuban Children's Refugee Program, 1961–1967, Box 3, NN3-363-095-001, NARA.

32. Dubinsky, *Babies without Borders*, 57–58.

33. "Child-care Institution Civil Rights Compliance Review," March or April 1974, OPP/CCP, Subject Files, Series E, Folder: Child Care Facilities: Licensing, 1967, OPPC.

34. BOW, "Address to the Annual Meeting of the Child Welfare League of America, May 23, 1963," BOW Papers, Personal Files, Conference & Workshops, Box 17, Folder: BOW Conference & Workshops, Child Welfare League of America Annual Meeting, Cleveland OH, May 1963, OPPC.

35. Cheris Brewer, *Questioning the Cuban Exile Model: Race, Gender, and Resettlement, 1959–1979* (El Paso: LFB Scholarly Publishing, 2010), 14.

36. HistoryMiami Museum, "Operation Pedro Pan."

37. "Heartbroken Cuban Parents Shipping Steady Stream of Children to U.S.," *Houston Chronicle*, May 27, 1962, 6, OPP/CCP, Newspaper Clippings, Folder: May 1962, OPPC.

38. Email correspondence with Ximena Valdivia, August 3, 2015.

39. "Inter-office memo, from James T. Haverty to BOW," January 18, 1963, OPP/CCP, Series D, Folder: Camp Matecumbe, 1963, OPPC.

40. "Memorandum to BOW from Dorothea F. Sullivan," June 19, 1964, OPP/CCP, Administrative Files, Series A, Folder: Memorandum, May–Dec 1964, OPPC.

5. The "Other Miami"

Epigraph: Alejandro Portes and Alex Stepick, *City on the Edge: The Transformation of Miami* (Berkeley: University of California Press, 1993), xi.

1. Interview with Marvin Dunn, July 29, 2015, Palmetto Bay, Miami.

2. Interview with Dunn.

3. N. D. B. Connolly, *A World More Concrete: Real Estate and the Remaking of Jim Crow South Florida* (Chicago: University of Chicago Press, 2014), 5, 102–3.

4. Mary Dudziak, *Cold War Civil Rights: Race and the Image of American Democracy* (Princeton NJ: Princeton University Press, 2000).

5. Sheila L. Croucher, *Imagining Miami: Ethnic Politics in a Postmodern World* (Charlottesville: University Press of Virginia, 1997), 25.

6. Joan Didion, *Miami* (New York: Simon & Schuster, 1987), 33.

7. Portes and Stepick, *City on the Edge*, 61–65.

8. Marvin Dunn, *Black Miami in the Twentieth Century* (Gainesville: University Press of Florida, 1997), 19–25; and Portes and Stepick, *City on the Edge*, 68–69.

9. Dunn, *Black Miami*, 7; and Portes and Stepick, *City on the Edge*, 70–71.

10. Dunn, *Black Miami*, 7, 14–15.

11. Dunn, *Black Miami*, 1–2.

12. Croucher, *Imagining Miami*, 30; Dunn, *Black Miami*, 16–19, 51, 57, 60; and Connolly, *World More Concrete*, 19–20, 24–25.

13. Dunn, *Black Miami*, 61, 73–75; and Portes and Stepick, *City on the Edge*, 81.

14. "The Great Commoner's Palace in Miami," Florida Irish Heritage Center, August 18, 2010, https://floridairishheritagecenter.wordpress.com/2010/08/18/the-great-commoners-palace-in-miami/; and David Rieff, *Going to Miami: Exiles, Tourists, and Refugees in the New America* (Boston: Little, Brown, 1987), 26.

15. Croucher, *Imagining Miami*, 26; and Dunn, *Black Miami*, 77, 117–24, 143.

16. Connolly, *World More Concrete*, 31, 40–41, 52, 86.

17. Kenya Dworkin y Méndez, introduction to *Black Cuban, Black American: A Memoir*, by Evelio Grillo (Houston TX: Arte Público Press, 2000), viii–ix.

18. Rolando Alvarez Estévez, *La emigración Cubana en Estados Unidos, 1868–1878* (Havana: Editorial de Ciencias Sociales, 1986); Louis A. Pérez Jr., "Cubans in Tampa: From Exiles to Immigrants, 1892–1901," *Florida Historical Quarterly* 57, no. 2 (1978): 129; and Louis A. Pérez Jr., *Cuba between Empires, 1878–1902* (Pittsburgh: University of Pittsburgh Press, 1998), 96.

19. Grillo, *Black Cuban*, x–xi, 6–13, 39.

20. Interview with Dunn; Glenn Garvin, Michael J. Sainato, and Lance Dixon, "Remembering Protest that Led to Opening First Beach for Black Miamians," *Miami Herald*, May 9, 2015; and Dunn, *Black Miami*, 131, 160.

21. Chanelle N. Rose, *The Struggle for Black Freedom in Miami: Civil Rights and America's Tourist Paradise, 1896–1968* (Baton Rouge: Louisiana State University Press, 2015), 45–46, 185.

22. Connolly, *World More Concrete*, 208; and Rose, *Struggle for Black Freedom*, 180–81.

23. Dunn, *Black Miami*, 151; Croucher, *Imagining Miami*, 28–30; and Rose, *Struggle for Black Freedom*, 171.

24. Dunn, *Black Miami*, 158, 164–69; and Croucher, *Imagining Miami*, 31.

25. Interview with Dunn.

26. Dunn, *Black Miami*, 171; and interview with Dunn.

27. Connolly, *World More Concrete*, 205–8.

28. Interview with Dunn.

29. Dunn, *Black Miami*, 224, 230–33, 238, 246–50, 267–92; and Chanelle Nyree Rose, "Beyond 1959: Cuban Exiles, Race, and Miami's Black Freedom Struggle," in *Civil Rights and Beyond: African American and Latino/a Activism in the Twentieth-Century United States*, ed. Brian D. Behnken (Athens: University of Georgia Press, 2016), 70.

30. Rose, *Struggle for Black Freedom*, 92, 95, 175.

31. Portes and Stepick, *City on the Edge*, 87–88; and Dunn, *Black Miami*, 162.

32. Rose, *Struggle for Black Freedom*, 163–64, 170–71.

33. Raymond A. Mohl, "Race and Space in the Modern City: Interstate-95 and the Black Community in Miami," in *Urban Policy in Twentieth-Century America*, ed. Arnold R. Hirsch and Raymond A. Mohl (New Brunswick NJ: Rutgers University Press, 1993), 101–2, 108–9.

34. Mohl, "Race and Space," in Hirsch and Mohl, *Urban Policy*, 101, 110–13, 117–18, 122–23, 125; and Connolly, *World More Concrete*, 2, 214.

35. Mohl, "Race and Space," in Hirsch and Mohl, *Urban Policy*, 130.

36. Dunn, *Black Miami*, 170.

37. Connolly, *World More Concrete*, 11–12, 75–76, 224.

38. Frank Legree, interview by Madison Davis Lacy Jr., December 13, 1989, Eyes on the Prize II, Washington University Digital Gateway Texts, http://digital.wustl.edu/e/eii/eiiweb/leg5427.0356.093marc_record _interviewee_process.html.

39. García, *Havana USA*, 29.

40. C. P. Trussell, "U.S. May Deliver Cuba Exiles Here," *New York Times*, December 14, 1961, 12.

41. "Miami Perturbed By Cuba Refugees," *New York Times*, October 21, 1961, 5.

42. "Cubans in Miami Are U.S. Concern," *New York Times*, October 21, 1962, 41; and Iraida López, *Impossible Returns: Narratives of the Cuban Diaspora* (Gainesville: University Press of Florida, 2015), 35.

43. "Miami Perturbed By Cuba Refugees," 5.

44. Casavantes Bradford, *Revolution Is for the Children*, 190, 200–201.

45. Rose, "Beyond 1959," in Behnken, *Civil Rights and Beyond*, 70–71.

46. Rose, *Struggle for Black Freedom*, 218.

47. Letter to Frank M. Craft from Wave L. Perry, October 17, 1962, Series 325, Box 1, Folder: Cuban Refugee Assistance Program Miscellaneous Correspondence, 1962, ff7, SAF.

48. Comptroller General of the United States, "Report to the Congress of the United States: Financial Assistance Provided to Ineligible Cuban Refugees in the Miami, Florida, Area," December 1964, 1, Series 325, Box 1, Folder: General Accounting Office, ff8, SAF.

49. "Cuba's Refugees: The Steady Flow to Miami Is Creating Problems," *New York Times*, January 28, 1962.

50. Masud-Piloto, *With Open Arms*, 62–83; and Cortés, *Cuban Refugee Programs*, 129–33, 286.

51. Casavantes Bradford, *Revolution Is for the Children*, 200–201.

52. Juanita Greene, "Don't Blame Exiles for Joblessness, Say Negro Clerics," *Miami Herald*, April 6, 1963, OPP/CCP, Newspaper Clippings, Folder: April 1963, OPPC.

53. McCandlish Phillips, "Miami Economy Strained as Cubans Hunt for Jobs," *New York Times*, April 3, 1961, 1; memorandum to Diocesan Resettlement Directors and Directors of Special Cuban Refugee Committees from John E. McCarthy, Director, Department of Immigration United States Catholic Conference, April 25, 1967, BOW Papers, Personal Files, Appointments, Box 6, Folder: "Commission on Cuban Refugees, 1967

Jan.–April," OPPC; and Félix Masud-Piloto, *From Welcomed Exiles to Illegal Immigrants: Cuban Migration to the U.S., 1959–1995* (Totowa: Rowman & Littlefield, 1995), 63.

54. John Britton, "Cuban Refugees Take Jobs from Fla. Negroes," *Jet*, March 21, 1963, 18, https://books.google.com/books?id=A7wDAAAAMBAJ&pg=PA16&dq=jet+cuba+negro&hl=en&sa=X&ved=0ahUKEwjF3Kbm7bXRAhVj4YMKHX9mBysQ6AEIJDAC#v=onepage&q=jet%20cuba%20negro&f=false.

55. Rose, *Struggle for Black Freedom*, 189, 191, 197.

56. Letter to Skillin from BOW, OPPC.

57. Britton, "Cuban Refugees Take Jobs," 14, 16.

58. Cortés, *Cuban Refugee Programs*, 274.

59. Britton, "Cuban Refugees Take Jobs," 18.

60. Britton, "Cuban Refugees Take Jobs," 114, 138, 287, 290.

61. Rose, "Beyond 1959," in Behnken, *Civil Rights and Beyond*, 68–69, 75–76.

62. Brewer, *Questioning the Cuban Exile Model*, 2–3, 12.

63. Interview with T. Willard Fair, June 21, 2016, Miami Urban League Central Office; and T. Willard Fair, "T. Willard Fair Was the 'Muhammad Ali of Black Dade County,'" *Miami Herald*, October 6, 2013.

64. Fair, "'Muhammad Ali of Black Dade County.'"

65. Interview with Fair.

66. Interview with Fair.

67. Interview with Dunn; and Dunn, *Black Miami*, 319–20.

68. Brewer, *Questioning the Cuban Exile Model*, 14.

69. Email correspondence with Simms.

70. Interview with Dunn.

71. R. Hart Phillips, "Miami Is Going Latin as Cubans Make Their Effect Felt in City," *New York Times*, March 18, 1962, 85.

72. Didion, *Miami*, 63.

73. Portes and Stepick, *City on the Edge*, 144; and letter to Skillin from BOW, OPPC.

74. Letter to BOW [no sender signature, probably Ray W. Davies, minister of LeJeune Presbyterian Church in Miami], October 25, 1965, BOW Papers, Personal Files, Correspondence, Box 20, Folder: BOW Correspondence, 1963–1965, OPPC.

75. Letter to Reverend Ray W. Davies, Minister of LeJeune Presbyterian Church in Miami, from BOW, October 26, 1965, BOW Papers, Personal Files, Correspondence, Box 20, Folder: BOW Correspondence, 1963–1965, OPPC.

6. Operation Pedro Pan in Cuba

1. Interview with Alvaro.
2. Interview with Alvaro; and email correspondence with Raul Alvaro, February 10, 2017.
3. Triay, *Fleeing Castro*, 2–9. The Bayamo pact was reported in *Time*, October 6, 1961.
4. Bravo, *Operación Peter Pan*, segment 2.
5. Shnookal, *Operation Pedro Pan*, 112–13.
6. Shnookal, *Operation Pedro Pan*, 105.
7. Shnookal, *Operation Pedro Pan*, 107–8.
8. Baker interview by Gonzalez-Pando, part 1, FIU CLHP.
9. Dulce María Iglesias de Martínez, "Mis Hijas Vinieron Solas en la Operación Peter Pan," accessed February 25, 2022, https://pedropanca .tripod.com/cubankidsfromthe60sexodus2/id16.html.
10. Shnookal, *Operation Pedro Pan*, 63–65.
11. Conde, *Operation Pedro Pan*, xi. For more on this history, see Dorothy Legarreta, *The Guernica Generation: Basque Refugee Children of the Spanish Civil War* (Reno: University of Nevada Press, 1984).
12. Dubinsky, *Babies without Borders*, 56.
13. Torres, *Lost Apple*, 4; and Conde, *Operation Pedro Pan*, xi–xii.
14. Laura Briggs, *Somebody's Children: The Politics of Transracial and Transnational Adoption* (Durham NC: Duke University Press, 2012), 150.
15. Gómez Cortés, *Operación Peter Pan*, 14; and Baker interview by Gonzalez-Pando, part 1, FIU CLHP.
16. Eire, *Waiting for Snow*, 270–71; and Gómez Cortés, *Operación Peter Pan*, 14.
17. María Vidal de Haymes, "Operation Pedro Pan: One Family's Journey to the U.S.," in *Poverty and Inequality in the Latin America-U.S. Borderlands: Implications of U.S. Interventions*, ed. Keith M. Kilty and Elizabeth A. Segal (New York: Hayworth Press, 2004), 119–23.
18. Baker, "Journey out of the Past."
19. Torres, *Lost Apple*, 4–5; Masud-Piloto, *With Open Arms*, 39; and Bryan O. Walsh, "Cuban Refugee Children," *Journal of Interamerican Studies and World Affairs* 13, no. 3/4 (July–October 1971): 381–94.
20. Gómez Cortés, *Operación Peter Pan*, 218.
21. Fabián Escalante, *The Cuba Project: CIA Covert Operations, 1960–1962*, trans. Maxine Shaw (New York: Ocean Press, 2004), 112.
22. Casavantes Bradford, *Revolution Is for the Children*, 151.

23. David Atlee Phillips, *The Night Watch* (New York: Atheneum, 1977), 35, 40–53, 60, 80–81.

24. Phillips, *Night Watch*, 86, 88, 90, 96–97; Dubinsky, *Babies without Borders*, 25–26; Torreira and Buajasán, *Operación Peter Pan*, 25–26, 90–91, 92n32, 93; Juan Carlos Rodríguez, *The Inevitable Battle: From the Bay of Pigs to Play Girón*, trans. Rose Ana Berbeo (Havana: Editorial Capitán San Luis, 2009), 56–57; and "American Radio in the Caribbean Counters Red Campaign in Cuba," *New York Times*, September 9, 1960, 1, 2.

25. Torres, *Lost Apple*, 43.

26. Portes and Stepick, *City on the Edge*, 126; Casavantes Bradford, *Revolution Is for the Children*, 152–53; García, *Havana USA*, 125–26; Jon Elliston, *Psywar on Cuba: The Declassified History of U.S. Anti-Castro Propaganda* (Melbourne: Ocean Press, 1999), 47; Rodríguez, *Inevitable Battle*, 2; Didion, *Miami*, 88–90, 167; and Lourdes Arguelles, "Cuban Miami: The Roots, Development, and Everyday Life of Emigré Enclave in the U.S. National Security State," *Contemporary Marxism* 5 (Summer 1982): 31.

27. Torres v. C.I.A., No. 98 C 149, 39 F.Supp.2d 960 (1999), http://www.leagle.com/decision/199999939FSupp2d960_1906; Torres v. C.I.A., No. 98 C 149, 29 F.Supp.2d 497 (1998), accessed July 30, 2017, http://www.leagle.com/decision/199852629FSupp2d497_1459; and Baker, "Journey out of the Past."

28. Torres, *Lost Apple*, 55, 89–93, 179–80, quote on p. 180.

29. Torreira and Buajasán, *Operación Peter Pan*.

30. Rodríguez, *Inevitable Battle*, 60–61.

31. Gómez Cortés, *Operación Peter Pan*, 7, 227, 229–30, 253, 256, 262–63.

32. Walsh, "Un Católico Americano," in de la Cuesta and Herrera, *Razón y pasión*, 26; Gómez Cortés, *Operación Peter Pan*, 210; and Baker, "Journey out of the Past."

33. Elliston, *Psywar on Cuba*, 3.

34. Gómez Cortés, *Operación Peter Pan*, 127, 129–32, 135–39.

35. Torreira and Buajasán, *Operación Peter Pan*, 191.

36. Bell, "Operation Pedro Pan," 10.

37. Conde, *Operation Pedro Pan*, 57, 65.

38. Torreira and Buajasán, *Operación Peter Pan*, 119–20, 157n10, 158, 197.

39. Rodríguez, *Inevitable Battle*, 62.

40. Ramón "Mongo" Grau Alsina and Valerie Ridderhoff, *Mongo Grau: Cuba desde 1930* (Madrid: Agualarga Editores, 1997), 9–11.

41. Grau and Ridderhoff, *Mongo Grau*, 32–33, 128–29, 134–38, 141.

42. Conde, *Operation Pedro Pan*, 61; and Torreira and Buajasán, *Operación Peter Pan*, 232–33.

43. Torres, *Lost Apple*, 79–80, 83–85; Conde, *Operation Pedro Pan*, 59–70; Blázquez and Sutton, "Operation Peter Pan"; Grau and Ridderhoff, *Mongo Grau*, 128, 137–39, 141, 146, 155–57, 239; and Shnookal, *Operation Pedro Pan*, 172.

44. Grau and Ridderhoff, *Mongo Grau*, 146, 149, 152–53.

45. Grau and Ridderhoff, *Mongo Grau*, 152–53.

46. Torres, *Lost Apple*, 131–32; and Grau and Ridderhoff, *Mongo Grau*, 157.

47. Gómez Cortés, *Operación Peter Pan*, 27–28.

48. "Memo to BOW from Unknown," April 24, 1962, OPP/CCP, Administrative Files, Series A, Folder: Memorandum, Feb–Aug 1962, OPPC.

49. Shnookal, *Operation Pedro Pan*, 169.

50. Gómez Cortés, *Operación Peter Pan*, 235–40, 242–43.

51. Triay, *Fleeing Castro*, 40; Torreira and Buajasán, *Operación Peter Pan*, 200–201; and Torres, *Lost Apple*, 134–36.

52. Baker interview by Gonzalez-Pando, part 2, FIU CLHP.

53. Gómez Cortés, *Operación Peter Pan*, 24, 223–24; Conde, *Operation Pedro Pan*, 59, 70; and Torres, *Lost Apple*, 71.

54. First Research Corporation, "Report on Accounting & Organization Study and Consultation in Connection with Cuban Children's Program," January 1962, 4, 6, Chart A, Appendix, BOW Papers, BOW Works by Others, Folder: Report on Accounting & Organization Study and Consultation in Connection with Cuban Children's Program 1962, OPPC.

55. Letter to Mike McCann from BOW, March 22, 1963, BOW Papers, Personal Files, Correspondence, Box 20, Folder: BOW Correspondence, 1963–1965, OPPC.

56. Letter to M. D. W. McCann Esq., M.B.E. from Walsh, January 4, 1967, BOW Papers, Personal Files, Correspondence, Box 20, Folder: BOW Correspondence, 1966–1967, OPPC.

57. Gómez Cortés, *Operación Peter Pan*, 222–23.

58. Torres, *Lost Apple*, 81–82, 135; Triay, *Fleeing Castro*, 36–37; Operation Pedro Pan Group, "History of Operation Pedro Pan"; and Gómez Cortés, *Operación Peter Pan*, 222–23, 245–52.

59. Torres, *Lost Apple*, 82; and Conde, *Operation Pedro Pan*, 62.

60. García, *Havana USA*, 24.

61. García, *Havana USA*, 25.

62. Torreira and Buajasán, *Operación Peter Pan*, 98, n. 41, 209; and Triay, *Fleeing Castro*, 40.

63. Conde, *Operation Pedro Pan*, 69; García, *Havana USA*, 25; Carol Rosenberg, "Ramón Grau, Organizer of Cuban Kids' Flight, Dies," *Miami Herald*, November 4, 1998, 1B, 4B; and Gómez Cortés, *Operación Peter Pan*, 25.

7. A Brief History of Intimate Ties

1. Interview with García.

2. Didion, *Miami*, 84.

3. Schoultz, *That Infernal Little Cuban Republic*, 18–19.

4. Transcript of the Platt Amendment (1903), accessed April 13, 2017, https://www.ourdocuments.gov/doc.php?doc=55&page=transcript.

5. Louis A. Pérez Jr., *On Becoming Cuban: Identity, Nationality, and Culture* (New York: Ecco Press, 1999), 37, 75–83.

6. Pérez, *On Becoming Cuban*, 18, 22, 30–32.

7. Pérez, *On Becoming Cuban*, 126–29.

8. Marial Iglesias Utset, *A Cultural History of Cuba during the U.S. Occupation, 1898–1902*, trans. Russ Davidson (Chapel Hill: University of North Carolina Press, 2011), 33–35, 50–51.

9. Iglesias Utset, *Cultural History of Cuba*, 1–3, 21–24.

10. Pérez, *On Becoming Cuban*, 221.

11. Robert Whitney, *State and Revolution in Cuba: Mass Mobilization and Political Change, 1920–1940* (Chapel Hill: University of North Carolina Press, 2000), 24; and Louis A. Pérez Jr., *Cuba under the Platt Amendment, 1902–1934* (Pittsburgh: University of Pittsburgh Press, 1986), 187–89.

12. Pérez, *On Becoming Cuban*, 359–61, 372–73.

13. Quote in Louis A. Pérez Jr., *Cuba in the American Imagination: Metaphor and the Imperial Ethos* (Chapel Hill: University of North Carolina Press, 2008), 100–101.

14. Schoultz, *That Infernal Little Cuban Republic*, 27.

15. Sumner Welles, *Relations between the United States and Cuba* (Washington DC: Government Printing Office, 1934), 3.

16. Schoultz, *That Infernal Little Cuban Republic*, 7

17. "Cuba: The First 100 Days," *Time*, April 20, 1959; and *Time*, October 3, 1960, cover.

18. Quoted in Richard E. Welch Jr., *Response to Revolution: The United States and the Cuban Revolution, 1959–1961* (Chapel Hill: University of North Carolina Press, 1985), 35.

19. Schoultz, *That Infernal Little Cuban Republic*, 90.

8. A National Test

1. García, "40 Years/40 Lessons (2)."
2. R. Hart Phillips, "Plan to Resettle Cuban Refugees across Nation Started in Miami," *New York Times*, January 6, 1962, 3.
3. Monsignor Walsh provided data to the subcommittee that became part of its files but not of the public transcript. "Cuban Refugee Problems," Hearings before the Subcommittee to Investigate Problems Connected with Refugees and Escapees, U.S. Senate, 87th Congress, December 6, 1961, in Cortés, *Cuban Refugee Programs*, 3–4, 7; and letter to BOW from Philip A. Hart, Chairman of Subcommittee on Refugees and Escapees, January 8, 1962, BOW Papers, Personal Files, Correspondence, Box 20, Folder I, BOW Correspondence, 1947–1962, OPPC.
4. Torres, *Lost Apple*, 123–24, 210–11.
5. Cortés, *Cuban Refugee Programs*, 12, 35–36, 45–48.
6. Torreira and Buajasán, *Operación Peter Pan*, 116–17.
7. "Senator Kennedy Greets Arriving Refugees," *Resettlement Re-cap*, April 1967, 1, Series 325, Box 2, Folder: Publications—Resettlement Re-cap CRA, ff1, SAF.
8. Keith Wheeler, "A Failure That We Must Recoup: 'Hell of a Beating' in Cuba," *Life*, April 28, 1961, 17–25.
9. "'Secret' Cuban Revolt Comes out in the Open," *Life*, April 14, 1961, 28–33.
10. International Rescue Committee advertisement, *Reader's Digest*, August 1961, 253.
11. "With Faith, and Parish Kindness, Refugees Succeed, Finding a Life of Freedom in Michigan," *Resettlement Re-cap*, March 1969, 1, Series 325, Box 2, Folder: Publications—Resettlement Re-cap CRA, ff1, SAF.
12. Letter from Norine B. Richey to Abraham Ribicoff, June 8, 1962, and letter to Norine B. Richey from Martha H. Hynning, July 24, 1962, Folder: June 1962, Refugee Problems, 1958–1962, RG 102, Records of the Children's Bureau, Central File, 1958–1962, Box 760, NN3-102-83-1, NARA.
13. Letter to Fern Pence from Ana Anders, July 26, 1961, Series 325, Box 1, Folder: Cuban Refugee—Reports, Letters, Newspaper Articles, ff5, SAF.
14. Letter to Fern Pence from Mirtha Sierra, August 11, 1961, Series 325, Box 1, Folder: Cuban Refugee—Reports, Letters, Newspaper Articles, ff5, SAF.
15. Letter to Fern M. Pence from Gustavo Alonso de la Torre, August 4, 1961, Series 325, Box 1, Folder: Cuban Refugee—Reports, Letters, Newspaper Articles, ff5, SAF.

16. Letter to John F. Kennedy from Gerardo Ameijeiras, August 30, 1962, Folder: August 1962, Refugee Problems, 1958–1962, RG 102, Records of the Children's Bureau, Central File, 1958–1962, Box 760, NN3-102-83-1, NARA.

17. Letter to Jacqueline Kennedy from José L. Hernández, August 24, 1962, and letter to José L. Hernández from Mildred Arnold, October 18, 1962, Folder: Aug. 1962, Refugee Problems, 1958–1962, RG 102, Records of the Children's Bureau, Central File, 1958–1962, Box 760, NN3-102-83-1, NARA.

18. Letter to Aurelio Pineiro from Robert Kennedy, March 12, 1963; letter to Aurelio Pineiro from Robert Kennedy, August 2, 1963; and letter to Robert Kennedy from Aurelio Pineiro, June 30, 1963—all in Folder: Cuban Refugee Children, Correspondence, RG 363, Records of the Social and Rehabilitation Service, Unaccompanied Cuban Children's Refugee Program, 1961–1967, Box 2, NN3-363-095-001, NARA.

19. Letters found in Folder: June 1962, Refugee Problems, 1958–1962, RG 102, Records of the Children's Bureau, Central File, 1958–1962, Box 760, NN3-102-83-1, NARA; and letter to Senator Paul Douglas from Vivian Poe, June 3, 1962, Folder: June 1962, Refugee Problems, 1958–1962, RG 102, Records of the Children's Bureau, Central File, 1958–1962, Box 760, NN3-102-83-1, NARA.

20. CWB, "Contract for Provision of Foster Care for Unaccompanied Cuban Refugee Children," n.d., 1961, Folder: Refugee Problems, 1958–1962, RG 102, Records of the Children's Bureau, Central File, 1958–1962, Box 761, NN3-102-83-1, NARA.

21. Letter to John F. Kennedy from Sally Oston, July 27, 1961, Folder: Refugee Problems, 1958–1962, RG 102, Records of the Children's Bureau, Central File, 1958–1962, Box 761, NN3-102-83-1, NARA.

22. Letter to Abraham Ribicoff from Alfred H. Schultz, July 6, 1962, and letter to Alfred H. Schultz from Mildred Arnold, August 27, 1962, Folder: Aug. 1962, Refugee Problems, 1958–1962, Records of the Children's Bureau, Central File, 1958–1962, Box 760, NN3-102-83-1, NARA.

23. Documents passim. Series 897, Box 1 (Correspondence with other states regarding placement of children, 1959–1970), Folder: Correspondence Colorado, SAF.

24. Letter to Frances Davis from Charles B. Rovin, Chief, Branch of Welfare at U.S. Dept of the Interior, Bureau of Indian Affairs, Series 897, Box 1 (Correspondence with other states regarding placement of children 1959–1970), Folder: Correspondence Arizona, SAF.

25. "Cuban Children Helped in Florida," 41.

26. Memorandum from Dorothea F. Sullivan to Joan Gross, December 3, 1963, OPP/CCP, Administrative Files, Series A, Folder: Memorandum, Sept–Dec 1963, OPPC.

27. Letter from P. H. Powers to Philip Bonsal, April 3, 1961, OPP/CCP, Subject Files, Series E, Folder: Powers, P. H., 1961, 1968, OPPC.

28. Letter from P. H. Powers to W. L. Mitchell, April 3, 1961, OPP/CCP, Subject Files, Series E, Folder: Powers, P. H., 1961, 1968, OPPC.

29. BOW, "A Statement Prepared by Father Bryan O. Walsh, Director, in Connection with Certain Criticisms of the Program Made by Miss P. H. Powers, of Havana, Cuba," n.d., OPP/CCP, Subject Files, Series E, Folder: Powers, P. H., 1961, 1968, OPPC.

30. Letter from Dorothy McCrary to BOW et al., July 31, 1962, OPP/CCP, Subject Files, Series E, Folder: CC Program History 1960–1967, 1980, OPPC.

31. Letter to BOW from Jesús Hazas, June 14, 1965, Folder: Cuban Refugee Children, Florida State Agency, Correspondence—General, January 1, 1965–December 31, 1965, RG 363, Records of the Social and Rehabilitation Service, Unaccompanied Cuban Children's Refugee Program, 1961–1967, Box 3, NN3-363-095-001, NARA.

9. Cold War Childhood

1. Personal interviews, Villa Maria, Muchachitas de: Polita Grau, Pury Lopez Santiago (1997 35th anniversary, 1962–97), FIU CLHP VHS 502, FISP005176, Special Collections; interview with Lopez Santiago; email correspondence with Lopez Santiago; and John Paul Rathbone, *The Sugar King of Havana: The Rise and Fall of Julio Lobo, Cuba's Last Tycoon* (New York: Penguin, 2010), 1, 12.

2. Kriste Lindenmeyer, "Children, the State, and the American Dream," in *Reinventing Childhood after World War II*, ed. Paula S. Fass and Michael Grossberg (Philadelphia: University of Pennsylvania Press, 2012), 94.

3. Holt, *Cold War Kids*, 5–6.

4. John E. B. Myers, *A History of Child Protection in America* (Philadelphia: Xlibris, 2004), 17.

5. Lori Askeland, "Informal Adoption, Apprentices, and Indentured Children in the Colonial Era and the New Republic, 1605–1850," in *Children and Youth in Adoption, Orphanages, and Foster Care: A Historical Handbook and Guide,* ed. Lori Askeland (Westport CT: Greenwood Press, 2006), 7–10, 14; Myers, *History of Child Protection*, 17, 37–42; and Ellen Herman, *Kinship by Design: A History of Adoption in the Modern United States* (Chicago: University of Chicago Press, 2008), 21.

6. Myers, *History of Child Protection*, 46–47, 51–52.

7. Marilyn Irvin Holt, "Adoption Reform, Orphan Trains, and Child-Saving, 1851–1929," in Askeland, *Children and Youth in Adoption*, 17–19, 21. Irvin Holt also points out that many children were of immigrants whose poor understanding of English led them to agree to relocation arrangements they did not fully understand. Thus, children were taken from these parents under specious conditions (p. 25). See also Herman, *Kinship by Design*, 24.

8. Paula S. Fass, *The End of American Childhood: A History of Parenting from Life on the Frontier to the Managed Child* (Princeton NJ: Princeton University Press, 2016), 86–95.

9. Myers, *History of Child Protection*, 78–80, 87, 101, 194.

10. Irvin Holt, "Adoption Reform," in Askeland, *Children and Youth in Adoption*, 23–25; and Herman, *Kinship by Design*, 56–58.

11. Fieldston, *Raising the World*, 14–16.

12. Myers, *History of Child Protection*, 197.

13. Dianne Creagh, "Science, Social Work, and Bureaucracy: Cautious Developments in Adoption and Foster Care, 1930–1969," in Askeland, *Children and Youth in Adoption*, 32–34.

14. Briggs, *Somebody's Children*, 131–36.

15. Fass, *Children of a New World*, 170.

16. Herman, *Kinship by Design*, 22.

17. Ressler, Boothby, and Steinbock, *Unaccompanied Children*, 198–200.

18. Fass, *End of American Childhood*, 106, 181, 182–84, 190–91.

19. Paula S. Fass, "The Child-Centered Family? New Rules in Postwar America," in Fass and Grossberg, *Reinventing Childhood*, 5, 10–12.

20. Holt, *Cold War Kids*, 85–86, 93, 114, 148.

21. Anita Casavantes Bradford, "Remembering Pedro Pan: Childhood and Collective Memory Making in Havana and Miami, 1960–2000," *Cuban Studies* 44, no. 1 (2016): 283–308.

22. Casavantes Bradford, *Revolution Is for the Children*.

23. Casavantes Bradford, *Revolution Is for the Children*, 96.

24. "Bertha and Harry Holt," The Adoption History Project, updated February 24, 2012, http://pages.uoregon.edu/adoption/people/holt.htm.

25. Dubinsky, *Babies without Borders*, 93–94; and Creagh, "Science, Social Work, and Bureaucracy," in Askeland, *Children and Youth in Adoption*, 39.

26. Briggs, *Somebody's Children*, 150.

27. Fieldston, *Raising the World*, 19, 55–56, 58, 82–83.

28. Myers, *History of Child Protection*, 206, 218–19, 280–83, 287.
29. Myers, *History of Child Protection*, 210–11, 296.
30. Creagh, "Science, Social Work, and Bureaucracy," in Askeland, *Children and Youth in Adoption*, 34, 36.
31. Fieldston, *Raising the World*, 106–7.
32. "Marshall D. Schechter, 'Observations on Adopted Children,' 1960," The Adoption History Project, updated February 24, 2012, http://pages .uoregon.edu/adoption/studies/SchechterOAC.htm.
33. Margaret Peacock, *Innocent Weapons: The Soviet and American Politics of Childhood in the Cold War* (Chapel Hill: University of North Carolina Press, 2014), 1.
34. Peacock, *Innocent Weapons*, 4.
35. Peacock, *Innocent Weapons*, 4–5, 42–43.
36. Fieldston, *Raising the World*, 98–103.
37. Elaine Tyler May, *Homeward Bound: Americans in the Cold War Era* (New York: Basic Books, 1988), 3, 13–14, 18–19.
38. "October 13, 1960: The Third Kennedy-Nixon Presidential Debate," Commission on Presidential Debates, accessed February 25, 2022, https:// www.debates.org/voter-education/debate-transcripts/october-13-1960 -debate-transcript/.
39. Christina Klein, *Cold War Orientalism: Asia in the Middlebrow Imagination, 1945–1961* (Berkeley: University of California Press, 2003), ch. 4, 144–52.
40. Jodi Kim, "An 'Orphan' with Two Mothers: Transnational and Transracial Adoption, the Cold War, and Contemporary Asian American Cultural Politics," *American Quarterly* 61, no. 4 (December 2009): 855–80.
41. R. Hart Phillips, "'Castro Freed Cuba from U.S.' Is 'Correct' Answer in Havana," *New York Times*, June 8, 1960, 12; and C. P. Trussell, "Abuse of Parents Charged to Cuba," *New York Times*, December 8, 1961, 24.
42. "Cubans in U.S. Seek Toys for Refugees," *New York Times*, November 29, 1961, 25.
43. Michelle Chase, *Revolution within the Revolution: Women and Gender Politics in Cuba, 1952–1962* (Chapel Hill: University of North Carolina Press, 2015), 1, 77–78.
44. Casavantes Bradford, *Revolution Is for the Children*, ch. 1.
45. Casavantes Bradford, *Revolution Is for the Children*, 48–49, 84.
46. Fidel Castro Ruz, "Otra vez Fidel Castro se dirige a los artistas," *Obra revolucionaria*, September 27, 1961, 18.
47. Castro Ruz, "Otra vez Fidel Castro," 23.

48. "Patria potestad y ensenanza privada," *Revolución*, October 28, 1960, 1, 6; "Crearán oficinas del registro civil," *Revolución*, October 4, 1960, 3; "Serán unidas en matrimonio cuatrocientas mil parejas," *Revolución*, November 22, 1960, 13; and Ricardo Solano, "Operación bautizo colectivo," *Bohemia*, September 17, 1961, 14–15.

49. Torreira and Buajasán, *Operación Peter Pan*, 310–11; and Fidel Castro, "Si de alguién se ha ocupado la revolución ha sido de los ninos," *Bohemia*, September 24, 1961, 70–75, 81.

50. Castro Ruz, "Otra vez Fidel Castro," 9–24.

51. Chase, *Revolution within the Revolution*, 61.

52. Chase, *Revolution within the Revolution*, 174–75.

53. Casavantes Bradford, *Revolution Is for the Children*, 40–41.

54. Casavantes Bradford, *Revolution Is for the Children*, 93–94.

55. Armando Hart, "La revolución y los problemas de la educación," *Cuba Socialista*, December 1961, 34.

56. Tomás Sena, "¡Hablan los Padres!," *Bohemia*, October 15, 1961, 16–18.

57. Elizabeth Sutherland, *The Youngest Revolution: A Personal Report on Cuba* (New York: Dial Press, 1969), 14.

58. Dubinsky, *Babies without Borders*, 26.

59. Maret and Aschkenas, "Operation Pedro Pan."

60. Dubinsky, *Babies without Borders*, 49.

61. Gómez Cortés, *Operación Peter Pan*, 188–89, 292.

62. Shnookal, *Operation Pedro Pan*, 114.

63. Conde, *Operation Pedro Pan*, 193.

64. Shnookal, *Operation Pedro Pan*, 204.

65. Conde, *Operation Pedro Pan*, 193–94.

66. Letter to "sir" [no addressee] from Marion Hill, October 10, 1962, Series 897, Box 2, Folder: Alabama-Connecticut Foster Parent Inquiries, SAF.

67. Letter to Frances Davis, Director, Division of Child Welfare FSDPW, from Mrs. Edward Gresham, Director, Bureau of Child Welfare at State of Alabama Dept. of Pensions and Security, August 29, 1961, Series 897, Box 1 (Correspondence with other states regarding placement of children 1959–1970), Folder: Correspondence Alabama, SAF.

68. Memorandum to Frances Davis from Louise A. Alpert, July 5, 1962, Series 897, Box 1 (Correspondence with other states regarding placement of children 1959–1970), Folder: Correspondence Arizona, SAF; and letter to Abraham Ribicoff from M. J. Ackerson, April 2, 1962, Series 897, Box 2, Folder: Delaware-Iowa Foster Parent Inquiries, SAF.

69. Memorandum from BOW to Dr. Sheppard, July 22, 1970, OPP/CCP, Subject Files, Series E, Folder: Adoption Policy, 1970–1972, OPPC.

70. "Refugee Children Placed throughout Diocese."

71. Jim Conner, "Young Refugees Here from Cuba," *Pueblo (CO) Star-Journal and Sunday Chieftain*, March 25, 1962, 1D, OPP/CCP, Newspaper Clippings, OPPC.

72. Mary Louise Wilkinson, "They Left Cuban Parents, Came to Miami Alone," *Miami News*, February 18, 1962, 3B, OPP/CCP, Newspaper Clippings, Folder: February 1962, OPPC.

73. Program for "White Christmas Snow," December 23, 1965, Folder: Cuban Refugee Children, Florida State Agency, Correspondence—General, January 1, 1965–December 31, 1965, RG 363, Records of the Social and Rehabilitation Service, Unaccompanied Cuban Children's Refugee Program, 1961–1967, Box 3, NN3-363-095-001, NARA.

74. Phillips, "14,072 Children," 2.

75. "Detroit Joining Drive to House Cuban Children," *Michigan Catholic*, March 15, 1962, 1.

76. Kathryn Close, "Cuban Children away from Home," in Cortés, *Cuban Refugee Programs*, 6–9.

77. U.S. Children's Bureau, "Cuba's Children in Exile," in Cortés, *Cuban Refugee Programs*, 8–9.

78. "Memo to Florida City House Parents and Social Workers from BOW," February 19, 1964, OPP/CCP, Administrative Files, Series D, Folder: Florida City Shelter, 1964–1966, OPPC.

79. Letter to BOW from Sullivan, October 26, 1962, OPPC.

80. Memo to Dorothea F. Sullivan from A. S. [?] Zahn, July 18, 1963, OPP/CCP, Administrative Files, Series A, Folder: Memorandum, Dorothea F. Sullivan, Director of Social Services, 1963–1964, OPPC.

81. Ferguson, "Unwanted Children Find Love."

82. Torres, *Lost Apple*, 3, 180–82.

83. Cliff Solway, *The Lost Apple* (English), produced by David Susskind, Talent Associates–Paramount Ltd, 1963, OPPC.

84. Letter to Dorothea Sullivan from Fred Wardenburg of Talent Associates, BOW Papers, Subject Files, Lo-Na, Box 32, Folder: The Lost Apple, 1963–1966, OPPC.

85. "WTVJ / Miami, 'The Day Ralph Renick Died,'" aired July 12, 1991, on WTVJ, https://www.youtube.com/watch?v=06U7uhK1YS4.

86. "The Plight of Pepito: Cuba's Lost Generation," July 27, 1961, WTVJ News Special Program, Louis Wolfson II Florida Moving Image Archive, OPPC.

10. For God and Country

1. Interview with Cepero.
2. William Inboden, *Religion and American Foreign Policy, 1945–1960: The Soul of Containment* (New York: Cambridge University Press, 2008), 5.
3. Inboden, *Religion and American Foreign Policy*, 1, 29, 58–59, 257.
4. Torreira and Buajasán, *Operación Pan*, 137; and Walsh, "Un Católico Americano," in de la Cuesta and Herrera, *Razón y pasión*, 26.
5. Shnookal, *Operation Pedro Pan*, 45.
6. John M. Kirk, *Between God and the Party: Religion and Politics in Revolutionary Cuba* (Tampa: University of South Florida Press, 1989), 26–30, 34–35, 40.
7. Kirk, *Between God and the Party*, 38, 53–56; and Casavantes Bradford, *Revolution Is for the Children*, 24–25.
8. Pérez, *On Becoming Cuban*, 55–60, 247–55; and Lillian Guerra, *Visions of Power in Cuba: Revolution, Redemption, and Resistance, 1959–1971* (Chapel Hill: University of North Carolina Press, 2012), 148.
9. Casavantes Bradford, *Revolution Is for the Children*, 35–36.
10. Pérez, *On Becoming Cuban*, 33–34, 400–404; and Triay, *Fleeing Castro*, 3.
11. Casavantes Bradford, *Revolution Is for the Children*, 40–41, 84, 99–107, 111–15, 185–87.
12. Kirk, *Between God and the Party*, 40–45.
13. Michael J. McNally, *Catholicism in South Florida, 1868–1968* (Gainesville: University of Florida Press, 1982), 128–29; Kirk, *Between God and the Party*, 46, 48–49, 51, 53, 65–67; and Margaret E. Crahan, "Cuba: Religion and Revolutionary Institutionalization," *Journal of Latin American Studies* 17, no. 2 (November 1985): 321.
14. Crahan, "Cuba," 323–25; and Guerra, *Visions of Power*, 94, 135.
15. Chase, *Revolution within the Revolution*, 46.
16. Kirk, *Between God and the Party*, 43, 68, 71, 77; and Guerra, *Visions of Power*, 112–16.
17. Crahan, "Cuba," 319–21.
18. Kirk, *Between God and the Party*, 82, 100.
19. Torreira and Buajasán, *Operación Peter Pan*, 7, 11–12, 17, 21, 292–95.
20. Kirk, *Between God and the Party*, 87; and Guerra, *Visions of Power*, 147.
21. Crahan, "Cuba," 328.
22. Guerra, *Visions of Power*, 94; Escalante, *Cuba Project*, 51; Rodríguez, *Inevitable Battle*, 28–29; Kirk, *Between God and the Party*, 84–86; R. Hart Phillips, "Cuban Cathedral Invaded by Mobs," *New York Times*,

November 14, 1960, 1, 5; "Havana Steps Up Attacks on Church," *New York Times*, September 13, 1961, 1, 23; "Cuba: The Awakening Church," *Time*, November 28, 1960, http://content.time.com/time/subscriber/article/0 ,33009,871833,00.html; "And Now the Children?," *Time*, October 6, 1961, http://www.time.com/time/magazine/article/0,9171,827800,00.html; and "Memorandum for General Taylor from Allen Dulles," March 10, 1961, 5, https://www.cia.gov/readingroom/document/0000481613.

23. Kirk, *Between God and the Party*, 95–99.

24. Kirk, *Between God and the Party*, 103, 112.

25. Casavantes Bradford, *Revolution Is for the Children*, 50, 88–90; McNally, *Catholicism in South Florida*, 131–33; and Castro, "Si de alguién se ha ocu- pado," 70–75, 81.

26. Letter to BOW from Coleman O. Carroll, Bishop of Miami, October 9, 1961, BOW Papers, Personal Files, Correspondence, Box 20, Folder: BOW Correspondence, 1947–1962, OPPC.

27. Operation Pedro Pan Group, "History of Operation Pedro Pan."

28. Escalante, *Cuba Project*, 153.

29. Crahan, "Cuba," 326–28.

30. Torreira and Buajasán, *Operación Peter Pan*, 21, 292–95.

31. Guerra, *Visions of Power*, 145.

32. Rodríguez, *Inevitable Battle*, 31.

33. Triay, *Fleeing Castro*, 4.

34. Shnookal, *Operation Pedro Pan*, 49.

35. "Raul Castro Declares Priests Called for Strike by Students," *New York Times*, February 8, 1961, 8; and Guerra, *Visions of Power*, 146.

36. Fidel Castro Ruiz, "Castro Radio and TV Interview," *Revolución*, Havana, July 6, 1961, LANIC (Latin American Network Information Center) Cas- tro Speech Data Base (CSDB): Speeches, Interviews, Articles, 1959–1966, http://lanic.utexas.edu/project/castro/db/1961/19610706.html; and "Cas- tro Scores Escambray Revolutionaries," Havana, January 28, 1961, LANIC CSDB: Speeches, Interviews, Articles, 1959–1966, http://lanic.utexas.edu /project/castro/db/1961/19610128.html.

37. R. Hart Phillips, "Cuba Opens Drive for Cane Cutters," *New York Times*, January 30, 1961, 10.

38. Conde, *Operation Pedro Pan*, 32; and McNally, *Catholicism in South Flor- ida*, 135–37.

39. Alejandro Anreus, "Catholic Cuba: From Las Casa to the Castros," *Commonweal*, August 2, 2016, https://www.commonwealmagazine.org /catholic-cuba.

40. Colleen McDannell, *The Spirit of Vatican II: A History of Catholic Reform in America* (New York: Basic Books, 2011), 23.

41. Thies Schulze, "Charles Edward Coughlin and the Vatican," in *The Culture of Catholicism in the United States*, ed. Saskia Hertlein and Hermann Josef Schnackertz, American Studies monograph series (Heidelberg: Universitätsverlag), vol. 213 (Winter 2012): 237.

42. David J. O'Brien, *The Renewal of American Catholicism* (New York: Oxford University Press, 1972), 45.

43. O'Brien, *Renewal of American Catholicism*, 6; McDannell, *Spirit of Vatican II*, 6, 35–36, 39, 45–47, 64; and Elizabeth A. Harris, "First Days of School, Decade by Decade," *New York Times*, September 8, 2015, https://www.nytimes.com/interactive/2015/09/08/nyregion/09first-day-school-new-york-city.html.

44. Triay, *Fleeing Castro*, 44.

45. Robert J. Alexander, "Light and Shadow in Castro's Cuba," *Christian Century*, May 25, 1960, 632–34; Everett C. Parker, "Miami's Real-Life Drama," *Christian Century*, October 11, 1961, 1209–12; "Refugee Cuban Children Need Homes," *Christian Century*, April 4, 1962, 417–18; and "Chicagoans Welcome Refugees from Cuba," *Christian Century*, April 4, 1962, 418.

46. David White, "Cuba: Beautiful and Violent," *Christian Century*, January 21, 1959, 74–76.

47. McDannell, *Spirit of Vatican II*, 68; and O'Brien, *Renewal of American Catholicism*, 4.

48. McNally, *Catholicism in South Florida*, 2, 4, 64, 71–72, 75–77, 97.

49. Catholic Charities of the Archdiocese of Miami, "Our History"; "The Catholic Church and the Cuban Refugee—Together at the Point of Crisis," n.d., BOW Papers, Personal Files, BOW Appointments, Catholic Welfare Bureau, Cuban Children's Program, 1963, 1969, Box 5, OPPC; "History, 1958–2018: Archbishop Coleman F. Carroll," Archdiocese of Miami, accessed June 1, 2018, https://www.miamiarch.org/CatholicDiocese.php?op=H_Carroll; and McNally, *Catholicism in South Florida*, 84, 100, 102, 115, 116–26, 143.

50. García, *Havana USA*, 19; and McNally, *Catholicism in South Florida*, 146, 177, 213–15.

51. Letter to Father Patrick Finneran, S.J. in Hong Kong from BOW, June 29, 1962, BOW Papers, Personal Files, Correspondence, Box 20, Folder: BOW Correspondence, 1947–1962, OPPC.

52. Letter to BOW from Carroll, OPPC.

53. Letter to BOW from Coleman O. Carroll, December 21, 1961, BOW Papers, Personal Files, Correspondence, Box 20, Folder I, BOW Correspondence, 1947–1962, OPPC.
54. Attebery, "From Havana to Montana," 63, 66, 68–69.
55. Letter to BOW from Pilar Caballero Arnaiz, August 12, 1961, BOW Papers, Personal Files, Correspondence, Box 20, Folder: BOW Correspondence, 1947–1962, OPPC.
56. Letter from Bishop Coleman O. Carroll to BOW, August 26, 1963, BOW Papers, Personal Files, BOW Appointments, Catholic Welfare Bureau, Cuban Children's Program, 1963, 1969, Box 5, OPPC.
57. BOW, "Recollection of Havana Trip—Msgr. Bryan O. Walsh," March 25, 1963, 9, 12, BOW Papers, Works by BOW, Box 44, Folder: Recollection of Havana Trip, 1965, OPPC.
58. Letter to Monsignor Enrique Perez Serantes from BOW, January 16, 1964, BOW Papers, Personal Files, Correspondence, Box 20, Folder: BOW Correspondence, 1963–1965, OPPC.
59. Kirk, *Between God and the Party*, 115.

11. Abuse

Epigraph: Proust, *Swann's Way*, 47.

1. Gómez Cortés, *Operación Peter Pan*, 61–66, 70–71; Bravo, *Operación Peter Pan*, segments 1 and 2; and Shnookal, *Operation Pedro Pan*, 152.
2. John Dorschner, "Operation Pedro Pan," Business Monday, insert *Miami Herald*, September 22, 2003, 27, OPP/CCP, Newspaper Clippings, OPPC.
3. Torres, *Lost Apple*, 163–64.
4. CWB, "A Manual for Foster Parents," n.d., OPP/CCP, Subject Files, Series E, Folder: Foster Home Care, 1961–1974, OPPC.
5. Gómez Cortés, *Operación Peter Pan*, 93, 98–101; Conde, *Operation Pedro Pan*, 155–57; and Bravo, *Operación Peter Pan*, segment 2.
6. Phone interview with Rodriguez.
7. Phone interview with Rodriguez.
8. Robert Rodriguez v. Archbishop John C. Favalora, Circuit Court of the 11th Judicial Circuit in and for Miami-Dade County, Florida, Case no. 0514163 CA 27, June 9, 2006, http://www.bishop-accountability.org/complaints/2006_06_09_Rodriguez_v_Miami_amended_re_Bryan_O_Walsh.pdf; and phone interview with Rodriguez.
9. Jay Weaver, "Cuban Refugee Who Accused Deceased Priest of Abuse Protests Case Dismissal," *Miami Herald*, September 14, 2009.

10. Third District Court of Appeal, State of Florida, No. 3D07-1931, Robert Rodriguez v. Archbishop John C. Favalora, April 8, 2009, https://case -law.vlex.com/vid/11-so-3d-393-614569447; and Jay Weaver, "A Cuban Refugee Who Came to Miami as Part of the Pedro Pan Relocation Program Protested the Dismissal of His Lawsuit Accusing a Revered Priest of Sexually Abusing Him," *Miami Herald*, September 15, 2009, http:// www.bishop-accountability.org/news2009/09_10/2009_09_15_Weaver _DismissalOf.htm.

11. The Roman Catholic Diocese of Helena, "List of Accused Personnel," accessed February 26, 2022, https://diocesehelena.org/list-of-accused -personnel/; and "Database of Publicly Accused Roman Catholic Priests, Nuns, Brothers, Deacons, and Seminarians," BishopAccounability .org, accessed June 30, 2019, https://bishop-accountability.org/priestdb /PriestDBbylastName-H.html.

12. Torres, *Lost Apple*, 168–70.

13. Jay Weaver, "Pedro Pan Memory Brings Suit against Priest for Alleged Abuse," *Miami Herald*, November 9, 2002, 3B; and "Database of Publicly Accused."

14. Gómez Cortés, *Operación Peter Pan*, 66.

15. Jay Weaver, "Lawsuit Claims Vatican, Archdiocese of Miami Knew of Priest's Troubled Past," *Miami Herald*, March 30, 2010, https://www.sun -sentinel.com/news/fl-xpm-2010-03-30-fl-priest-sex-abuse-20100330 -story.html.

16. Phone interview with Rodriguez.

12. Vaults of Oblivion

Epigraph: Proust, *Swann's Way*, 46.

1. Interview with Riopedre.

2. Cristina García, *Dreaming in Cuban* (New York: Ballantine, 1992), 97.

3. García, *Dreaming in Cuban*, 138.

4. Quoted in Matthew Frye Jacobson, "Americanists at Work and at Play," *American Quarterly* 62, no. 2 (June 2010): 342.

5. Pérez Firmat, *Life on the Hyphen*, 25, 44, 53.

6. Conde, *Operation Pedro Pan*, 204–5.

7. Eire, *Learning to Die*, 16, 194.

8. Joyce Carol Oates, "Not All There," *New Yorker*, February 13 and 20, 2017, 93–94.

9. Paul Ricoeur, *Memory, History, Forgetting*, trans. Kathleen Blamey and David Pellauer (Chicago: University of Chicago Press, 2004), 87.

10. Interview with Lopez Santiago; and email correspondence with Lopez Santiago.

11. Memo to All Social Work Supervisors from Dorothea F. Sullivan, August 31, 1964, OPP/CCP, Administrative Files, Series A, Folder: Memorandum, Dorothea F. Sullivan, Director of Social Services, 1963–1964, OPPC.

12. Ruth Leys, *Trauma: A Genealogy* (Chicago: University of Chicago Press, 2000), 3; and D. Fassin and R. Rechtman, *The Empire of Trauma: An Inquiry into the Condition of Victimhood*, trans. Rachel Gomme (Princeton NJ: Princeton University Press, 2009), 30–31.

13. Cathy Caruth, *Unclaimed Experience: Trauma, Narrative, and History* (Baltimore: Johns Hopkins University Press, 1996), 1–2.

14. Leys, *Trauma*, 2, 19–20, 22, 33.

15. Jenny Edkins, *Trauma and the Memory of Politics* (Cambridge: Cambridge University Press, 2003), 4.

16. Jeffrey Alexander, *Cultural Trauma and Collective Identity* (Berkeley: University of California Press, 2004), 1, 8, 10, 12.

17. Interview with Diaz Dash; and email correspondence with Diaz Dash.

18. Interview with Azel.

19. Mario Ramon Garcia, "Pedagogical Bibliography of Literary Naturalism" (PhD diss., University of Miami, 1976), https://scholarship.miami .edu/esploro/outputs/doctoral/Pedagogical-Bibliography-Of-Literary -Naturalism/991031447361902976?institution=01UOML_INST?; and interview with García.

20. García, "40 Years/40 Lessons (2)."

21. Interview with García.

22. Interview with Azel.

23. Interview with García.

13. Bittersweet Reunions

1. Interview with Diaz Dash; and email correspondence with Diaz Dash.

2. Bravo, *Operación Peter Pan*, segment 1.

3. Memorandum to All Participating Agencies, November 20, 1963, OPP/CCP, Administrative Files, Series A, Folder: Memorandum, Sept–Dec 1963, OPPC.

4. Conde, *Operation Pedro Pan*, 172; and García, *Havana USA*, 35, 37.

5. Conde, *Operation Pedro Pan*, 176–78; "1,170 More Cuban Refugees Reach Florida on Freighter," *New York Times*, January 26, 1963, 3; and "Refugee Bargain with Cubans Ends," *New York Times*, July 4, 1963, 2.

6. Didion, *Miami*, 126–28.

7. Torres, *Lost Apple*, 193–96.

8. Letter from HEW to State Agencies Administering Public Assistance Plans and Child Welfare Programs, May 3, 1963, OPP/CCP, Subject Files, Series E, Folder: HEW, OPPC.

9. Letter to Senator George Smathers from Beth Thompson, June 26, 1962, Folder: June 1962, Refugee Problems, 1958–1962, RG 102, Records of the Children's Bureau, Central File, 1958–1962, Box 760, NN3-102-83-1, NARA.

10. HEW, Bureau of Family Services and Children's Bureau, "Cuban Refugee Program," 1–2, SAF.

11. Memorandum from Dorothea Sullivan to BOW, March 12, 1965, OPP/CCP, Subject Files, Series E, Folder: Discharge of Children, 1962–1965, OPPC.

12. Pedro Pan Collection, CHC0350, Box 1, Folder 5, Villaverde Rodriguez Family, 1961–65, Operation Pedro Pan Files, CHC.

13. Bravo, *Operación Peter Pan*, segment 2.

14. HistoryMiami Museum, "Operation Pedro Pan."

15. Interview with García.

16. García, "40 Years/40 Lessons (2)."

17. Brewer, *Questioning the Cuban Exile Model*, 127–29.

18. Conde, *Operation Pedro Pan*, 182–83.

19. Torres, *Land of Mirrors*, 90–91.

20. Conde, *Operation Pedro Pan*, 189–90.

21. Gómez Cortés, *Operación Peter Pan*, 33–38.

22. Phone interview with Rodriguez.

23. Eire, *Waiting for Snow*, 369.

24. "Memorandum to All Participating Agencies, Cuban Children's Program from BOW," March 16, 1964, OPP/CCP, Administrative Files, Series A, Folder: Memorandum, Jan–April 1964, OPPC.

25. Memorandum from Dorothea F. Sullivan to Margaret Condon et al., January 20, 1966, and memorandum from Dorothea F. Sullivan to All Social Work Supervisors, OPP/CCP, Subject Files, Series E, Folder: Continuation of Care, 1966, OPPC.

26. Gómez Cortés, *Operación Peter Pan*, 177–85.

27. Memorandum from BOW to Reverend Administrators, Social Service Supervisors et al., October 19, 1962, OPP/CCP, Subject Files, Series E, Folder: Return of Children to Cuba, 1962–1964, OPPC; memo from Dorothea F. Sullivan, (no recipients) January 29, 1964, OPP/CCP, Administrative Files, Series A, Folder: Memorandum, Jan–April 1964, OPPC; and "Memorandum to Katherine Daly et al. from Dorothea F. Sullivan," July

24, 1964, OPP/CCP, Administrative Files, Series A, Folder: Memorandum, May–Dec 1964, OPPC.

28. Mary Louise Wilkinson, "Cuba Mom Threatens Suit for Children," *Miami News*, September 15, 1965, 10A, OPP/CCP, Newspaper Clippings, Folder: September 1965, OPPC.

29. CWB, "Return of Children to Parents in Cuba, April 1964," OPP/CCP, Subject Files, Series E, Folder: Return of Children to Cuba, 1962–1964, OPPC.

30. "Memorandum to Social Workers, Cuban Division, CWB, Inc. from BOW," November 14, 1961, OPP/CCP, Administrative Files, Series A, Folder: Memorandum 1961, OPPC.

31. Memorandum to State Public Welfare Administrators and Child Welfare Directors from Arnold, SAF.

32. Folder: Cuban Refugee Children, Policy, Registration at Refugee Center, RG 363, Records of the Social and Rehabilitation Service, Unaccompanied Cuban Children's Refugee Program, 1961–1967, Box 3, NN3-363-095-001, NARA.

33. Monsignor Bryan O. Walsh, "The History of Operation Pedro Pan," March 1, 2001, BishopAccountability.org, March 1, 2001, http://www .bishop-accountability.org/news5/2001_03_01_Walsh_TheHistory.htm.

34. Walsh, "History of Operation Pedro Pan."

35. Interview with Arenas.

36. Catholic Charities of Staten Island, "Our Mission," accessed February 26, 2022, https://www.cc-si.org/about/.

37. Interview with Arenas.

38. Conde, *Operation Pedro Pan*, 191–92.

14. Putting the Program to Bed

1. Conde, *Operation Pedro Pan*, 179–80; García, *Havana USA*, 43; Torres, *Lost Apple*, 206–11; and Cortina and de Valle, "Exodus Unleashes a Flood," 1A, 8A.

2. Letter to McCann from BOW, January 4, 1967, BOW Papers, Personal Files, Correspondence, Box 20, Folder I, BOW Correspondence, 1966–1967, OPPC.

3. Jesús Arboleya Cervera, *Cuba y los cubanoamericanos: El fenómeno migratorio cubano* (Havana: Fondo Editorial Casa de las Américas, 2013), 28.

4. Masud-Piloto, *With Open Arms*, 57–62.

5. Lucille Batson, "Telephone Conversation with Frances Davis (6/3/66)," June 3, 1966, Folder: Cuban Refugee Children, Florida State Agency,

Correspondence—General, January 1, 1966–December 31, 1967, RG 363, Records of the Social and Rehabilitation Service, Unaccompanied Cuban Children's Refugee Program, 1961–1967, Box 3, NN3-363-095-001, NARA.

6. Operation Pedro Pan Group, "History of Operation Pedro Pan."

7. Letter to James O. Woods from Frances Davis, Director of Division of Child Welfare at Florida State Department of Public Welfare, March 10, 1966, Series 897, Box 2, Folder: Alabama-Connecticut Foster Parent Inquiries, SAF.

8. Katherine Oriez, "'They Come to Us in Their Darkest Hour,'" *Our Sunday Visitor*, January 9, 1966, 8, OPP/CCP, Newspaper Clippings, OPPC.

9. "Location of Accompanied Cuban Children outside of Florida," July 31, 1966, OPP/CCP, Administrative Files, Series D, Folder: Agency Lists, 1962–1963, OPPC.

10. Memorandum to Diocesan Resettlement Directors and Directors of Special Cuban Refugee Committees from John E. McCarthy, Director, Department of Immigration United States Catholic Conference, April 25, 1967, BOW Papers, Personal Files, Appointments, Box 6, Folder: "Commission on Cuban Refugees, 1967 Jan.–April," OPPC.

11. CWB, "Memorandum to All Contracting Agencies," OPPC.

12. "Agency Closings," n.d. (probably 1967), OPP/CCP, Series D, Folder: Agencies, Closing, 1966–1967, OPPC.

13. Letter from BOW to Reverend James F. Scherer, January 25, 1967, OPP/CCP, Series D, Folder: Agencies, Closing, 1966–1967, OPPC.

14. Letter from BOW to Most Reverend Paul J. Hallinan, D.D., January 25, 1967, OPP/CCP, Series D, Folder: Agencies, Closing, 1966–1967, OPPC.

15. BOW, "Cuban Refugee Children," OPPC.

16. García, *Havana USA*, 44–45.

17. Memorandum "Proposal to Phase Out the Cuban Refugee Program" to State Agencies Administering Approved Public Assistance Plans from John L. Costa, Commissioner, Assistance Payments Administration, within HEW, May 22, 1972, Series 325, Box 2, Folder: HEW-Releases, ff9, SAF.

18. George Volsky, "U.S. Cuban Refugee Program Split by Reports of Director's Political Activity," *New York Times*, May 10, 1976, https://www.nytimes.com/1976/05/10/archives/us-cuban-refugee-program-split-by-reports-of-directors-political.html.

19. Memorandum from April 10, 1973, to State Administrators and Other Interested Organizations and Agencies, "Notice of Intention to Phase Out Federal Reimbursement to States under the Migration and Refugee Assistance Act of 1962 (P.L. 87–510)," from Philip J. Rutledge of HEW, Series 325, Box 2, Folder: CRA Program Correspondence-HEW-1972, ff15, SAF.

20. AP, "Cuban Refugee Unit Closing in Miami after Two Decades," *New York Times*, September 8, 1981, https://www.nytimes.com/1981/09/08/us/cuban-refugee-unit-closing-in-miami-after-two-decades.html.

21. Memorandum from BOW to Archbishop Carroll, September 11, 1972, OPP/CCP, Subject Files, Series E, Folder: Cuban Children's Program, 1961–1977, OPPC.

22. Memorandum from BOW to Frances Davis, September 18, 1972, OPP/CCP, Subject Files, Series E, Folder: Cuban Children's Program: Phase out, 1972–1978, OPPC.

23. Memo to Dorothy McCrary from Pete O'Connor, n.d. (probably May 1976), OPP/CCP, Administrative Files, Series A, Folder: Memorandum, 1970s, OPPC.

24. Donahue, "100s Thank Priest," 5; and Marjorie L. Donahue, "Operation Pedro Pan: How Thousands of Children Shuffled under Castro's Nose," *The Voice*, March 3, 1978, 4, OPP/CCP, Newspaper Clippings, Folder: 1970s, OPPC.

25. Bea L. Hines, "Se retira héroe de refugiados de Pedro Pan," *Nuevo Herald*, January 10, 1996, 1C, 6C

26. Triay, *Mariel Boatlift*, 25–26, 49–51.

27. Triay, *Mariel Boatlift*, 56–59, 148, 161.

28. Marie Salazar, "Many Are Alone . . . but Free," *The Voice* 22, no. 6 (May 9, 1980): 3.

29. Interview with Dunn.

30. Triay, *Mariel Boatlift*, xvi.

31. Interview with Arenas.

32. Interview with García.

33. Masud-Piloto, *From Welcomed Exiles*, xxiv; and Edward M. Kennedy, "Refugee Act of 1980," *International Migration Review* 15, nos. 1–2 (1981): 141–42.

34. Triay, *Mariel Boatlift*, 146.

35. Salazar, "Many Are Alone," 3.

36. Marjorie L. Donohue, "Children's Program Starting Up Again," *The Voice* 22, no. 6 (May 9, 1980).

37. State of Florida Department of Health and Rehabilitative Services, "Report of Disbursements," July 1, 1980–June 30, 1981, OPP/CCP, Subject Files, Series E, Folder: Cuban Children's Program: Phase out, 1980–1981, OPPC.

38. Letter from BOW to Victor Palmieri, August 7, 1980, OPP/CCP, Subject Files, Series E, Folder: Cuban Children's Program II, 1980–1982, OPPC.

39. Contract for Provision of Foster and/or Group Care for Unaccompanied Cuban Refugee Children, July 1, 1980, Bethany Residence, OPP/CCP, Subject Files, Series E, Folder: Cuban Children's Program: Phase out, 1980–1981, OPPC.
40. Contract for Provision of Foster and/or Group Care, OPPC.
41. Letter from BOW to Archbishop Edward A. McCarthy, October 21, 1980, OPP/CCP, Subject Files, Series E, Folder: Cuban Children's Program II, 1980–1982, OPPC.
42. Letter from Mercedes Scopetta, PhD, et al. to Archbishop Edward A. McCarthy, September 10, 1980, OPP/CCP, Subject Files, Series E, Folder: Cuban Children's Program II, 1980–1982, OPPC.
43. Triay, *Mariel Boatlift*, 146–47.
44. Catholic Service Bureau, Inc., "Unaccompanied Cuban Minors Project," 1980, 1, 2, OPP/CCP, Subject Files, Series E, Folder: Cuban Children's Program II, 1980–1982, OPPC.
45. Donohue, "Children's Program Starting." It is not clear if García-Rubio was removed from the church for pedophilia or homosexuality, since in the 1960s when these charges first came to light, the categories did not carry the specificity they do today. See Weaver, "Lawsuit Claims Vatican."
46. Masud-Piloto, *From Welcomed Exiles*, 84, 86.
47. "Memo from Barbara A. Cruse [Dir. Of Child Welfare] to Archdiocesan Director," June 23, 1981, OPP/CCP, Series D, Folder: Boystown, August 1966, OPPC.
48. OPP/CCP, Administrative Files, Series D, Folder: Cuban Boys' Home: Mariel Boatlift, 1980–1981; letter to Barbara Cruse, Director of Child Welfare, Catholic Service Bureau, from Angela Hernandez, December 16, 1980, OPP/CCP, Administrative Files, Series D, Folder: Cuban Boys' Home: Mariel Boatlift, 1980–1981; letter to Oswaldo Lambert from BOW, June 9, 1981, OPP/CCP, Administrative Files, Series D, Folder: Cuban Boys' Home: Mariel Boatlift, 1980–1981, OPPC; BOW, "Cuban Refugee Children," November 3, 1987, unpublished manuscript, 2, 6, BOW Papers, BOW Works, Folder: Cuban Refugee Children 1987, OPPC; and letter from Lloydine McGuinn to John P. McLaughlin, July 17, 1981, OPP/CCP, Subject Files, Series E, Folder: Cuban Children's Program: Phase out, 1980–1981, OPPC.
49. Letters to BOW from Ramón Grau Alsina, April 20, 1978, and May 15, 1979, BOW Papers, Personal Files, Correspondence, Box 22, Folder: BOW Correspondence, Correspondence from Public Figures, 1961–1992, OPPC.

50. Letter to BOW from Jeb Bush, November 10, 2001, BOW Papers, Personal Files, Correspondence, Box 22, Folder: BOW Correspondence, Correspondence from Public Figures, 1961–1992, OPPC.

51. Gómez Cortés, *Operación Peter Pan*, 85.

52. Ana Rodriguez-Soto, "Msgr. Walsh Remembered," *Florida Catholic* (Miami edition), January 3, 2002, A1, A3, OPP/CCP, Newspaper Clippings, OPPC.

53. Conde, *Operation Pedro Pan*, 213.

54. Josh Replogle, "Lawmakers: Children Being Well Cared for in Catholic Center," AP News, June 25, 2018, https://apnews.com /5a456662e7aa4dbea98dc80b5f804ce5.

55. Casavantes Bradford, "Remembering Pedro Pan," 294–95.

15. The Politics of Exile Identity

1. Interview with Lopez Santiago; and email correspondence with Lopez Santiago.

2. García, *Havana USA*, 114.

3. García, *Havana USA*, 84.

4. Arboleya, *Cuba y los cubanoamericanos*, 27–28; and Oates, "Not All There," 93.

5. BOW, "The Community Looks at the Problem," paper presented at National Resettlement Conference for Cuban Refugees, January 30, 1961, 1, 5, BOW Papers, Personal Files Conferences & Workshops, Folder: National Conference on Resettlement of Cuban Refugees, Miami, January 1961, OPPC.

6. Marc Caputo, "Life's Tale Gives Martinez a Chance to Make History," *Miami Herald*, August 1, 2004.

7. García, "40 Years/40 Lessons (2)."

8. Torres, *Lost Apple*, 9–10.

9. García, *Havana USA*, 8; Geoffrey Tomb, "City Makes World Affairs Its Business," *Miami Herald*, May 2, 1983, 1C, 2C; and Didion, *Miami*, 134–36.

10. Conde, *Operation Pedro Pan*, 159.

11. Raquel Garcia, "Las Muchachitas de Villa Maria: A Cuban Sisterhood of the Yellow Roses of Texas," Island Media Group, last updated May 19, 2021, https://www.islandernews.com/civic_corner/las-muchachitas-de -villa-maria-a-cuban-sisterhood-of-the-yellow-roses-of-texas/article _848e0ef4-4aaa-11e9-9889-e3ae450d9998.html.

12. Personal interviews, Grau, Lopez Santiago, FIU CLHP VHS 502, Special Collections.

13. Interviews with the Muchachita Group, Miami, August 21, 2014.

14. Interview with Alvaro.

15. Attebery, "From Havana to Montana," 73.

16. HistoryMiami Museum, "Operation Pedro Pan."

17. HistoryMiami Museum, "Operation Pedro Pan."

18. Brewer, *Questioning the Cuban Exile Model*, ix–xii.

19. García, *Havana USA*, 84.

20. García, *Dreaming in Cuban*, 250, 255.

21. Ruth Behar, ed., *Bridges to Cuba/Puentes a Cuba* (Ann Arbor: University of Michigan Press, 1995), 6–7.

22. Interview with García.

23. Interview with Alvaro.

24. Interview with Alvaro.

25. Interview with Diaz Dash; and email correspondence with Diaz Dash.

26. Interview with Arenas.

27. Interview with Lopez Santiago; and email correspondence with Lopez Santiago.

28. Personal interviews, Grau, Lopez Santiago, FIU CLHP VHS 502, Special Collections; interview with Lopez Santiago; and email correspondence with Lopez Santiago.

29. Interview with Lopez Santiago; and email correspondence with Lopez Santiago.

30. Eleanor Blau, "Earl Robinson, 81, a Composer of Labor Movement Songs, Dies," *New York Times*, July 23, 1991, https://www.nytimes.com/1991/07/23 /obituaries/earl-robinson-81-a-composer-of-labor-movement-songs-dies.html.

31. Interview with Lopez Santiago; and email correspondence with Lopez Santiago.

16. The Return

1. Interview with Diaz Dash; email correspondence with Diaz Dash; and interview with Cepero.

2. Phone interview with Rodriguez.

3. Eire, *Waiting for Snow*, 51; and Eire, *Waiting for Snow* (Free Press, 2006 edition), 390.

4. López, *Impossible Returns*, 1–2, 5–6, 13–14, 121–22, ch. 4.

5. Didion, *Miami*, 118, 121.

6. Torres, *Lost Apple*, 217–21; Masud-Piloto, *With Open Arms*, 73–74; Conde, *Operation Pedro Pan*, 194–97; Gómez Cortés, *Operación Peter Pan*, 152–

53, 174–75; Casavantes Bradford, "Remembering Pedro Pan," 293; and Didion, *Miami*, 123.

7. Traver, "Memories of Cuba."

8. Bell, "Operation Pedro Pan," 9.

9. Torres, *Lost Apple*, 15, 217, 220, 226.

10. Torres, *Land of Mirrors*, 8.

11. Torres, *Land of Mirrors*, 37–38.

12. Gómez Cortés, *Operación Peter Pan*, 21–22, 46.

13. Bravo, *Operación Peter Pan*, segments 1 and 2; Estela Bravo, *Operación Peter Pan: Volando de Vuelta a Cuba*, segment 3, accessed August 20, 2014, https://www.youtube.com/watch?v=-leaz35_SZ4; and Estela Bravo, *Operación Peter Pan: Volando de Vuelta a Cuba*, segment 4, July 17, 2012, https://www.youtube.com/watch?v=-leaz35_SZ4.

14. Bravo, *Operación Peter Pan*, segment 3.

15. Gómez Cortés, *Operación Peter Pan*, 111, 122, 125.

16. Gómez Cortés, *Operación Peter Pan*, 114–15, 122–23.

17. Iraida H. López, "'. . . And There Is Only My Imagination Where Our History Should Be': An Interview with Cristina García," in Behar, *Bridges to Cuba*, 104.

18. Email correspondence with Simms.

19. Interview with Lopez Santiago; and email correspondence with Lopez Santiago.

20. Interview with Arenas.

21. Interview with García.

22. Interview with Azel.

23. Interview with Riopedre.

Conclusion

1. Karen DeYoung, "Court Order Sought for Elian's Return to Father," *Washington Post*, April 15, 2000, https://www.washingtonpost.com/archive/politics/2000/04/15/court-order-sought-for-elians-return-to-father/1c92d263-22e6-4cb8-873c-e937b9afae21/.

2. Sandy Grady, "Elian Belongs to His Dad: He's Become a Victim of Bad U.S. Policy," *Philadelphia Daily News*, January 12, 2000.

3. William J. Clinton, "Remarks on the Fiscal Year 2001 Federal Budget and an Exchange with Reporters," White House briefing room, January 25, 2000, https://www.presidency.ucsb.edu/documents/remarks-the-fiscal-year-2001-federal-budget-and-exchange-with-reporters.

4. President William J. Clinton, interview with Dan Rather, CBS News, April 6, 2000, https://www.govinfo.gov/content/pkg/PPP-2000-book1/pdf/PPP-2000-book1-doc-pg644-2.pdf.

5. "Elian Interview Sparks Miami Row," BBC News, September 30, 2005, http://news.bbc.co.uk/1/hi/world/americas/4299294.stm.

6. Luis Noe-Bustamante, Antonio Flores, and Sono Shah, "Facts on Hispanics of Cuban Origin in the United States, 2017," PewResearch Center, September 16, 2019, https://www.pewresearch.org/hispanic/fact-sheet/u-s-hispanics-facts-on-cuban-origin-latinos/.

7. Arboleya, *Cuba y los cubanoamericanos*, 164; and Lillian Guerra, "Fear and Loathing in Havana and Miami," *New York Times*, February 17, 2020, https://www.nytimes.com/2020/02/17/opinion/international-world/cuba-identity-castro.html?searchResultPosition=1.

8. Noe-Bustamante, Flores, and Shah, "Facts on Hispanics of Cuban Origin."

9. Marc Caputo, "Poll: Obama Got Big Share of Cuban American Vote, Won among Other Hispanics in Florida," *Miami Herald*, November 8, 2012.

10. Arboleya, *Cuba y los cubanoamericanos*, 254.

11. Sarah Moreno, "Thousands of Cuban Exiles Are Exploring an Unusual Option: Returning to Cuba to Live," *Miami Herald*, March 12, 2018.

12. Daniela Fernández, "Young Cuban Americans Have the Power to Reject Republicans and Turn Florida Blue," *Miami Herald*, January 7, 2020.

13. Karen DeYoung, "More than 100 House Democrats Urge Biden to Implement Changes in Cuba Policy," *Washington Post*, December 16, 2021, https://www.washingtonpost.com/national-security/cuba-biden-letter/2021/12/16/7d4d9152-5e8c-11ec-8665-aed48580f911_story.html.

14. UNHCR (United Nations High Commissioner for Refugees), "Global Trends: Forced Displacement in 2017" (Geneva: UNHCR, 2018), 2–3, https://www.unhcr.org/5b27be547.pdf.

15. Amnesty International, "The World's Refugees in Numbers," accessed May 20, 2019, https://www.amnesty.org/en/what-we-do/refugees-asylum-seekers-and-migrants/global-refugee-crisis-statistics-and-facts/; and Phillip Connor and Jens Manuel Krogstad, "For the First Time, U.S. Resettles Fewer Refugees than the Rest of the World," Pew Research Center, July 5, 2018, https://www.pewresearch.org/fact-tank/2018/07/05/for-the-first-time-u-s-resettles-fewer-refugees-than-the-rest-of-the-world/.

16. Michael D. Shear and Zolan Kanno-Youngs, "Trump Slashes Refugee Cap to 18,000, Curtailing U.S. Role as Haven," *New York Times*, Septem-

ber 26, 2019, https://www.nytimes.com/2019/09/26/us/politics/trump
-refugees.html.

17. Matthew Haag, "Thousands of Immigrant Children Said They Were Sexually Abused in U.S. Detention Centers, Report Says," *New York Times*, February 27, 2019, https://www.nytimes.com/2019/02/27/us/immigrant
-children-sexual-abuse.html?searchResultPosition=1.

18. Meagan Flynn, "Detained Migrant Children Got No Toothbrush, No Soap, No Sleep. It's No Problem, Government Argues," *Washington Post*, June 21, 2019, https://www.washingtonpost.com/nation/2019/06
/21/detained-migrant-children-no-toothbrush-soap-sleep/?utm_term=
.435ff6e95488.

19. Darryl Forges, "Homestead Child Migrant Detention Facility Shutting Down," NBCMiami.com, October 28, 2019, https://www.nbcmiami
.com/news/local/homestead-detention-center-will-not-have-contract
-renewed-reports/2021336/.

20. "Not Just Cubans: Many Latinos Now Call Miami Home," NBCNews.com, March 4, 2014, https://www.nbcnews.com/news/latino/not-just-cubans
-many-latinos-now-call-miami-home-n37241.

21. Interview with Dunn.

22. Interview with García.

23. Gerald Fogarty, "The Catholic Church in the United States since 1960: From Triumph to Turmoil," in *The Culture of Catholicism in the United States*, ed. Saskia Hertlein and Hermann Josef Schnackertz, American Studies monograph series (Heidelberg: Universitätsverlag), vol. 213 (Winter 2012): 8.

24. Gustavo Pérez Firmat, *Next Year in Cuba: A Cubano's Coming-of-Age in America* (New York: Anchor Books, 1995), 86.

25. Ricoeur, *Memory, History, Forgetting*, 21, 36, 57, 80–81, 121–22, 498.

26. Interview with Diaz Dash; and email correspondence with Diaz Dash.

INDEX

Page numbers in italics refer to illustrations.

abuses: of children, 120–21, 147; Daniel Harrington and, 48–50, 146, 150; in foster care, 148–49, 158; by nuns or priests, 50, 52–53, 58, 148, 167, 191; at Opa-locka, 38; at shelters, 170. *See also* sexual abuse

adjustment problems: crying in, 29, 105, 158, 166, 169; familial love absence and, 23, 33, 40; placement for, 35

adoption: Americans for overseas, 18, 108, 120–21, 123; against Cold War, 121–24; of OPP child, 128–29, 167; OPP not including, 128–29; in United States, 116

Alba, María, 124

Alexander, Jeffrey, 157

Alvarez, Lissette, as Pedro Pan, 51–52

Alvarez, Olguita, as Pedro Pan, 51–52

Alvaro, Raul, as Pedro Pan, 17, 84–85, 183, 186

Ameijeiras, Gerardo, as Pedro Pan, 110

American Chamber of Commerce Plan, 14

Americanization: assimilation expectations as, 36, 106, 130, 132, 158; automobiles and television in, 55–56; with citizenship, 172; of Cubans, 44, 153; CWB rules for, 33–

34; dress requirements and, 36, 48; Eloy Cepero on, 133; John Kennedy assassination and, 160; language challenges in, 158, 160, 165, 188; religious schools for, 136; sentimentalism for, 129; trauma of, 63

Americans: on communism, 106, 108–9, 124, 129–30; for Cuban children, 128; on Cuban entitlements, 111; on families, 122–23; on Marielitos, 178; overseas adoptions by, 18, 108, 120–21, 123; on refugees, 199–200; sentimentalism for, 129

Antonio Maceo Brigade, 191–92

Aquino, Sixto, as Pedro Pan, 15, 28

Aquino, Vivian, as Pedro Pan, 15, 28

Árbenz Guzmán, Jacobo, 32, 89

Ardavin, Tony, as Pedro Pan, 58

Arenas, José: as Pedro Pan, 53, 55–56, 169–71, 176, 187; on returning, 194

Arnaiz, Pilar Caballero, 146

Arnaz, Desi, 153

Arnold, Mildred, 62, 110–11

Artime, Manuel, 90

assimilation expectations, 36, 106, 130, 132, 158

Auerbach, Frank, 15, 17

Azel, José: on exile or immigrant terminology, 195; on Fidel Castro, 2; language and poetry by, 160; as Pedro Pan, 55

Baker, James, 13; on age restriction, 17; Bryan Walsh and, 14–15; on CIA, 96; on Cuban children rumors, 87–88; Ferré House and, 28; Leopoldina Grau Alsina and, 96; passports and, 16, 94; on patria potestad document, 87; Penny Powers and, 97; Ruston Academy and, 14, 28, 92, 94, 96–97, 136
Baker Hall, 50–51
balseros (rafters), 197
Baryshnikov, Mikhail, 56
Batista, Fulgencio: Cubans on, 14, 40, 84, 98, 124, 137; Fidel Castro on officials and, 41, 99, 138, 163; opposition to, 14
Batson, Lucille, 110, 113–14
Bay of Pigs: CIA and, 32; Fidel Castro after, 99–100, 139; John Kennedy and, 89; José Miró Cardona on, 91; United States and, 90, 99, 106, 108, 163; visas after, 20, 52, 94
Behar, Ruth, as Pedro Pan, 185
Biden, Joe, 199
Blacks, 121; on Cubans, 7, 59–60, 70, 74–78, 82–83; Cubans as, 58–59, 63, 81–82; on democracy, 77; education lack for, 68, 75, 80–81; on interstate highway, 72–73; Jews allying with, 80; Marvin Dunn on Cubans and, 81–82, 175; in Miami, 67–69, 71, 201; Opa-locka and, 71, 80, 82; racial violence on, 72; shelters against, 64; T. Willard Fair for, 79–80
boats, 8–9, 16, 172, 175, 177–78, 196–97
Boissevain, Maria, 94

Brace, Charles Loring, 116
Brondel Hall, 49, 85, 146, 183
Brooks, Luther L., 73–74
Buajasán Marrawi, José, 91, 98
Buck, Pearl S., 120
Burger, Warren, 55–56
Bush, Jeb, 178

Caballero, Miguel, 22
Camp Kendall. *See* Kendall Camp
Camp Matecumbe. *See* Matecumbe Camp
Candler, Warren Akin, 133
Canler, Ed, as Pedro Pan, 29, 33, 164, 193
Cardona, José Miró, 20, 90–91, 105–6
Carroll, Coleman: on Cuban refugees, 145–46; on one large camp, 32; on Opa-locka, 29, 32; sex abuse knowledge by, 150; T. Willard Fair on, 80; on visas, 15–16
Carter, Jimmy, 69, 174–76, 191
Castano, Jay, as Pedro Pan, 40–42
Castro, Fidel: on anti-communism, 139; on Batista officials, 41, 99, 138, 163; after Bay of Pigs, 99–100, 139; Bryan Walsh on, 140; on Catholic Christianity, 137–40; Catholic Church on, 86, 201; CIA on, 89, 96, 103–4; Cuban Americans on, 3–5, 10–11, 99; Cubans on, 3–5, 90; as dead, 190; on democracy, 138; on Elián González, 197–98; on families and children, 125–26, 136; José Azel on, 2; as masculine, 125; passage allowed by, 172, 174; on patria potestad document, 125–

27; promises by, 84–85; Rescate assassination plot on, 96; responsibility of, for journey, 131, 187; schools shut by, 87, 100, 126–27, 136; United States and, 1, 17, 84, 92, 103; on wealth and capitalism, 125–26

Castro, Raúl, 198–99, 201

Castro Cuba: Carlos Eire on, 190; private school closings by, 2, 87, 136, 138, 140–41; U.S. family Cold War with, 123–24, 200; for women, 124

Catholic Church: abuse and, 50, 52–53, 58, 148, 167, 191; on Castro government, 86, 201; on communism, 138–39, 142–43, 146; in Cuba, 135, 137–38, 141; Cubans on, 137; Fidel Castro against, 137–40; John Kennedy and, 134; on OPP, 140; for Pedro Pans, 4–5; sexual crime and, 149–50, 201; in United States, 141–44

Catholic Welfare Bureau (CWB): Americanization rules by, 33–34; Brondel Hall of, 49, 85, 146, 183; of Bryan Walsh, 24, 111; Camp Kendall run by, 22; as childcare agency, 14–15; on child disabilities, 38; child readmission in, 168–69; with Dade County, 13, 22, 25; ending of, 178; finances and, 45, 54; with Florida, 26; Florida City apartments by, 30; foster care and, 3, 18, 25; George Guarch of, 23–24; on homosexuality, 34–35; on integration, 59, 62–63; numbers taken by, 27–28, 53, 172–73; Opa-locka by, 32; parental legal

custody and, 168; on return to Cuba, 167; school support by, 13–14; on separation, 113, 155, 164, 169; supervision by, 64; trauma and, 155, 191; for unaccompanied children, 27–28; U.S. payments to, 45–46; visa waivers from, 41, 98, 146

CCF. See Christian Children's Fund (CCF)

CCP. See Cuban Children's Program (CCP)

Central American child detainees, 200

Central Intelligence Agency (CIA): for counterrevolutionaries, 85; Cuban Catholics and, 139; on Fidel Castro, 89, 96, 103–4; involvement of, 89–90; on Jacobo Árbenz Guzmán, 32; OPP by, 91–93, 96; Radio Swan by, 90–92, 96, 140; Zenith Technical Enterprises of, 90

Cepero, Eloy, as Pedro Pan, 56–57, 60, 133, 189

Chase, Michelle, 124

Che. See Guevara, Ernesto (Che)

children, 18; abuse of, 120–21, 147; crime and, 51, 53, 170; as homeless, 116–18, 120; United States on, 115–18; violence against, 64, 177; world premium on, 119

Children's Bureau (U.S.): creation of, 117–18; Dorothy McCrary to, 113; for nonsectarian and Protestant children, 25; numbers taken by, 27–28

Chinese Cubans, 63

Chirino, Willy: as Pedro Pan, 166, 178; on St. Raphael's, 33

Chovel, Elly: at Florida City and foster homes, 31; as Pedro Pan, 17, 88, 192

Christian Children's Fund (CCF), 120

CIA. *See* Central Intelligence Agency (CIA)

citizenship, 180; Americanization with, 172; for Cubans, 172, 198; oath of, 56; for Pedro Pans, 5, 7

civil rights: changes from, 70–71; Cuban children and, 5; U.S. violence against, 6

Clinton, Bill, 196–98, 201

Cold War: adoption and Pedro Pans against, 121–24; Americans on, 106, 108–9, 124, 129–30; Cuba and United States in family, 123–24, 200; division of, 4; Elián González resurrecting, 196–98; and faith, 133–34; Miami-Dade County in, 106; OPP from, 100; and racism, 66; and religion, 142; standards, 34; United States on, 18–19, 66, 108, 121–24, 198, 200

communism: Americans on, 106, 108–9, 124, 129–30; Bryan Walsh on, 4–5, 86–87, 134, 145; Catholic Church on, 138–39, 142–43, 146; Fidel Castro on anti-, 139; Jay Castano on, 40–42; Protestantism on, 142–43; trauma and anti-, 157; United States on children and, 4–5, 86–87, 134, 145; white identity from Cuban anti-, 78

Conde, Yvonne, 30, 154

Coughlin, Charles, 141

counterrevolutionaries, 1, 85

Craft, Frank M., 18, 26, 62, 75

Crahan, Margaret, 140

Crespo, Ramón Torreira, 91

crime: blame for, 64, 78, 119, 175; Catholic Church and sexual, 149–50, 201; children and, 51, 53, 170; Cuban children and, 47, 51, 64, 78, 177

Crouch, Stanley, 66–67

CRP. *See* Cuban Refugee Program (CRP)

Cuba: Catholic Church in, 135, 137–38, 141; education in, 81, 136; emotions on visiting, 160–61, 166–68, 189–90; on family, 119; family Cold War of, with United States, 123–24, 200; Havana Syndrome in, 199; María de los Angeles Torres on, 192–93; migration and, 5–6, 14, 18, 46, 78; Protestantism in, 135, 137; racism and, 59–60, 62, 102–3, 105; return hopes for, 162, 180; return to, 160–61, 166–68, 189; Ruston Academy in, 14, 28, 92, 94, 96–97, 136; United States controlling, 100–103. *See also* Castro Cuba

Cuban Americans: exile and, 181–82; on Fidel Castro, 3–5, 10–11, 99; history conflict by, 184–86; Latino differences with, 198; on Marielitos, 175–76; master narrative for, 157; memories of, 152–53; Miami and, 184–88; return and identity of, 190; volunteer numbers of, 25

Cuban Boys' Home, 30, 33, 174, 178

Cuban children, 24; adoption of, 128–29, 167; adult reunions by, 182–84; agencies returning, 47; Americans for, 128; cognitive abnormalities of, 35; crime and, 47, 51, 64, 78, 177; crying by, 29, 105, 158, 166, 169; education of, 14, 44, 93; Fidel Castro on families and, 125–26; group homes for, 24, 28, 45–47, 53, 59, 118; historical memories of, 8–11, 13, 84; master narrative for, 157; to Miami, 1, 73–74, 186–87; as 1.5 generation, 154, 158, 160, 166, 185, 190–91; parental fear for, 85–88; parental separation trauma for, 87–88, 152, 155–57; parent letters by, 111–12; parents on Soviet Union and, 41, 87–88, 122, 126, 136, 140; parents reclaiming, 162–65; as readmitted, 168–69; and "special needs" terminology, 130; sponsorship of, 120; as unaccompanied, 1–3, 17, 27–28, 176–77; as unclaimed, 24, 27–28, 44; United States on communism and, 1, 88, 129–30; worry of, for parents, 113–14. *See also* foster care; shelters

Cuban Children's Program (CCP): age and financial assistance in, 10, 164; ages in, 16–18; Bryan Walsh directing, 146; Cuban children in, 1–2; departures in, 1–2, 23, 84, 128; history of, 8; numbers of, 8–9, 44, 207n24; Phase II, 176; plan and money for, 14–15; for unaccompanied Cuban children, 17; unclaimed children in, 24, 27–28; years of, 7. *See also* Operation Pedro Pan (OPP)

Cuban Children's Services, 174

Cuban Girls' Home, 36

Cuban Marist Brothers, 37–38

Cuban Missile Crisis, 97, 110; flights after, 8, 99, 163, 187; Pedro Pan locations after, 32; refugees before, 75; reunion before, 29, 164

Cuban Refugee Children's Program, 26

Cuban Refugee Committee, 18

Cuban Refugee Emergency Center, 19–20, 27, 105, 131–32

Cuban Refugee Program (CRP), 19–20, 25, 106, 164

Cuban Revolutionary Council, 90–91

Cubans: Americanization of, 44, 153; as Blacks, 58–59, 63, 81–82; Blacks on, 7, 59–60, 70, 74–78, 82–83; on Catholic Church, 137; Coleman Carroll on refugees as, 145–46; and Cuba return expectations, 7, 21; English language challenges and, 102, 157; entitlements and, 75–76, 78, 111; exit permits for, 20; on Fidel Castro, 3–5, 90; on Fulgencio Batista, 14, 40, 84, 98, 124, 137; as Jewish, 25; Marvin Dunn on Blacks and, 81–82, 175; into Miami, 6–7; Miami rejecting, 158; on OPP, 127; in United States, 165–66; United States accepting, 105; United States on childlike, 103–4, 124–25; United States on Soviet Union and, 4, 6, 18, 66, 90; and white access, 78; on whiteness and Blackness, 69–70

Cuervo, Teté, 95, 98

CWB. *See* Catholic Welfare Bureau (CWB)

Dash, Mercedes Diaz: family reunion for, 162; Miami and, 186–87; as Pedro Pan, 1, 128, 157–58, 159, 189, 202

Davis, Frances, 26, 35, 128

de Giquel, Serafina Lastra, 95, 97

de la Portilla, Berta, 97

del Toro, Sara de Odio, 95

democracy: Blacks on, 77; Cold War and, 18–19, 121–22, 198; Cuba migration testing, 5–6, 14, 18, 46, 78; Fidel Castro on, 138

Department of Health, Education, and Welfare (HEW): for CRP, 25; Florida and, 25; John Kennedy and, 19–20; numbers taken by, 9; for OPP, 2, 173; on segregated institutions, 61–62

DeSantis, Ron, 199

de Varona Loredo, Manuel Antonio, 96

Devereux School, 35, 50–51, 149

Didion, Joan, 67, 82, 191

Displaced Persons Act (1948), 18

Don Bosco Boys' Home, 44

Dreaming in Cuban (C. García), 152–53

dress requirements, 36, 48

Dubinsky, Karen, 8

Dulles, Allen, 104, 139

Dunn, Marvin: on Blacks and Cubans, 81–82, 175; on Florida childhood, 65–66, 80; politics and, 80, 201; on racism, 68, 71

Echeverría, José Antonio, 137

education: Blacks lacking, 68, 75, 80–81; in Castro Cuba, 87, 100, 126–27, 136; and Castro Cuba private school closings, 2, 87, 136, 138, 140–41; in Cuba, 81, 136; of Cuban children, 14, 44, 93; and Protestantism in Cuba, 135; as segregated, 75, 81; in special facilities, 36–37

Eire, Carlos: on Castro Cuba, 190; as Pedro Pan, 26, 55, 59–60, 88, 167; on refugee ethics, 154

Eisenhower, Dwight, 18–19, 89–90, 119, 134

Elliston, Jon, 92

emotional disturbances: homes for, 51; institutions for, 50–51; list of, 39–40; over-treatment of, 39; rates of, 38

entitlements: Americans on Cuban, 111; Blacks on, 75–76; for Cuban children, 10, 164; Cubans and, 75–76, 78; ending of, 173–74; lack of, 44–45; spreading of, 75

exile: Cuban Americans and, 181–82; emotions of, 190–91; as identity, 180, 186; influence of, 201–2; Pedro Pans on, 202; return or, 190; trauma of, 154–55

"expat" as term, 180–81

Fair, T. Willard, 79–80

Fajardo, Eloisa, 25

families: absence and, 23, 33, 40; Americans on, 122–23; Fidel Castro on children and, 125–26, 136; Operation Matrimony for, 126; reunion with, 169, 173; social salvation by, 119–20

Fass, Paula, 8, 117

Federal Bureau of Investigation (FBI), 17–18, 75–76, 78–79

Feo, Hilda, 95
Ferré, Maurice, 28, 95, 175, 182, 201
Ferré House, 28
Figueroa, Gabriel Orozco, as Pedro Pan, 92
Finlay, Carlos, 97
Finlay, Francisco, 97
Fitzpatrick, John J., 37
Flanagan, James, 48–49
Florida, 2, 25; Africans and Seminole Indians in, 67; Blacks and interstate highway in, 72–73; Catholic Church in, 143–45; on children, 18; civil rights in, 70; history of, 67–68; Marvin Dunn on, 65–66, 80; numbers taken by, 27–28; refugee responsibility by, 26; refugee television program of, 107; on sexual abuse allegations, 149–50; Spain in early, 67
Florida City, 30–31, 31, 34
Fong, Oscar, as Pedro Pan, 49–50, 49
Fong, Reinaldo, as Pedro Pan, 49–50, 49
"Forja" (self-published pamphlet), 40
Fort McCoy, 177
foster care, 47; abuse in, 148–49, 158; Bryan Walsh favoring, 130; conditions in, 28, 148; costs of, 28; in CWB group homes, 3, 18, 25; group homes, orphanages, and, 118; in homes, 5, 24–25; in JFCS and UHIAS, 3, 18, 25; in 1950s, 118; numbers in, 53; payments to, 45–46; segregation and, 62; trauma in, 157
Freedom Flights, 172, 180
Freud, Sigmund, 156

García, Cristina, 152–53, 185, 194
García, María Cristina, 180
García, Mario R.: on Miami Cubans, 185, 201; as Pedro Pan, 52–53, 57, 105, 160, 165, 176; on refugee status, 181; on returning, 193–94
García-Rubio, Ernesto, 150, 178, 246n45
Garzón, Carolina, 38
Giquel, Sergio, 97
González, Elián, 196–98
González, Flora, 193–94
González, Juan Miguel, 196
Gore, Al, 197
Granado, Alfredo, as Pedro Pan, 52
Granado, Betty, as Pedro Pan, 52
Grau Alsina, Leopoldina (Polita), 93–94, 96, 98
Grau Alsina, Ramón (Mongo), 93–96, 98
Greene, Juanita, 76
Grillo, Evelio, 69–70
Gromyko, Andrei, 134
group homes, 118; children in, 24; costs of, 28; foster home to, 47; numbers in, 53; payments to, 45–46; segregation in, 59
Guarch, George, 23–24, 63, 97
Guerra, Lillian, 138, 198
Guerrero, Joaquín, 150, 213n47
Guevara, Ernesto (Che), 90, 192

Hale, Robert F., 16
Harnett, Margaret, 63
Harrington, Daniel B., 48–50, 146, 150
Havana Syndrome, 199
Haymes, María Vidal de, as Pedro Pan, 88

Hernandez, José L., as Pedro Pan, 110

HEW. *See* Department of Health, Education, and Welfare (HEW)

High, Robert King, 76–77, 106

Hine, Lewis, 117

Hispanics, 63

Holt, Bertha, 120

Holt, Harry, 120

homosexuality, 34–35, 147–48

Hoover, J. Edgar, 18

Hungarian Refugee Relief Program, 18–19

Hurley, Joseph Patrick, 28, 143–44

identity of Cuban Americans, 190

Inboden, William, 134

Jamaica, 16, 51, 166

Jesuit Boys' Home, 29

Jewish Family and Children's Service (JFCS): Dorothy McCrary to, 113; foster care in, 3, 18, 25; numbers taken by, 26–28; Ruth Behar and, 185

Jews: as Black allies, 80; Cubans as, 25; racial violence against, 72

JFCS. *See* Jewish Family and Children's Service (JFCS)

Jim Crow, 6, 68, 70–72

Johnson, Lyndon B., 8, 76, 106, 172

Juliano, Rosario Diaz, *159*

Kendall Camp: as children's home, 22, 41–42, 51, 128, 164; conditions at, 28, 37, 148–49; hunger strike at, 52; sexual abuse at, 150

Kennedy, Jacqueline, 110

Kennedy, John F., 4, 19–20, 76, 89, 160; as Catholic, 134; Cuban Americans on, 99; hospitality by, 105, 196; people writing to, 110–11

Kennedy, Robert, 110, 163

Kennedy, Ted, 106

Khrushchev, Nikita, 103, 122, 131

King, Martin Luther, Jr., 8, 78–79

KLM Airlines, 16, 97, 148, 155

Korean orphans, 120

Ku Klux Klan, 68, 141

Lange, Dorothea, 118

language challenges: and Americanization, 158, 160, 165, 188; of Cubans with English, 102, 157; English class provision for, 145; English studies for, 22, 55–56, 63, 81, 136; friction over, 75, 81, 158; as hampering, 70, 232n7; punishment for, 39, 52–53; translations for, 33

Lansdale, Edward, 91

Lazell, Arthur, 20, 105, *109*

Legree, Frank, 73, *74*

Lincoln Hall, 35

López, Alex, as Pedro Pan, 147, 150

López, Iraida, 190–91

López, Pepito, 131–32

Lopez, Pury: family reunion for, 187–88; as Pedro Pan, 31, 180, 187, 194; resettlement for, 43, 55; tale by, 115, 155

The Lost Apple (Susskind), 130–31, 148

Madariaga, María Dolores, as Pedro Pan, 33

Mansfield, Mike, 48, 50

Marielitos, 175–78

Martí, José, 100–101, 124, 138

Martínez, Elizabeth Sutherland, 126–27
Martínez, Mel, as Pedro Pan, 13, 181
Martínez Ybor, Vicente, 69
master narrative, 157
Masvidal, Raul, 99
Matecumbe Camp, 85, 144, 213n47; boys gymnastics routine at, 41; Bryan Walsh at, 29, 48; conditions at, 28–29, 37, 39–40, 50; dining hall problems at, 40; homosexuality and, 34–35, 147–48; neighbor complaints on, 64; overcrowding at, 111, 147, 169; photos at, 47, 48; routine at, 33, 42, 58; sexual abuse at, 148, 150
May, Elaine Tyler, 122
McCrary, Dorothy, 26, 113, 174
McGregor, Robert, 16
McKinley, William, 99, 105
Mediavilla, Maximiliano, 36–37, 47, 213n47
memories: of Cuban Americans, 152–53; Cuban children with historical, 8–11, 13, 84; separation and, 40–42, 87–88, 152
Méndez, Francisco, as Pedro Pan, 167
Mendieta, Ana, as Pedro Pan, 51
Mendieta, Raquel, as Pedro Pan, 51
Menéndez, Pedro, as Pedro Pan, 13
Mexico: as destination, 87; as route, 57, 94, 163, 167, 172, 186; unaccompanied children through, 3
Miami: Blacks in, 67–69, 71, 201; Cuban Americans and, 184–88; Cuban children to, 1, 73–74, 186–87; Cuban Refugee Committee of, 18; Cuban Refugee Emergency Center in, 19; Cuban rejection by, 158; Cuban Revolution building of modern, 200; Cubans into, 6–7; culture of, 66–67; Dade County and, 13, 22, 25, 106; integration in, 66, 71–72; interstate highway to, 72–73; OPP exhibits in, 184; as Pan-American destination, 6; racism and, 6–7, 65, 68, 71, 75–76, 78
Mikoyan, Anastas, 100, 138–39
Mission of the Immaculate Virgin, 53
Mitchell, William, 26, 112
Mongo. See Grau Alsina, Ramón (Mongo)
Monje, Juan, as Pedro Pan, 191–92
Monroe Doctrine, 4
Montalban, Carlos, 130–31
Montana, xi, 6, 39, 48, 49, 85, 86, 145, 146
Morton, Beatriz López, 95
Mount Loretto orphanage, 53, 170
Movement of Revolutionary Recovery, 90
Mukherjee, Bharati, 153
"mulatto" as term, 61
Myer, Dillon S., 20

National Association of Black Social Workers, 121
Navarro, Miguel Estades, 37
Nixon, Richard, 122–23, 173
Nuñez, Julio, as Pedro Pan, 58
Núñez, Marta, 92

Oates, Joyce Carol, 154, 180–81
Obama, Barack, 3, 186, 198–99, 201
O'Brien, David J., 141

Ochoa, Marina, 162

O'Connor, Pete, 174

Oettinger, Katherine Brownell, 26–27, 142

O'Farrill de la Campa, Albertina, 97–98

1.5 generation, 154, 158, 160, 166, 185, 190–91

Opa-locka: abuse at, 38; Blacks and, 71, 80, 82; for boys, 32, 32, 92, 177; boys to, 39, 56; Bryan Walsh on, 32–33; Coleman Carroll on, 29, 32; consolidation to, 29; Cuban Marist Brothers at, 37–38; haircut sentences at, 36; Jesuits at, 37; as military base, 17, 90–91; Miró Cardona and, 90–91; numbers at, 33; sexual abuse at, 147, 149; violence at, 36–37

Operación Peter Pan (Bravo), 193

Operation Babylift, 192

Operation Christian Humanism, 138

Operation Matrimony, 126

Operation Pedro Pan (OPP), 89; definition of, 9; legality of, 168; naming of, 13, 43; number of children in, 2, 172–73. *See also specific subjects*

Operation Pedro Pan Foundation, 179

OPP. *See* Operation Pedro Pan (OPP)

orphanages, 53, 116, 118, 170, 232n7

Palá, Francisco, 28, 40

Pan American (Pan Am) Airways: flights on, 17, 57, 98; as sponsoring airline, 1, 15–16, 39, 57

parents: advice for, 118; children reclaimed by, 162–65; children writing to, 111–12; child worry about, 113–14; Cuban children separated from, 87–88, 152, 155–57; and CWB and legal custody, 168; fear of, for children, 85–88; on Soviet Union and children, 41, 87–88, 122, 126, 136, 140, 147

patria potestad: document on, 85–87, 91, 148, 167, 198; Fidel Castro on, 125–27; Mongo on, 96; political freedom or, 198

Peacock, Margaret, 122

Pence, Fern, 109–10

Pérez, Lucila, 108

Pérez, Oscar, 108

Pérez Firmat, Gustavo, 153, 201–2

Pérez Serantes, Enrique, 137, 139, 146

Perry, Wave L., 26, 75

Phillips, David Atlee, 89–91

Pineiro, Aurelio, as Pedro Pan, 110

"The Plight of Pepito" (special report), 131

Polita. *See* Grau Alsina, Leopoldina (Polita)

Portes, Carlos, as Pedro Pan, 56

post-traumatic stress disorder (PTSD), 156

Powers, Penny, 94–97, 112–13

Prieto, Antonio, as Pedro Pan, 171

Protestantism: capitalism and, 135–36; Children's Bureau and, 25; on communism, 142–43; in Cuba, 135, 137

Proust, Marcel, 1–2, 147, 151–52

Pruna, Fernando, 22

PTSD. *See* post-traumatic stress disorder (PTSD)

punishments, 37, 38–39

racial integration: CWB on, 59, 62–
63; Dorothea Sullivan on, 61, 64;
in Miami, 66, 71–72
racism: Cold War and, 66; Cuba and,
59–60, 62; Cubans on, 69–70;
delinquency and, 119; experiences
of, 58–60, 62–63, 161, 170; against
Frank Legree, 73, 74; Hispanics
and, 63; integration and, 59, 62–
63, 66, 71–72; Jim Crow and, 6,
68, 70–72; Miami and, 6–7, 65,
68, 71, 75–76, 78; mulatto and,
61; Pedro Pans and, 5–6, 130, 183;
segregation and, 59, 61–62, 71, 75,
78, 81; of United States, against
Cuba, 102–3, 105; U.S. childcare
and institutional, 121; violence of,
68–69
Radio Swan, 90–92, 96, 140
rafters. See *balseros* (rafters)
Randall House, 50–51
Range, M. Athalie, 73, 81
Rasputin, Grigori, 94
Refugee Act (1980), 176
Refugee Relief Act, 18
refugees, 18–19; Americans on,
199–200; crisis of, 13; Cubans as,
145–46; ethics and, 154; as non-
white, 58–59; *Resettlement Re-cap*
on, 108, 109; sexual abuse against,
200; as tag, 51, 180–81; United
States on, 18, 26, 176; world numbers of, 199
Regalado, Tomás, as Pedro Pan, 164
religion: child shelters by, 46; and
Cold War, 133–34, 142; and
placements, 25. See also Catholic
Church; Protestantism

Remembrance of Things Past
(Proust), 2
Renick, Ralph, 43, 131–32
Reno, Janet, 196–97, 201
Rescate (Rescue), 96
resettlement: choices in, 113; of
Cubans, 44, 153; destinations for,
216n9; hospitality and challenges
in, 106, 108; of Marielitos, 177;
number of children in, 46; for
Pury Lopez, 43, 55; violent experiences in, 52–53
Resettlement Re-cap, 108, 109
resistance activities, 40
return, 194; of children, 47; and
Cuba visits, 160–61, 166–68,
189–90; as disloyalty, 189–90, 192;
and exile, 190; expectations of,
for Cubans, 7, 21; hopes for, 162,
180; Mayda Riopedre on, 195; by
1.5 generation, 190–91; by Pedro
Pans, 192–93; wholeness from,
192–93
reunion: of Cuban children with
adult, 182–84; before Cuban Missile Crisis, 29, 164; with families,
169, 173; fortitude and persistence
for, 166–67; Freedom Flights for,
172, 180; for Mercedes Diaz Dash,
162; for Pury Lopez and family,
187–88; as unpredictable, 164–65,
171
Ribicoff, Abraham, 19–20, 29, 44,
48, 128
Ricoeur, Paul, 155, 202
Riis, Jacob, 117
Riopedre, Mayda: family changes
for, 152; as Pedro Pan, 22–23; on
returning, 195; to shelter, 28, 60

Rivero, Manuel Ray, 20

Rodríguez, Justo, as Pedro Pan, 171

Rodríguez, Villaverde, 164

Rodriguez Diaz, Roberto: on Cuba visits, 189; as Pedro Pan, 1, 59–60, 148–51, 166–67

Romero, María Cristina, as Pedro Pan, 50

Roosevelt, Franklin, 99, 105, 141

Roosevelt, Theodore, 117

Ros-Lehtinen, Ileana, 93

Rovin, Charles, 111

Rubio, Marco, 185

Ruston Academy, 14, 28, 92, 94, 96–97, 136

Samet, Seymour, 6, 78

Santiago, Pury Lopez. See Lopez, Pury

Schechter, Marshall, 121

Scott, Rick, 199

segregation, 59, 61–62, 71, 75, 78, 81

separation: CWB on, 113, 155, 164, 169; memories and, 87–88, 152; for younger children, 56

sexual abuse, 148; by Catholic clergy, 149–50, 201; child detention with, 200; Coleman Carroll on, 150; Ernesto García-Rubio and, 150, 178, 246n45; at Opa-locka, 147, 149

Shallow, Charles, 46

shelters, 60; abuses at, 170; adults working in, 7–8; anti-Negro feeling at, 64; on Blacks, 64; Catholic orders and, 22; children in, 3, 24; children returned to, 47; conditions in, 28; geographical distribution of, 45; payments to, 45–46;

by religion, 46; as transitional, 44; trauma in, 157; for unclaimed children, 24, 27–28

Shnookal, Deborah, 87, 127

Sierra, Mirtha, 109–10

Simms, Gerardo, as Pedro Pan, 55, 81–82, 194

Smirnoff, Yakov, 56

Smith, Gilbert, 98

Smith, McGregor, 56, 133

Social Security Administration, 26

Socorrás, Carlos Prío, 96

Sosa, Candi, as Pedro Pan, 148, 193

Soto, Emilio, as Pedro Pan, 53

Soviet Union. See Union of Soviet Socialist Republics (USSR)

Spain: accent of, 41; children taken from, 87; Cuba and, 100–101, 125–26, 135, 139–40, 187; in early Florida, 67; routes through, 16–17, 98, 115, 162–63, 169, 172

Spengler, Eusebio Leal, 127

Spock, Benjamin, 118

Stalin, Joseph, 134

State Department (U.S.), 2

St. Benedict's College, 45

Stern, Thalia, 72

St. Joseph's Home, 49, 57, 112, 145, 146

St. Joseph's Villa, 15, 28

St. Raphael's Hall, 29, 37, 213n47

St. Vincent's Orphanage, 43–44

Sullivan, Dorothea, 34, 35–36, 61, 64, 213n47

Susskind, David, 130–31, 148

Thomas, Alicia, 95

Thomas, John Frederick, 78, 106

Torrado, Osvaldo Dorticós, 139

Torres, María de los Angeles: on Cuba, 192–93; as OPP scholar, 91, 98, 150, 166, 181–82, 184; as Pedro Pan, 60

Torres, Oscar, as Pedro Pan, 50

transport modes. See boats; KLM Airlines; Pan American (Pan Am) Airways

trauma: of Americanization, 63; for Cuban children, 87–88, 152, 155–57; as cultural, 156–57; CWB and, 155, 191; of exile, 154–55; research on, 155–56

Triay, Victor, 25–26, 175

Truman, Harry, 134

Trump, Donald, 3, 178, 199–200

UHIAS. See United Hebrew Immigrant Aid Society (UHIAS)

unaccompanied children: Bryan Walsh on, 176–77; CCP for, 17; of Central America, 3; of Cuba, 1–2; CWB for, 27–28; among Marielitos, 176; Mexico and, 3

Unaccompanied Cuban Children's Program. See Cuban Children's Program (CCP)

unclaimed children, 24, 27–28, 44

Union of Soviet Socialist Republics (USSR): Fidel Castro and, 103, 126; parents on children and, 41, 87–88, 122, 126, 136, 140; sugar purchases by, 100; United States on, 56, 103, 121–22, 131, 134; United States on Cubans and, 4, 6, 18, 66, 90; visitors from, 100, 138

United Hebrew Immigrant Aid Society (UHIAS): as child agency, 25; Dorothy McCrary to, 113; foster care in, 3, 18, 25; numbers with, 26–28

United States: adoption in, 116; American and Cuban letters to, 110–11; Bay of Pigs and, 90, 99, 106, 108, 163; and Catholic Church, 141–44; on childlike Cubans, 103–4, 124–25; on children, 115–18; child welfare inadequacy in, 120–21; on civil rights, 6; on Cold War, 18–19, 66, 108, 121–24, 198, 200; on communism and children, 1, 88, 129–30; on Cuba, 100–103; and Cuban counterrevolutionary efforts, 90; Cubans accepted by, 105; on Cubans and Soviet Union, 4, 6, 18, 66, 90; Cubans in, 165–66; departments of, involved in OPP, 2–3; on faith, 133–34; on family, 119–20; on Fidel Castro, 1, 17, 84, 92, 103; and payments to CWB, 45–46; Pedro Pan public knowledge in, 43–44; racism of, 66, 102–3, 105; on refugees, 18, 26, 176; on Soviet Union, 56, 103, 121–22, 131, 134; on unaccompanied children, 1–3. See also Americanization

USSR. See Union of Soviet Socialist Republics (USSR)

Utset, Marial Iglesias, 102

Valdés, Nelson, as Pedro Pan, 51–52, 191

Valdivia, Carmen, as Pedro Pan, 29

Venceremos Brigades, 192

Vilano, Mari, as Pedro Pan, 166

violence: from administrators, 52–53; against Blacks and Jews, 72; against children, 64, 177; at Opa-locka, 36–37; of racism, 68–69

visas: after Bay of Pigs, 20, 52, 94; changing of, 23–24; Coleman Carroll on, 15–16; CWB for waivers and, 41, 98, 146; for students, 14–15, 20; and waiver numbers, 17, 20–21, 44, 163; as waivers, 15–16

Voorhees, Tracy S., 18–19

Wallenberg, Raoul, 93

Walsh, Bryan O.: as CCP director, 146; on CIA, 92; on communism, 4–5, 86–87, 134, 145; crime reports to, 64; on Cubans and economy, 82–83; CWB of, 24, 111; data from, 229n3; death of, 178; on Fidel Castro and Catholics, 140; for Florida growth, 145; for foster care, 130; Frank Auerbach and, 17; as fulcrum, 26–27; on home assignments, 47; on humanitarian aid, 88–89; on Hungarian refugees, 19; on indefinite future, 53–54; Matecumbe Camp and, 29, 48; money raised by, 14–15; on Opa-locka, 32–33; on Pedro Pan beginnings, 13, 43; and Penny Powers, 112–13; on Phase II unaccompanied boys, 176–77; press release from, 44; on "refugee" as term, 181; on Robert King High, 77; on school dismissals, 37; on segregated institutions, 61–62; St. Benedict's College visit by, 45; on unapproved facilities, 111

W. Harry Smith Agency, 15, 95, 98

white privilege, 60

Wilhelm, Silvia, as Pedro Pan, 13, 166

Wise, Marshall, 76

women, 38; Cuba freeing, 124; OPP camaraderie among, 182–83; OPP role for, 95

work skills provision, 44

Year of Education (1961), 87, 126–27, 136

Zenith Technical Enterprises, 90

Zoloth, Shirley, 72